EMPLOYMENT TRII REMEDIES HANDBOOK

2021-22 Edition

General Editor

Benjamin Gray, Littleton Chambers

Forewords

The Honourable Mr Justice Choudhury
President of the Employment Appeal Tribunal

Judge Barry Clarke
President Employment Tribunals (England & Wales)

Judge Shona Simon
President Employment Tribunals (Scotland)

BATH PUBLISHING

First edition: Published April 2014

Subsequent editions published 2015 and annually thereafter

Eighth edition published July 2021

ISBN 978-1-9163023-7-2

Text © Bath Publishing Limited

Typography © Bath Publishing Limited

Bath Publishing Limited
27 Charmouth Road
Bath
BA1 3LJ
Tel: 01225 577810

email: info@bathpublishing.co.uk
www.bathpublishing.co.uk

Bath Publishing Limited is a company registered in England: 5209173
Registered Office: As above

FOREWORD BY THE HON. MR JUSTICE CHOUDHURY (from the 2020/21 edition)

A significant proportion of appeals heard in the Employment Appeal Tribunal are based on, or include, remedy issues. That reflects the fact that remedy issues are often the most difficult aspect of any employment claim. That is perhaps hardly surprising given the huge number of variables and the complex case law that has developed in this field. It is therefore a great relief for an adviser, whether at first instance or on appeal, to have to hand a reliable handbook to guide one through the maze of regulatory provisions and cases to provide an accurate idea of what the remedy should be, or at least the range within which the remedy should lie.

This text, now in its eighth year, is just such a handbook. Written by an experienced practitioner from a specialist employment law set, the handbook is an accessible and user-friendly guide which will appeal to a wide range of readers from seasoned representatives to those facing an employment dispute for the first time. Its accessibility lies in its clear presentation, where case law references are concise and manageable. Its user-friendliness lies in its alphabetic ordering of topics and (in the e-version) its hyperlinked cross-references. There is probably no other remedies guide where one can locate the key principles relating to 'zero-hours contracts' (an important topic for these times) as quickly as I managed to do with Mr Gray's book! One of the best means of understanding how relevant principles are to be applied is by worked examples, and this book has an abundance of those in almost every chapter. The examples are well thought out and based on the kinds of 'real life' scenarios that litigants are likely to face. There is also a substantial section on costs awards in the Employment Tribunal, the risks of which are sometimes underestimated in what is intended to be a predominantly costs-free jurisdiction.

The handbook is a valuable contribution to this complex and rapidly developing area of law and will no doubt continue to be for many editions to come.

The Hon. Mr Justice Choudhury

President

Employment Appeal Tribunal

June 2020

FOREWORD BY JUDGE BARRY CLARKE (from the 2020/21 edition)

It is a pleasure to follow the practice of my predecessor as President of Employment Tribunals in England and Wales, Judge Brian Doyle, by contributing a foreword to the latest edition of the Employment Tribunal Remedies Handbook.

Before I became a judge, I would regularly provide training to newly qualified employment lawyers. Sometimes I would invite delegates to offer me examples of the first question they would ask a new or prospective claimant client. A range of reasonable responses (to coin a phrase) would follow. Those more inclined to focus on procedure would suggest: "*Have you brought a copy of your contract of employment with you?*" Those who saw themselves in the vanguard of worker protection would propose: "*What principle is at stake here?*" Those with honed communication skills might ask: "*How can I help?*" Those with time to spare might suggest: "*Starting from the beginning, tell me why you've come to see me*". Those already thinking of setting up their own law firms would reveal themselves, by suggesting: "*Can you make a payment on account of costs?*"

None of these answers is necessarily wrong, and it is no doubt good for the legal marketplace that it is populated by people with different skills and different styles. Sooner rather than later, however, there is one question that must be asked. It is the issue upon which all participants in Employment Tribunal litigation, whether claimants, respondents or representatives, must be swift to focus. It is also the question that a judge will want answered during a preliminary hearing held for case management purposes, or at the outset of the main hearing. That question is this: "*What do you want to achieve?*"

All litigants must apply their minds to the remedy they seek. Litigation is often a long journey, so it must be right, before setting off, to decide the destination. It is surprising then that, on many occasions, the look on a person's face suggests that they simply haven't given it any thought. The understandable wish to lay blame or to escape it, or the emotional aspects of the case, may have distracted them from taking a cold, hard, rational look at the case.

There are all sorts of things that people wish to achieve in Employment Tribunal litigation. When I ask the question, the answers in a typical month would include at least some of the following: the chance to have "my day in court"; vindication; a desire to restore a reputation or minimise the damage to it; the wish to "be listened to"; to make sure "no one goes through what I have been through"; and the wish to be seen "not to give in easily" or to "set a precedent". All are valid and, in the right case, might get some airtime. However, except where making recommendations in discrimination cases, Employment Tribunal litigation is principally about the provision of financial compensation to those who win their cases. That being so, the question "what do you want to achieve?" must quickly become "what is this case worth?"

That is why question 9 on the ET1 claim form is drafted as it is. The heading is "What do you want if your claim is successful?" But question 9.2 gets to the heart of it: "What compensation or remedy are you seeking?"

To the many lawyers and litigants who will read this handbook, the answer is not "To be confirmed", whether it is written on the ET1 or on a subsequent schedule of loss. My instinct is that this answer is given so often because people fear arithmetic or worry that they are not good at it. That is understandable, because the answer might be complex. What if the claimant only wins part of the claim? What types of loss might result in compensation? How far into the future might loss be awarded? How should an award for injury to feelings be calculated? What effect does interest, taxation or recoupment have on the award? How might pension loss be compensated? Will any costs be recovered?

While an editor's work is never truly done in this fast-moving field, Mr Gray's work gets as close as any, and this handbook benefits enormously from its user-friendly design and the sophisticated companion online toolkit. Together, they can give parties and practitioners considerable confidence that they have accounted for all types of financial remedy and the variables that might inflate or deflate them. They can also give judges confidence that the remedy has been calculated as fairly and as accurately as possible.

Judge Barry Clarke

President, Employment Tribunals (England & Wales)

June 2020

FOREWORD BY JUDGE SHONA SIMON (from the 2020/21 edition)

It is easy to assume that because, in Great Britain, the power to make primary and secondary employment legislation resides almost entirely with the UK Government and Parliament, employment law must therefore be uniform in that territorial area. Whilst employment law is indeed largely the same in England, Wales and Scotland, those who make the assumption that it is exactly so fall into a trap, set for those who fail to undertake the legal research that should be done by those operating their legal practice on a cross border basis. Nowhere is that trap more dangerous than in the law governing remedies in Employment Tribunals.

By way of example, those practising on a cross border basis need to know that the discount rate to be taken into account when future loss is being calculated differs as between England and Wales (currently -0.25%) and Scotland (-0.75%). Similarly, income tax rates are different. Furthermore, although the interest rate on damages is currently the same both sides of the border that has not always been the position nor will it necessarily be so in the future as the rates used are those which apply in the respective civil courts systems: these are fixed by different mechanisms.

When it comes to quantification of damages generally, Employment Tribunals in Scotland will apply principles of Scots law. Further discussion about why this is so can be found at *https://www.judiciary.uk/wp-content/uploads/2017/07/vento-consultation-response-20170904.pdf*. This means, of course, that a degree of care requires to be taken when making submissions about principles which can be derived from case law; the professional embarrassment which will flow from citing Court of Appeal decisions on quantification of damages to a Scottish Employment Tribunal, only to be told (I would hope gently and diplomatically) that the principle in question forms no part of Scots law, should not be underestimated.

Help though is at hand, when navigating this difficult terrain, in the form of the Employment Tribunal Remedies Handbook. Care has been taken by the General Editor to ensure that these cross border differences are drawn to the attention of the reader, making this a reference work which will be of considerable assistance, irrespective of whether those consulting it are pleading their case before an Employment Tribunal in England and Wales, on the one hand, or in Scotland, on the other.

Judge Shona Simon

President, Employment Tribunals (Scotland)

June 2020

INTRODUCTION

Welcome to the new edition of the Employment Tribunal Remedies Handbook which once again is packed with information about the calculation of remedy in employment claims. Now into its 8th year, the Handbook is rapidly gaining a reputation as the 'go-to' resource when calculating remedy and has even been relied on by the EAT.

The handbook is an invaluable tool for potential claimants and respondents from before proceedings have been brought through to all stages of later litigation. It is as important as ever that potential claimants understand what their claims might be worth before embarking on employment tribunal litigation. It is also useful for respondents to a potential claim to know, for example, what their liabilities could be before undertaking disciplinary proceedings or a redundancy exercise. And with Early Conciliation now compulsory, both parties benefit from having the key remedy information available to enable them to reach a compromise.

All of this means that the information contained in the Employment Tribunal Remedies Handbook is essential at any stage of a dispute where the assessment and valuation of remedies is a possibility.

Each employment right that can be enforced in an employment tribunal is summarised, followed by the principles that will be applied to any remedies. For example, the common claims of unfair dismissal, discrimination and detriment are covered, and also all the numerous less litigated rights such as time off for study and training and the right of a TUPE transferee to be notified of employee liability information. For each such entry, the nature of any award is set out, such as the route to calculate a basic award or the principles that will be applied to calculate a compensatory award.

There are also separate entries for each element of a remedy and the principles used in its calculation, such as mitigation, loss of chance, tax and termination payments, grossing up, order of adjustments, recoupment, the definition of a week's pay, and many other elements of a remedy calculation. Each entry is cross-referenced to others, so it is possible to start anywhere in the book when a specific issue arises, not just at the particular right that is being enforced.

The text is supported by worked examples, to show clearly how the law is applied. 39 essential tables are included with up to date information on caps, limitation periods, Ogden tables, National Minimum Wage rates and much more, so that the information needed is always to hand.

What's new in the 2021-22 edition?

The book has been updated to include the latest limits and caps, changes in legislation and recent case law. Apart from the new figures, the main changes are set out below:

- **ACAS Code and Protected Disclosures**: The EAT's decision in *Ikejiaku v British Institute of Technology Ltd* UKEAT/0243/19 identifies that a Protected Disclosure made to an employer is likely to amount to a Grievance within the meaning of the ACAS Code. Failure to respond appropriately may therefore result in an uplift of any compensation.

- **Costs**: Employment Tribunals have the power to cap the amount of costs recoverable on Detailed Assessment (*Kuwait Oil Company v al-Tarkait* [2020] EWCA Civ 1752).

- **Fixed Term Contracts**: Provisions allowing an employee to resign on notice in the event of a repudiatory breach by their employer are unlikely to displace the common law right to damages for the duration of the contract (or any other period of notice) without clear wording to this effect – *Hall v London Lions Basketball Club (UK) Ltd* UKEAT/0273/19.

- **Holiday Pay**: The EAT's interpretation of *King v The Sash Window Workshop Ltd* EUECJ C-214/16 in *Smith v Pimlico Plumbers Ltd* UKEAT/0211/19 has been incorporated into this edition.

- **Injury to Feelings**: A Fourth Addendum has been released to the Presidential Guidance on awards under this heading, and the figures for each band have been updated accordingly.

- **Reinstatement and Re-Engagement**:

  - Interest is not payable on a sum due under a re-engagement order where the employer declines to re-engage the employee (*Fortheringhame v Barclays Services Ltd* UKEAT/0208/19).

  - The EAT has provided further guidance on what amounts to "practicability" in respect of such orders in *Kelly v PGA European Tour* [2021] EWCA Civ 559.

- **Causation**: Further guidance on whether and to what extent dismissal from subsequent employment breaks the chain of causation has been provided by the EAT in *Hakim v The Scottish Trade Unions Congress* UKEATS/0047/19.

- **Pension Loss**: The Principles for compensating pension loss have been updated.

- **TUPE**: Where a claim for failure to inform and consult is brought by "affected employees", then compensation will only be awarded to those employees who are actually parties to the case (*Ferguson and ors v Astrea Asset Management Ltd* UKEAT/0139/19). This case also calls into question the approach to protective awards set out in *Susie Radin Ltd v GMB & ors* [2004] ICR 893.

- **COVID**: Various changes have been made to reflect the impact of COVID legislation in this area.

As always, any comments or suggestions for improvement or additions for subsequent editions are most welcome. Please forward any comments to the publishers at info@bathpublishing.co.uk.

Benjamin Gray

Littleton Chambers

July 2021

Benjamin Gray is a barrister at Littleton Chambers. He advises and represents both employees and employers in all stages of employment litigation and dispute resolution across the full spectrum of employment law. Benjamin was appointed to the Attorney General's C Panel of Junior Counsel to the Crown in February 2017. He is also a co-author of Bloomsbury's *Termination of Employment*.

Contents

Contents

Table of Cases

Table of Statutes

Table of Statutory Instruments

ACAS (The Advisory, Conciliation and Arbitration Service)

(see also *Adjustments and order of adjustments*)

An award for compensation can be increased or reduced, by up to 25%, if the employer/employee (but not worker – see *Local Government Yorkshire & Humber v Shah* UKEAT/0587/11/ZT) has unreasonably failed to comply with a relevant code of practice relating to the resolution of disputes (see s207(A) TULRC(A) 1992). A relevant code of practice will have been issued either by ACAS or the Secretary of State under ss199 to 206 TULR(C)A. At present ACAS *Code of Practice 1: Disciplinary and Grievance Procedures* (2015) is the only relevant code of practice.

The ACAS Code is not engaged unless a grievance is raised in writing and therefore the ACAS uplift is not available if a grievance is raised orally (see *The Cadogan Hotel Partners Ltd v Ozog* UKEAT/0001/14/DM, paragraph 52). 'Grievance' is defined by the Code as *'concerns, problems or complaints that employees raise with their employers'*, and appears to be construed broadly (*Ikejiaku v British Institute of Technology Ltd* UKEAT/0243/19).

The full list of tribunal jurisdictions to which s207A applies is detailed in Schedule A2 of TULR(C)A:

- s120 and s127 EA 2010 (discrimination etc in work cases);
- s145A TULR(C)A 1992 (inducements relating to union membership or activities);
- s145B TULR(C)A 1992 (inducements relating to collective bargaining);
- s146 TULR(C)A 1992 (detriment in relation to union membership and activities);
- Paragraph 156 of Schedule A1 TULR(C)A 1992 (detriment in relation to union recognition rights);
- s23 ERA 1996 (unauthorised deductions and payments);
- s48 ERA 1996 (detriment in employment);
- s111 ERA 1996 (unfair dismissal, but see below);
- s163 ERA 1996 (redundancy payments);
- s24 NMWA 1998 (detriment in relation to national minimum wage);
- The Employment Tribunals Extension of Jurisdiction (England and Wales) Order 1994 (SI 1994/1623) (breach of employment contract and termination);
- The Employment Tribunals Extension of Jurisdiction (Scotland) Order 1994 (SI 1994/1624) (corresponding provision for Scotland);
- Regulation 30 of the Working Time Regulations 1998 (SI 1998/1833) (breach of regulations);
- Regulation 32 of the Transnational Information and Consultation of Employees Regulations 1999 (SI 1999/3323) (detriment relating to European Works Councils);
- Regulation 45 of the European Public Limited-Liability Company Regulations 2004 (SI 2004/2326) (detriment in employment);
- Regulation 33 of the Information and Consultation of Employees Regulations 2004 (SI 2004/3426) (detriment in employment);
- Paragraph 8 of the Schedule to the Occupational and Personal Pension Schemes (Consultation by Employers and Miscellaneous Amendment) Regulations 2006 (SI 2006/349) (detriment in employment);
- Regulation 34 of the European Cooperative Society (Involvement of Employees) Regulations 2006 (SI 2006/2059) (detriment in relation to involvement in a European Cooperative Society);
- Regulation 17 of the Cross-border Railway Services (Working Time) Regulations 2008 (SI 2008/1660) (breach of regulations);
- Regulation 9 of the Employment Relations Act 1999 (Blacklists) Regulations 2010 (SI 2010/493) (detriment connected with prohibited list).

Ill health capability dismissals

The ACAS Code's disciplinary provisions only apply in cases where there is *'culpable conduct'* or performance correction or punishment (*Holmes v Qinetiq Ltd* UKEAT/0206/15). In *Holmes,* the claimant was dismissed because of ill-health. No disciplinary procedure was invoked because, apart from the effects of his illness, the claimant was able to perform the job of security guard and there was no suggestion that his conduct or performance gave rise to a disciplinary situation or involved culpable conduct. That meant the employer was not required to follow the ACAS Code of Practice on Disciplinary and Grievance Procedures and the uplift under s207A(2) was not available.

Capability cases involving poor performance are capable of falling within the Code, but only where such performance involves *'culpable conduct'*. The Code does not apply to a capability dismissal arising from ill-health or sickness absence *'and nothing more'*.

Dismissal for Some Other Substantial Reason (SOSR)

In *Phoenix House Ltd v Stockman & Anor* UKEAT/0264/15/DM the EAT held that the disciplinary section of the ACAS Code, and therefore the ACAS uplift, does not apply to dismissals for some other substantial reason where 'misconduct is not alleged and capacity is not in issue'. Mitting J rejected the provisional view expressed by Laing J in *Hussain v Jury's Inn Group Ltd* UKEAT/0283/15/JOJ said that there were 'pointers in both directions' on this issue, holding that 'clear words in the Code' were needed for the ACAS adjustment to apply, and this was not the case in dismissals for Some Other Substantial Reason.

Absolute value

When making an adjustment under these provisions, a Tribunal must take account of the absolute value of a given uplift, rather than just the percentage value. Failure to do so when the award yields 'a significantly large amount in absolute terms' is an error of law (*Acetrip Ltd v Dogra* UKEAT/0238/18/BA). Although *Dogra* was concerned with uplifts, it seems logical that the same principle will also apply to a reduction in compensation.

Order of Adjustments: Where a compensatory award for unfair dismissal falls to be adjusted for unreasonable failure to comply with a relevant code of practice, the adjustment is applied immediately before any reduction for contributory conduct (s123(6)) or reduction due to the receipt of an enhanced redundancy payment in excess of the basic award (s123(7)) (see s124A(a) and *Basic award, Compensatory award, Contributory conduct, Redundancy*).

Example 1

An ex-employee is awarded a basic award of £2,000, a compensatory award of £3,000 and damages for breach of contract of £500. The employer is found to have unreasonably failed to comply with a relevant code of practice and an uplift of 25% is applied to the applicable awards. The calculation would be as follows:

The basic award remains as £2,000 because the uplift does not apply to this award.

The compensatory award is now £3,000 x 1.25 = £3,750

The damages for wrongful dismissal are now £500 x 1.25 = £625

Example 2

An ex-employee would be awarded a basic award of £2,000, a compensatory award of £3,000 and damages for breach of contract of £500. However, he received an enhanced redundancy payment of £2,500. The employee is found to have unreasonably failed to comply with a relevant code of practice and a deduction of 25% is applied to the applicable awards. The calculation would be as follows:

The basic award is reduced to zero because of the enhanced redundancy payment, but there remains £500 of enhanced redundancy payment to put into the

calculation of the compensatory award: £2,500 - £2,000 = £500

The compensatory award is now (£3,000 x 0.75) - £500 = £1,750

The damages for wrongful dismissal are now £500 x 0.75 = £375

Statutory authorities: ERA 1996 *s123(6), 123(7)* and *s124A(a)*; TULR(C)A *Schedule A2*

Relevant case law: *Acetrip Ltd v Dogra* UKEAT/0238/18/BA; *Holmes v Qinetiq Ltd* UKEAT/0206/15/BA; *Local Government Yorkshire & Humber v Shah* UKEAT/0587/11/ZT; *Phoenix House Ltd v Stockman & Anor* UKEAT/0264/15/DM

Accelerated/decelerated receipt

(see also *Adjustments and order of adjustments; Table 38*)

Accelerated receipt

If an award is made to a claimant to compensate for future losses, they are in fact receiving the money before they would have received it if they had not been dismissed. The idea behind the discount for accelerated receipt, therefore, is to take into account any interest that might in fact be earned on this money if it were invested as a lump sum, when it would not ordinarily have been available to the claimant to do so.

A discount for accelerated receipt can be made on awards for future loss, including the compensatory award and an award for financial losses in a discrimination claim. The reduction will only apply to future losses, such as future income and benefits.

No discount will need to be applied if the award for future loss is relatively small, as will often be the case (see *Les Ambassadeurs Club v Bainda* [1982] IRLR 5).

There is no established route to calculate the appropriate reduction. Tribunals sometimes merely apply a single percentage adjustment to recognise accelerated receipt. However, in *Bentwood Bros (Manchester) Ltd v Shepherd* [2003] IRLR 364 the Court of Appeal overturned a decision to make a single 5% reduction for an award that covered 10 years' loss. It will always be necessary for a tribunal to set out the method it has used and its reasons for using it.

Decelerated receipt

Melia v Magna Kansei Ltd [2005] EWCA Civ 1547 holds that in principle an uplift can be applied for decelerated, or delayed, receipt to ensure that past and future losses are treated consistently.

those in England and Wales, are not legally bound by the decision of the Court of Appeal in *De Souza*. The President of the Employment Tribunals (Scotland) has said that the relevant awards in Scotland should be uprated in line with *De Souza* but employment judges in Scotland would be entitled to come to a different view on the matter and to quantify awards accordingly. Employment Judges should, if they decline to apply the *Simmons v Castle* uplift, set out their reasons for so doing.

Other relevant factors

Proof of injury: It is not inevitable that a tribunal will award an injury to feelings award where it is permitted to, though it is very unusual for no such award to be made. It is necessary for the individual to prove the nature of the injury to feelings and its extent, though this could be at its simplest the fact that a claimant has stated he was upset by his dismissal (see *Murray v Powertech (Scotland) Ltd* [1992] IRLR 257 and *Ministry of Defence v Cannock* [1994] ICR 918). The evidence a claimant will want to produce is the material which shows the impact of the discrimination on any subjective feelings of upset, frustration, worry, anxiety, mental distress, fear, grief, anguish, humiliation, unhappiness, stress and depression. For example, this might include evidence about the impact the discrimination has had on relationships with colleagues, friends and family and any particular difficulties caused by the discrimination. Such evidence might include medical evidence, but where the injury to feelings amounts to a mental illness such as depression, the claimant might well consider seeking an award for personal injury in addition to injury to feelings.

Double recovery: Where an individual is awarded sums both for injury to feelings and personal injury (e.g. depression) caused by the discrimination, the injury to feelings and personal injury awards must compensate for different injuries and not overlap. The consequence is that for example where discrimination has caused a period of depression, either the injury to feelings award or the personal injuries award will be less than would be appropriate if only one of the awards had been made**.**

Claimant's knowledge: It is not necessary for an injury to feelings award to be made that the claimant's injured feelings are caused by his knowledge that he has been discriminated against, contrary to the interpretation given to *Skyrail Oceanic Ltd v Coleman* [1981] IRLR 398. The EAT in *Taylor v XLN Telecom Ltd* [2010] IRLR 49 held that the calculation of the remedy for discrimination is the same as in other torts, and that knowledge of the discriminator's motives was not necessary for recovery of injury to feelings. The EAT nevertheless observed that the distress and humiliation suffered by a claimant will generally be greater where the discrimination has

been overt or the claimant appreciates at the time that the motivation was discriminatory.

Separate awards for separate grounds of discrimination: Where an individual has suffered a number of acts of discrimination, some caused by one protected ground, e.g. race, others by another protected ground, e.g. disability, the tribunal should make separate awards for each protected ground, as each is a separate wrong giving a right to damages (see *Al Jumard v Clywd Leisure Ltd* [2008] IRLR 345). However, where the discriminatory acts overlap as they arise from the same set of facts, such as where a dismissal is on grounds of both race and disability, a tribunal will not be expected to separate the injury to feelings and attribute parts to each form of discrimination. This may not necessarily result in an increased award compared to the situation where all the acts of discrimination are caused by one protected characteristic, as the tribunal must always have regard to the proportionality of the overall figure awarded for injury to feelings.

Future contingencies: Where the discriminatory act, such as a dismissal, would have occurred at some point in the future for legitimate reasons in any event, it is not appropriate to reduce the injury to feelings award to reflect that future possibility. The award reflects the injury to feelings caused by the knowledge that the reason for the act was discrimination, which cannot be offset by the fact that a lawful dismissal may have been carried out in any event (see *O'Donoghue v Redcar and Cleveland Borough Council* [2001] IRLR 615).

Adjustments: Interest can be awarded on the sum for injury to feelings (see *Interest*). Tribunals are required to consider interest whether or not an application has been made by a party (see *Komeng v Creative Support Ltd* UKEAT/0275/18/JOJ).

Reg 6(1)(a) of the Industrial Tribunals (Interest on Awards in Discrimination Cases) Regulations 1996 provides that the period over which interest accrues begins with the date of the discrimination and ends on the date the tribunal calculates compensation.

A percentage increase or reduction up to a maximum of 25% can be applied to reflect a failure by the employer or employee to comply with the ACAS disciplinary code of practice (see *ACAS*).

A *Polkey*-type deduction should not be applied to the award, even if the claimant would have been fairly dismissed at a date soon afterwards (*O'Donoghue v Redcar and Cleveland Borough Council* [2001] IRLR 615).

Tax: Awards for injury to feelings unrelated to termination of employment are tax-free, as are such awards related to the termination of employment prior to 6 April 2018 (*Moorthy v HMRC* [2018] EWCA Civ 847). However, from 6 April 2018, any compensation for injury to feelings in a termination payment will be taxable to the extent that the £30,000 'allowance' has been exceeded, following an amendment to s406 ITEPA 2003, except where the compensation is for a psychiatric injury.

Recoupment: N/A

Relevant case law: *A v HM Revenue & Customs* [2009]; *Al Jumard v Clwyd Leisure Ltd* [2008] IRLR 345; *De Souza v Vinci Construction UK Limited* UKEAT/0328/14/DXA; *De Souza v Vinci Construction (UK) Ltd* [2017] EWCA Civ 879; *Dunnachie v Kingston upon Hull City Council* [2004] UKHL 36; *Ministry of Defence v Cannock* [1994] ICR 918; *Moorthy v The Commissioners for Her Majesty's Revenue & Customs* [2014] UKFTT 834 (TC); *Moorthy v Revenue & Customs* [2016] UKUT 13 (TCC); *Moorthy v HMRC* [2018] EWCA Civ 847; *Murray v Powertech (Scotland) Ltd* [1992] IRLR 257; *O'Donoghue v Redcar and Cleveland Borough Council* [2001] IRLR 615; *Prison Service v Johnson* [1997] IRLR 162; *Gomes v Higher Level Care Ltd* [2018] EWCA Civ 418; *Grange v Abellio London Ltd* UKEAT/0304/17/JOJ; *Komeng v Creative Support Ltd* UKEAT/0275/18/JOJ; *Skyrail Oceanic Ltd v Coleman* [1981] IRLR 398; *Taylor v XLN Telecom Ltd* [2010] IRLR 49; *Vento v Chief Constable of West Yorkshire Police* [2002] EWCA Civ 1871; *Voith Turbo Ltd v Stowe* [2005] IRLR 228

Insolvency

The Redundancy Payments Service ("RPS") operates a scheme whereby the National Insurance Fund ("NIF") will make certain payments to ex-employees of an insolvent employer where certain conditions are satisfied (see ss182 to 190 ERA 1996). The ex-employee must make a claim to the RPS, who may make payments for a limited amount of the debts of the employer to the ex-employee. The debts covered are (s184):

- any arrears of pay in respect of one or more weeks, capped at 8 weeks (this includes Equal Pay claims);

- statutory notice pay;

- up to 6 weeks holiday pay accruing over the 12 months before 'the appropriate date';

- any basic award for unfair dismissal; and

- any reasonable sum by way of reimbursement of the whole or part of any fee or premium paid by an apprentice or articled clerk.

Unpaid maternity pay, paternity pay or sick pay cannot be claimed from the RPS under the insolvency rules. Maternity pay should be claimed from HMRC and sick pay from the DWP.

Sections 184(2) to 184(6) define what may amount to arrears of pay (which includes amongst other matters

a guarantee payment and a protective award), what amounts to holiday pay and what may amount to 'a reasonable sum'.

Sums due under a Sex Equality Clause (i.e. an Equal Pay claim) amount to 'arrears of pay' within the meaning of ss182 and 184 (*Graysons Restaurants Ltd v Jones and Ors* [2019] EWCA Civ 725).

The debts must have been due on 'the appropriate date' which is defined in s185, and depending on the nature of the debt may be the date of the formal insolvency of the employer, the date of termination of employment or the date on which the award was made (for example if the debt is the basic award or an unpaid protective award).

Where an individual has applied to the Redundancy Payments Service for payment, but it has not been made, or payment has not been made in full he can make a claim to the employment tribunal (s188 ERA 1996).

Under s124 Pension Schemes Act 1993 there is a comparable scheme for requesting (and enforcing) payment from the NIF for unpaid pension contributions.

Remedy: Where a tribunal upholds a claim for payment, the tribunal will make a declaration to that effect stating the amount that ought to be paid to the ex-employee from the NIF.

Calculation of remedy

Various limits apply to the entitlement of the ex-employee to be paid certain debts:

- Arrears of pay are limited to 8 weeks, with each week capped at £544 (or an appropriate proportion of that if the debt arises from part of a week) (ss184 and 186 ERA 1996);

- Statutory notice pay is anyway capped at 12 weeks, and each week is capped at £544 (or an appropriate proportion of that if the debt arises from part of a week) (ss184 and 186 ERA 1996);

- Holiday pay is limited to 6 weeks, with each week capped at £544 (or an appropriate proportion of that if the debt arises from part of a week) (ss184 and s186 ERA 1996).

Gross or net: Gross. A week's pay as defined in ss220 to 229 ERA 1996 applies (see *Week's pay*).

Limit on a week's pay: £544 (see *Table 1* for historical rates).

Limit on number of weeks: See individual limits above.

Any maximum or minimum: Maximum = £4,352 (arrears) + £6,528 (notice pay) + £16,320 (basic award/ redundancy) + £3,264 (holiday pay) = £30,464; No minimum

Adjustments: None

Mitigation: The nature of the underlying debt will determine whether the duty to mitigate applies. For example, the ex-employee is under a duty to mitigate their loss for failure to pay wages for the length of the statutory notice period, but there is no duty to mitigate loss in relation to a protective award or a basic award (see *Mitigation* and *Protective award*).

Any state benefits that have been received, or could have been claimed, will be deducted (see the Government's webpage on '*Your rights if your employer is insolvent*').

Tax: Any arrears of pay/protective award and accrued holiday pay will have income tax and national insurance deducted at the basic rate. 'Notional' tax, equivalent to the basic rate, will be deducted from compensation for failure to give statutory notice (this tax is not actually paid to HMRC but may be claimed back by the employee if their total income for the year is less than their personal allowance). The basic award will not be taxed at all unless it exceeds £30,000, which will in practice never happen because of the statutory limit.

Recoupment: Recoupment does not apply. Any state benefits received will be deducted from the award.

Statutory authorities: ERA 1996 *ss182 to 190*; Pension Schemes Act 1993 *s124*; TULR(C)A 1992 *s188*

Relevant case law: *Graysons Restaurants Ltd v Jones and Ors* [2019] EWCA Civ 725

Insurance

Under the Third Parties (Rights Against Insurers) Act 2010, where a person has insurance cover against a particular liability, or becomes insolvent, the rights under that insurance contract covering that liability transfer to the relevant claimant. That claimant can then bring a claim against the insurer directly before having established the liability in question (but will have to establish the liability before the right itself can be enforced). The EAT has held in *Watson v Hemingway Design Ltd (in liquidation) and others* [2019] UKEAT/0007/19 that Employment Tribunals have jurisdiction to hear such proceedings.

Interest

(see also *Discrimination; Financial penalties on employers; Injury to feelings; Table 12*)

There are two different situations in which interest is available on a tribunal award. First, where a tribunal award has not been paid interest accrues on the unpaid sum (see *Interest on unpaid compensation*). Secondly, a tribunal is able to award interest in discrimination claims brought under the EA 2010 as part of its award of compensation, to compensate for the fact

that compensation has been awarded after the loss compensated for has been suffered (see *Interest on discrimination awards*).

Interest on discrimination awards

A tribunal is able to award interest on awards of compensation made in discrimination claims brought under s124(2)(b) EA 2010, to compensate for the fact that compensation has been awarded after the relevant loss has been suffered (see s139 EA 2010, EA 2010 (Commencement No 4 etc) Order SI 2010/2317 and IT(IADC) Regs 1996).

The tribunal may award interest to the following types of discrimination award:

- Past financial loss;
- Injury to feelings;
- Aggravated and exemplary damages; and
- Physical and psychiatric injury.

Since a tribunal cannot award interest on past loss within a compensatory award for unfair dismissal, where an unfair dismissal is also a discriminatory dismissal, tribunals will often compensate such losses under the discrimination legislation.

Calculation: Interest is calculated as simple interest accruing from day to day (Reg 3(1)).

Interest rate: Until 29 July 2013 the interest rate to be applied in England and Wales was that prescribed for the special investment account under rule 27(1) of the Court Funds Rules 1987. The interest rate until 29 July 2013 was 0.5%. For claims presented on or after 29 July 2013 the relevant interest rate is that specified in s17 of the Judgments Act 1838 (see The Employment Tribunals (Interest on Awards in Discrimination Cases) (Amendment) Regulations 2013).

The interest rate now to be applied is 8% (see *Table 12* for a list of interest rates). It is important to note that, although the interest rate is currently the same in England and Wales and in Scotland, that has not always been the position nor will it necessarily be so in the future.

If the rate of interest changes during the period over which interest is calculated, the tribunal may use such median or average of those rates as seems to it appropriate, in the interests of simplicity (see The Industrial Tribunals (Interest on Awards in Discrimination Cases) Regulations 1996 Reg 3(3)).

Period of calculation, injury to feelings: interest is awarded on injury to feelings awards from the date of the act of discrimination complained of until the date on which the tribunal calculates the compensation (see Reg 6(1)(a) IT(IADC) Regs 1996).

Period of calculation, all other sums: interest is

awarded on all sums other than injury to feelings awards from the mid-point of the date of the act of discrimination complained of and the date the tribunal calculates the award (Reg 6(1)(b) IT(IADC) Regs 1996). The mid-point date is the date half way through the period between the date of the discrimination complained of and the date the tribunal calculates the award (Reg 4 IT(IADC) Regs 1996).

Period of calculation, early payment: where payment of any of the sums attracting interest has already been made by the respondent, the date of payment is taken as the date of calculation of the award for those particular sums (Reg 6(2) IT(IADC) Regs 1996).

Period of calculation, serious injustice discretion: where a tribunal considers that serious injustice would be caused if interest were to be calculated according to the approaches above, it can calculate interest on such different periods as it considers appropriate (Reg 6(3) IT(IADC) Regs 1996). See *Ministry of Defence v Cannock* [1994] IRLR 509, where interest was awarded over a longer period than provided for by the regulations due to the long period since the loss was incurred.

Interest cannot be awarded in respect of future loss or loss arising before the discrimination complained of (Reg 5 IT(IADC) Regs 1996). This reflects the broad principle behind the award of interest which is that it is compensation to the successful claimant for the loss they have suffered by virtue of not having received payment of the award at the date of the loss suffered.

Worked examples

Interest on past loss
Interest runs from the 'mid-point' date to the date of calculation. The mid-point is calculated as the date halfway between the date of the discriminatory act and ending on the calculation date (usually the judgment date). Interest accrues from day to day and is simple rather than compound.

Interest = (number of days from discriminatory act date to calculation date x 1/2 x interest rate x 1/100 x 1/365 x compensatory award (after all adjustments have been made - see *Adjustments and order of adjustments*).

Example 1

Compensation award = £20,000

Discriminatory date = 01/04/2019

Calculation date = 05/02/2021

Interest rate = 8%

Number of days between discriminatory date and calculation date = 676 inclusive

Interest = 676 ÷ 2 x 0.08 x 1/365 x 20,000 = £1,481.64

(the number of days have been divided by 2 because of the mid-point rule)

Interest on Injury to feelings
Interest runs from the date of the discriminatory act to the date of calculation. Interest accrues from day to day and is simple rather than compound.

Example 2

Injury to feelings award = £5,000

Discriminatory date = 01/04/2019

Calculation date = 05/02/2021

Interest rate = 8%

Number of days = 676 inclusive

Interest = 676 x 0.08 x 1/365 x 5,000 = £740.82

Interest on Physical and psychiatric injury and Aggravated damages
Interest on physical and psychiatric injury runs from the 'mid-point' date to the date of calculation. The mid-point date is calculated as the date half way between the discriminatory act and the calculation date (usually the judgment date). Interest accrues from day to day and is simple rather than compound.

The calculation works in exactly the same way as that for interest on past loss.

Any maximum or minimum: There is no minimum, and interest does not have to be awarded if the tribunal considers it would be unjust to do so (Reg 2). The maximum would be determined by the interest rate in force during the relevant period.

Adjustments: Interest is calculated after the final adjustments have been made to the award and after enhanced redundancy has been deducted (see *Adjustments and order of adjustments*).

Tax: Interest is awarded on the net loss suffered by the individual, see *Bentwood Bros (Manchester) Ltd v Shepherd* [2003] IRLR 364. Any grossing up, if required, will apply after interest has been calculated (see *Grossing up*).

Recoupment: The recoupment regulations do not apply to discrimination claims and hence they will not apply to any interest awarded.

Statutory authorities: *Court Funds Rules 1987 r27(1); Judgments Act 1838 s17; The Employment Tribunals (Interest on Awards in Discrimination Cases) (Amendment) Regulations 2013; The Industrial Tribunals (Interest on Awards in Discrimination Cases) Regulations 1996 Reg 3(3)*

Interest on unpaid compensation

If the employer fails to pay the compensation that has been awarded to the claimant within a certain prescribed time period, interest will accrue on unpaid sums. Interest is calculated as simple interest accruing from day to day.

In both discriminatory and non-discriminatory cases interest will start accruing from the date of the judgment but no interest will be payable if the award is paid within 14 days of the judgment.

Any sums withheld on account of the recoupment regulations will not accrue interest.

Interest is not payable on a sum due under a re-engagement order where the employer declines to re-engage the employee (*Fotheringhame v Barclays Services Ltd* UKEAT/0208/19/BA). It is likely that the same principle applies to an order for reinstatement.

Interim relief

Where a claim for unfair dismissal is brought, and where it is alleged that the reason or principal reason for the dismissal was for one of a number of protected reasons, the claimant may claim interim relief. Specific procedural rules apply, including that the claim must be brought within 7 days of the effective date of termination (see ss161 to 163 TULR(C)A 1992 and ss128 to 129 ERA 1996). The protected reasons are:

- Relating to enforcement of rights given to shop and betting shop workers, s100(1)(a) and (b) (see s128(1)(a)(i));

- Relating to acting as a representative under the WTR 1998, s101A(d) (see s128(1)(a)(i));

- Relating to performing the functions of a pensions trustee, s102(1) (see s128(1)(a)(i));

- Performing the functions of an employee representative, s103 (see s128(1)(a)(i));

- Making a protected disclosure, s103A (see s128(1)(a)(i));

- Relating to action over trade union recognition, para 161(2) Sch 1A TULR(C)A 1992 (see s128(1)(a)(ii));

- Relating to blacklisting, s104F(1) (see s128(1)(b));

- Membership of a trade union, participating in its activities, or making use of trade union services, s152(1)(a), (b) and (c) TULR(C)A 1992 (see s161(1) TULR(C)A 1992);

- Refusing to accept an offer to give up membership or collective bargaining rights, s152(bb) TULR(C)A 1992 (see s161(1) TULR(C)A 1992).

Remedy: If at the hearing of an application for interim relief it appears to the tribunal that the claim for unfair dismissal is likely to succeed (defined as a '"*pretty good" chance of succeeding*' in *Taplin v C Shippam Ltd* [1978] ICR 1068), the tribunal will announce its findings and explain to the parties its powers and how it can exercise them.

The tribunal must be persuaded that *all* elements of an automatic unfair dismissal claim are likely to succeed before granting interim relief. This includes, for example, any issue of employee status or whether there was a dismissal at all (see *Hancock v Ter-Berg and another* UKEAT/0138/19/BA).

If the employer is willing, pending the final determination of the unfair dismissal complaint, the tribunal can order that the employee be reinstated or re-engaged. Otherwise, the tribunal will make an order that the contract of employment is continued. Such an order has the effect that, until the unfair dismissal complaint is determined, the contract of employment continues for the purposes of pay, seniority, pension rights and similar matters, and for continuity of employment.

Either party may apply to the tribunal for the revocation or variation of such an order on the grounds that there has been a relevant change in circumstances (see s165 TULR(C)A 1992 and s131 ERA 1992).

If a claimant makes a complaint, and the tribunal finds, that the employer has failed to comply with an order for reinstatement or re-engagement, the tribunal will make an order for the continuation of the contract of employment and such compensation as it considers just and equitable in all the circumstances having regard to the infringement of the order and the loss suffered as a consequence.

If a claimant makes a complaint, and the tribunal finds, that the employer has failed to comply with an order for the continuation of the contract of employment, it will make an order for such compensation as it considers just and equitable in all the circumstances having regard to the infringement of the order and the loss suffered as a consequence (see s166 TULR(C)A or s132 ERA 1996).

If an ET makes an order for the continuation of the contract of employment at an interim relief hearing, and subsequently at the full hearing the claimant loses and the respondent is successful, it is unlikely that the claimant will have to repay the interim relief payments (see *Initial Textile Services v Rendell* [1991] UKEAT 383/91/230).

Gross or net: The award of any unpaid salary will be made gross under the continuing contract of employment and subject to PAYE (but see *Tax* below).

Tax: Payments under an interim relief order are

taxable as payments in connection with termination of employment under s401 **not** in full as earnings under s62 ITEPA (see also *Tax and termination payments*). See *Turullols v HMRC* where the First Tier Tribunal held that the claimant, who was found to have been unfairly dismissed, could claim back the tax that had been paid on the salary payments made under the interim relief order because they were payments in connection with the termination of her employment and therefore should have been tax-free up to £30,000. This would also have been the case even if the ET had ruled that the dismissal was fair.

Cap: There is no statutory cap, and this award falls outside the compensatory award (see s166 TULR(C)A 1992 and s132 ERA 196).

Statutory authorities: ERA 1996 *ss128 to 132*; TULR(C)A 1992 *ss161 to 166*

Relevant case law: *Hancock v Ter-Berg and another UKEAT/0138/19/BA; Initial Textile Services v Rendell* [1991] UKEAT 383/91/230; *Taplin v C Shippam Ltd* [1978] ICR 1068; *Turullols v Revenue & Customs* [2014] UKFTT 672 (TC)

Itemised pay statement

A worker has the right to be given by his employer, at or before the time at which any payment of wages or salary is made to him, a written itemised pay statement (s8 ERA 1996). Where an employer does not give a worker a statement as required (either because the employer gives the worker no statement or because the statement the employer gives does not comply with what is required), the worker may require a reference to be made to an employment tribunal to determine what particulars ought to have been included or referred to in a statement so as to comply with the requirements of the section concerned.

Calculation: Where the tribunal finds that an itemised pay statement has not been given to the worker and further that any unnotified deductions have been made from the pay of the worker during the period of 13 weeks immediately preceding the date of the application for the reference (whether or not the deductions were made in breach of the contract of employment), the tribunal may order the employer to pay the worker a sum not exceeding the aggregate of the unnotified deductions so made (s12(4) ERA 1996).

Gross or net: Gross

Limit on a week's pay: None

Limit on number of weeks: 13

Any maximum or minimum: None

Adjustments: N/A

Tax: The employer will deduct tax and national insurance as normal if the worker is still employed. However, if the worker is no longer in employment, the worker will be responsible for declaring this income on their self-assessment.

Statutory authorities: ERA 1996 *ss8* and *12(4)*

Job seekers allowance

(see also *Recoupment*)

There are 3 types of job seekers allowance (JSA):

- Contribution-based where the claimant has paid enough national insurance contributions during their employment;
- 'New style' JSA, also based on NI contributions;
- Income-based, where the claimant has not paid enough national contributions as an employee but was on a low wage. Universal Credit has replaced income-based JSA for most people.

Receipt of job seeker's allowance should be treated in 2 different ways, depending on whether the claim is for damages for wrongful dismissal or compensation for unfair dismissal.

Damages

Credit should be given for any job seekers allowance received during the damages period and during the statutory notice period. However, as with other state benefits, it could be argued that full credit should not be given if the employee did not receive their statutory notice period or payment in lieu, because they would exhaust their entitlement to state benefits sooner than they would have done if they had received their statutory notice.

Compensatory award

Job seekers allowance is not deducted from the compensatory award but is instead subject to the recoupment regulations (see *Recoupment*).

Adjustments: See *Recoupment* (Prescribed element)

Cap: See *Recoupment* (Prescribed element)

Recoupment: Only for compensation for unfair dismissal. Recoupment does not apply to wrongful dismissal.

Statutory authorities: The Employment Protection (Recoupment of Jobseeker's Allowance and Income Support) Regulations 1996

Judicial assessment and mediation

These two forms of Alternative Dispute Resolution are offered by tribunals in appropriate cases, and expressly considered at case management Preliminary Hearings.

Judicial Assessment

The principles and protocol are set out in the *Presidential Guidance – Rule 3 – Protocol on Judicial Assessment*.

Assessment is to take place at the first case management preliminary hearing, only after the identification of the issues and the making of case management orders. It is considered suitable for most cases and parties are encouraged to inform the tribunal in advance of their wish to undergo this procedure. Both parties must consent, and the process is strictly confidential. It is also free.

The assessment consists of a provisional Early Neutral Evaluation of the merits of liability and/or remedy by an Employment Judge.

Although Judicial Assessment has been around for some time, it does not appear to be used much in practice. At the first case management preliminary hearing there is usually a substantial gap between the parties on the facts, and the tribunal will either not have a copy of the documents that might shed light on the dispute, or not be able to adjudicate a dispute of oral evidence. The decision has to be made by a time-pressed judge who is unlikely to have all relevant factual material to hand. The risk of such a process is that an erroneous judicial assessment may render a dispute more intractable by locking the parties into an erroneous assessment of their cases.

From a remedy perspective, Judicial Assessment may be suitable where one party has unrealistic views of the quantum of their case that are easily identifiable without the need to resolve complex questions of fact or significant conflicts of evidence.

Judicial Mediation

This is a free service conducted by an Employment Judge over the course of a single day at the Employment Tribunal. Following an initial opening session, the parties sit in separate rooms and a Judge conducts 'shuttle diplomacy' between them.

Judicial Mediators tend to be facilitative rather than evaluative, focusing on relaying each party's position to the other side, and testing the realism of each party's position. The aim is to help each side understand the other's position, identify common ground and seek agreement.

The mediation is conducted on a Without Prejudice

basis with the Judicial Mediator having no further involvement in the case following the mediation.

Although there are no formal criteria for Judicial Mediation, it tends to be offered in cases lasting more than 3 days and/or where there is a continuing employment relationship between the parties (these requirements have been relaxed during the Covid-19 pandemic). The tribunal has to be satisfied that the mediation has a real prospect of success.

Leave for family and domestic reasons, maternity, paternity, adoption, shared parental: see *Detriment; Parental bereavement leave; Time off (various)*

Limitation period

This is the maximum period allowed between the act complained of and when the claim should be lodged at the ET (see *Table 18*).

Loss of chance

Once a tribunal has upheld a complaint of unlawful treatment such as discrimination or unfair dismissal, it is necessary for it to assess the remedy available to the claimant. Where the remedy includes an award to compensate for financial loss, it will be necessary to identify the sums the claimant would have received had the unlawful conduct not taken place. For a dismissal, in a straightforward case this will be the salary that would have been earned by the claimant.

In assessing the loss suffered by the claimant, the tribunal will take into account the chance of events having occurred following the unlawful act, and determine the award on the basis of the loss of that chance. For example, if there was a 25% chance that an individual would have been dismissed fairly in any event 6 months after their unlawful dismissal, the tribunal will calculate the losses suffered after that date as 75% of salary etc. that would have been earned had the individual remained in employment after that event.

Another example would be an individual who had, say, a 50% chance of being promoted shortly after their unlawful dismissal, where the tribunal could award future losses based on 50% of the increased salary to reflect the chance of it having been obtained (see *O'Donoghue v Redcar and Cleveland Borough Council* [2001] IRLR 615 and *Ministry of Defence v Wheeler* [1998] IRLR 23).

Where the chance of a future event is very high, or very low, the tribunal may well treat the chance as 100% or

0% as appropriate (see *Timothy James Consulting Ltd v Wilton* UKEAT/0082/14/DXA). There is no guideline cut off for such marginal chances.

The *Polkey* reduction is an example of this approach in the unfair dismissal context (see *Polkey*), but in considering the future actions of the employer the tribunal will take account of the actions of a reasonable employer (see *Abbey National v Formso* [1999] ICR 222). In discrimination cases the tribunal will seek to determine the future conduct of the actual employer. It will require evidence to demonstrate the chances of future events occurring (see *Wardle v Credit Agricole Corporate & Investment Bank* [2011] IRLR 604 and *Chagger v Abbey National plc & Anor* [2010] IRLR 47). Statistical evidence may well be relevant and admissible (see *Vento v Chief Constable of West Yorkshire Police* [2003] ICR 318).

Marginal tax rate

(see also *Grossing up*)

The marginal tax rate is a single tax rate that could be applied to a claimant's award when grossing up (see *Grossing up*). When deciding on the marginal tax rate, account should be taken of the claimant's personal tax free allowance (which can be found from their tax code at the date of dismissal), earnings already received in that tax year (including since dismissal), the relevant tax thresholds (see *Table 7*, *Table 8* and *Table 9*) and any other income the claimant may earn in the remainder of that tax year. The calculations are straightforward if a single tax rate is used but this is not always the appropriate approach.

Differential tax rates

Different tax rates may apply to different elements of the award (see *Yorkshire Housing Ltd v Cuerden* [2010] UKEAT/0397/09). However, the calculations are not straightforward and there is the added complication of a tapering personal allowance for earnings/tribunal awards between £100,000 and £125,140 (for the tax year 2021/22). See *Grossing up* for worked examples where differential tax rates are used.

Tax year

The relevant tax year for grossing up is the year the award is received by the claimant. Any adjustment to the award in subsequent tax years (e.g. upon reconsideration of a judgment) should be grossed up by reference to that subsequent tax year (*PA Finlay & Co Ltd v Finlay* UKEAT/0260/14).

Maternity Equality Clause

Women on maternity leave must receive any increases in pay due to them at the time they would have received them, had they not been on maternity leave and their pay, when they return, must reflect the increases they would have had, had they not been absent. The Maternity Equality Clause (s73 EA 2010) modifies the woman's contract so that her maternity related pay is increased in line with any actual increase in pay, or any increase that she would have been paid had she not been on maternity leave.

The tribunal has jurisdiction to determine a complaint relating to breach of an equality clause under s127 EA 2010.

Remedy: Arrears of up to 6 years' actual pay may be ordered (s132 EA 2010).

Gross or net: Gross

Limit on a week's pay: None

Limit on number of years: 6

Any maximum or minimum: None

Tax: Taxable under s62 ITEPA 2003.

Statutory authorities: EA 2010 ss73, 127 and 132

Maternity: see *Detriment; Maternity Equality Clause; Unfair dismissal; Table 16*

Maximum compensatory award: see *Statutory cap*

Minimum wage: see *National Minimum Wage*

Misconduct: see *Contributory conduct*

Money purchase pension scheme: see *Pension loss*

Mitigation

It is a fundamental principle that any claimant will be expected to mitigate the losses they suffer as a result of an unlawful act by giving credit, for example for earnings in a new job (mitigation in fact), and that the tribunal will not make an award to cover losses that could reasonably have been avoided (mitigation in law). For example, an unfairly dismissed employee is expected to search for other work, and will not recover losses beyond a date by which the tribunal concludes the individual ought reasonably to have been able to find new employment at a similar rate of pay. Such an individual may be awarded the difference between the salary of a lower paid new job, and their previous salary, for a period until the tribunal concludes they could reasonably have found similarly well paid work.

The claimant is expected to take reasonable steps to minimise the losses suffered as a consequence of the unlawful act. The burden of proving a failure to mitigate is on the respondent (*Fyfe v Scientific Furnishing Ltd* [1989] IRLR 331). It is insufficient for a respondent merely to show that the claimant failed to take a step that it was reasonable for them to take: rather, the respondent has to prove that the claimant acted unreasonably. There is a difference between acting reasonably and not acting unreasonably. If the claimant has failed to take a reasonable step, the respondent has to show that any such failure was *unreasonable* (*Wright v Silverline Car Caledonia Ltd* UKEATS/0008/16). The tribunal will consider:

1) what steps the claimant should have taken to mitigate his or her losses;

2) whether it was *un*reasonable for the claimant to have failed to take any such steps; and

3) if so, the date from which an alternative income would have been obtained.

A percentage reduction to compensation may be applied as an alternative, but only '*where the facts are so uncertain*' that it is a more logical approach than applying an end date. A tribunal that adopts this method '*should be in a position to justify the adoption of a crude approach*', and risks being overturned on appeal: *Hakim v The Scottish Trade Unions Congress* UKEATS/0047/19/SS.

A summary of the relevant principles can be found in *Cooper Contracting Ltd v Lindsey* UKEAT/0184/15/JOJ at paragraph 16.

The duty arises only after dismissal, so a failure to take up an alternative job offer made before that date will not constitute a failure to mitigate. It may be reasonable to attempt to mitigate loss by setting up a new business or becoming self-employed (see *Cooper Contracting Ltd v Lindsey* UKEAT/0184/15/JOJ and *Gardiner-Hill v Roland Berger Technics Ltd* [1982] IRLR 498) or by retraining (see *Sealy v Avon Aluminium Co Ltd* UKEAT/515/78, *Holroyd v Gravure Cylinders Ltd* [1984] IRLR 259 and *Orthet Ltd v Vince-Cain* [2004] IRLR 857).

The question of reasonableness is to be determined by the tribunal itself, with the claimant's wishes and views simply one of the factors in its analysis. Tribunals are encouraged not to apply too demanding a standard of the claimant.

Mitigation and 'good industrial relations practice'

An unfairly dismissed employee will not need to give credit for earnings received from a new job during the notice period where good industrial relations practice would have required payment in lieu of notice to the employee (see *Norton Tool Co Ltd v Tewson* [1973] All ER 183 and *Voith Turbo Ltd v Stowe* [2005] IRLR 228). However, the principle does not apply to constructive dismissal (*Stuart Peters Ltd v Bell* [2009] IRLR 941).

Dismissal from subsequent employment

Dismissal from a new job does not automatically break the chain of causation. Where, for example, a new job only partially mitigates an employee's loss of earnings, dismissal from that job may not sever the causal link between the respondent's act and the difference in earnings. A tribunal may therefore continue to award the difference in earnings between the old job and the new job after the claimant has left the new job (provided he or she is not earning more elsewhere): *Hakim v The Scottish Trade Unions Congress* UKEATS/0047/19/SS.

Mitigation and receipt of pension

In *Knapton v ECC Card Clothing Ltd* [2006] IRLR 756 the EAT held that credit does not need to be given for the early receipt of pension following dismissal, as it is deferred wages not a sum analogous to incapacity benefit which would be brought into account. However, if an individual is dismissed after the date when the pension can be drawn and there is no reduction in the value of the pension by being drawn at dismissal, it may be that a failure to draw the pension would be seen as a failure to mitigate a loss, and a sum for which the ex-employer should receive credit.

National Insurance Contributions

An unemployed person may receive Class 1 National Insurance credits to fill any gaps in their national insurance contributions (these contributions are automatically made if the person claims JSA). However, Reg 7(1) of The Social Security (Unemployment, Sickness and Invalidity Benefit) Regulations 1983 SI 1983/1598 states that if the person has received compensation for unfair dismissal, they are not entitled to receive national insurance contributions for the same period. If the person is unemployed for a long time, this could affect their entitlement to a state pension and other state benefits. The loss of NI contributions can therefore be claimed from the employer as a head of loss. The amount of compensation is fixed by reference to the weekly Class 3 NIC rate which is currently £15.40 per week (tax year 2021/22).

Remedy: Compensation per week = weekly Class 3 NIC rate.

Limit on a week's pay: The Class 3 NIC rate

Limit on number of weeks: None

Any maximum or minimum: None

Adjustments: Loss of NIC will form part of the compensatory award or damages and thus will be adjusted along with these awards.

Recoupment: Recoupment does not apply to this head of loss.

Statutory authorities: Social Security (Unemployment, Sickness and Invalidity Benefit) Regulations 1983 (SI 1983/1598) *Reg 7(1)*

National Living Wage: see *National Minimum Wage*

National Minimum Wage

(see also *Unlawful deductions from wages; Table 15*)

A broad range of workers are entitled to receive the national minimum wage. The rate depends upon the age of the worker and whether they qualify for an apprentice rate or, if an agricultural worker, the agricultural minimum wage (see *Table 15*). Calculating the pay received for the purposes of assessing whether the national minimum wage has been paid may in some cases be complex. An employer must keep sufficient records to show that workers who qualify have been paid the national minimum wage (Reg 38(1) NMWR 1999 and s9 and s31 NMWA 1998), and a worker is entitled to inspect those records (s10 NMWA).

There are four main routes by which an individual may enforce NMW rights:

1) A worker may bring a claim to the ET for unlawful deductions from wages (s17 NMWA 1998) (see *Unlawful deductions from wages*);

2) It is automatically unfair to dismiss a worker because he has asserted his right to the NMW or might qualify for the NMW (s104A ERA 1996) (see *Unfair dismissal*);

3) Under s23(1) NMWA 1998, a worker has the right not to be subjected to any detriment by any act or failure to act for specified reasons relating to the NMW (see *Detriment*);

4) A worker may bring a claim to the ET that his or her employer has refused access to records in accordance with s10 NMWA 1998 (s11 NMWA 1998).

Living accommodation

When an employer charges a worker for living accommodation the charge must be taken into account by comparing it to the worker's accommodation

offset calculated using the accommodation offset rate (currently £8.36 per day or £58.52 per week, 2021/22 tax year). If the charge is higher than the accommodation offset, then any excess amount above the accommodation offset will reduce the worker's national minimum wage pay.

If the accommodation charge is at or below the offset rate, it does not have an effect on the worker's pay.

If the accommodation is free, the offset rate is added to the worker's pay.

Although the EAT in *HMRC v Ant Marketing Ltd* UKEAT/0051/19/OO concluded that accommodation provided by a separate company was not provided by 'the employer', and therefore not subject to this offset, Choudhury P went on to hold that this conclusion was the result of the 'narrow basis' upon which the appeal was brought. He went on to conclude, in *obiter* remarks that are likely to be highly persuasive, that '*had the issue in this appeal been whether or not an employer could be said to be a provider of accommodation, even though it is not the owner or landlord in such accommodation, I would have unhesitatingly answered in the affirmative.*'

No other kind of company benefit (e.g. food, a car, childcare vouchers) count towards the National Minimum Wage.

Penalty for not paying NMW

HMRC can impose a penalty on employers if they are found not to have paid the NMW. Penalties for non-payment were doubled from 1 April 2016, from 100% of arrears owed to 200%, although these will be halved if paid within 14 days. The maximum penalty is £20,000 per worker.

Remedy for failing to pay the NMW

If a worker who is entitled to be paid the NMW is paid less than the NMW, the worker is entitled to be paid the difference between the relevant remuneration received by the worker for the pay reference period; and the relevant remuneration which the worker would have received for that period had he been remunerated by the employer at a rate equal to the NMW (s17 NMWA 1998).

Living accommodation provided by the employer should be taken into account when assessing the employer's liability (see Regs 30(d) and 36(1) NMWR 1999 and *Eastern Eye (Plymouth) Ltd v Hassan & Anor* UKEAT/0383/14/DA).

Remedy for refusal to permit access to records

Where a tribunal finds a complaint under s11 well founded, it will make a declaration to that effect and will make an award of 80 times the hourly minimum wage in force at the date when the award is made (s11(2) NMWA 1998).

If the claimant's employment is transferred under the Transfer of Undertakings (Protection of Employment) Regulations 2006, the obligation to maintain records under the NMWA transfers to the transferee (see *Mears Homecare Ltd v Bradburn and others* UKEAT/0170/18/JOJ).

Gross or net: Gross

Limit on number of years: 2 years for any claim presented on or after 8 January 2015, otherwise none. Although *Coletta v Bath Hill Court (Bournemouth) Property Management Ltd* UKEAT/0200/17/RN has held that there is no temporal cap on the recovery of a series of deduction of wages, the Deductions from Wages (Limitation) Regulations 2014 (SI 2014/3322) (which came into force after the events in *Coletta*) place a 2-year limit on claims for unlawful deductions from wages involving pay.

Tax: It is likely that this award will not be subject to tax, and should be characterised as a punishment or fine, not earnings or a payment connected to termination.

Statutory authorities: NMWA 1998 ss10 and 11; NMWR 1999 Regs 30(d), 36(1) and 38(1)

Relevant case law: *Coletta v Bath Hill Court (Bournemouth) Property Management Ltd* UKEAT/0200/17/RN; *Eastern Eye (Plymouth) Ltd v Hassan & Anor* UKEAT/0383/14/DA; *HMRC v Ant Marketing Ltd* UKEAT/0051/19/OO; *Mears Homecare Ltd v Bradburn and others* UKEAT/0170/18/JOJ

Net weekly pay

(see also *Gourley principle; Gross weekly pay; Week's pay*)

This is the figure used to calculate the actual net loss to the claimant in a number of awards. This will often be the gross weekly pay less tax and NI, and may also be less employer's pension contributions and other benefits if the value of the loss of those benefits is calculated separately, which is often the approach used. Some awards are calculated on gross weekly pay, for example where an employer is ordered to pay unpaid remuneration (where tax will be deducted at source upon payment in the usual way). The following awards use net weekly pay as the basis of the loss:

- Compensatory award;

- Damages for wrongful dismissal;

- Financial losses suffered as a result of unlawful discrimination.

Non-recoupable state benefits

(see also *Recoupment*)

The state benefits of job seekers allowance and income support, income-related employment support allowance and universal credit are subject to recoupment under the *Employment Protection (Recoupment of Jobseeker's Allowance and Income Support) Regulations 1996* (SI 1996/2349). The Regulations provide that, where a monetary award is made by the tribunal, it must identify any part of that award that constitutes the prescribed element (past loss of earnings) and the period to which it relates.

Other benefits, benefits awarded outside of the 'prescribed period', or benefits received in relation to awards that do not fall within the recoupment provisions are non-recoupable benefits.

Housing benefit, which can also be the subject of claw-back provisions, should not be deducted from any award for loss of earnings (*Olayemi v Athena Medical Centre and Anor* UKEAT/0140/15).

Normal working hours: see *Week's pay*

Notice pay

(see also *Breach of contract; Contractual notice period; Effective date of termination; Garden leave; Statutory notice period; Table 14*)

If an employee gives or is given notice of termination of their employment, they will usually be entitled to their normal pay during this period of notice. Four general approaches can be taken to whether the individual works their notice period and how they are paid:

1) The employee works their notice and gets paid their normal wage;

2) The employee is placed on garden leave, in which case they do not actually work during their notice but the employment contract is still in force and they get paid as normal;

3) The employee does not work their notice period, the contract is terminated earlier, and instead receives a payment equivalent to what would have been earned during this period (payment in lieu of notice or PILON);

4) The employee does not work during the notice period, and does not get paid all or some of their normal wage for the notice period.

In the fourth example, the employee may be entitled to compensation for breach of the obligation to be paid under the contract.

Occupational pension scheme: see *Pension loss*

Order of adjustments: see *Adjustments and order of adjustments*

Overtime: see *Compensatory award; Holiday pay; Week's pay; APPENDIX 3*

Parental bereavement leave

The *Parental Bereavement Leave Regulations 2020* (which came into force on 6 April 2020) implement a new statutory entitlement under the *Parental Bereavement (Leave and Pay) Act 2018* to Parental Bereavement Leave and Pay for employed parents who lose a child on or after 6 April 2020. The legislation gives bereaved parents who are employees at least a right to time off work to grieve.

Specifically:

- The Parental Bereavement Leave Regulations 2020 implemented a new entitlement for bereaved parents who are employees to two weeks' leave from their job; and

- The Statutory Parental Bereavement Pay (General) Regulations 2020 implemented a new entitlement for bereaved parents who meet certain eligibility criteria to receive a statutory payment whilst absent from work. This is paid at either the statutory flat rate of £151.97 per week for 2021/22, or 90% of average earnings calculated over a set reference period, whichever is the lower.

An employee is entitled under section 47C(1) of the ERA 1996 Act not to be subjected to any detriment by any act, or any deliberate failure to act, by an employer because they took or sought to take parental bereavement leave.

Parental leave

(see also *Detriment; Parental bereavement leave*)

Parents with at least one year's service are permitted to take up to 18 weeks' unpaid leave before a child's 18th birthday.

A system of Shared Parental Leave applies to births and adoptions from 5 April 2015 onwards.

An employee may present a complaint to an employment tribunal that his employer:

a) has unreasonably postponed a period of parental leave requested by the employee; or

b) has prevented or attempted to prevent the employee from taking parental leave (s80 ERA 1996).

Remedy: By s80(4) ERA 1996 the amount of compensation shall be such as the tribunal considers just and equitable in all the circumstances having regard to:

a) the employer's behaviour; and

b) any loss sustained by the employee which is attributable to the matters complained of.

Gross or net: Whether this is paid gross or net will depend on whether payment amounts to earnings or some other loss.

Limit on a week's pay: None

Limit on number of weeks: No, except in relation to the amount of leave the employee is entitled to by statute.

Any maximum or minimum: None

Adjustments: None

Tax: The tax treatment of any award is unclear. To the extent that the sum awarded is compensation for lost earnings, it is likely to be taxed under s62 ITEPA 2003 (see *Tax and termination payments*).

Recoupment: N/A

Statutory authorities: ERA 1996 *s80*

Part-time worker protection

A worker working part time has the right not to be treated by his employer less favourably than the employer treats a comparable permanent employee, on the ground that the worker is a part time worker, either as regards the terms of his contract; or by being subjected to any other detriment by any act, or deliberate failure to act, of his employer. Less favourable treatment will be permitted where it can be objectively justified. In assessing whether a part time worker has been less favourably treated, the tribunal will apply the pro rata principle unless that is inappropriate (Reg 5 PTW(PLFT) Regs 2000).

A worker has the right to request written reasons for any treatment which he or she considers might infringe the Reg 5 right, and is entitled to be provided with such a statement within 21 days of the request (Reg 6(1) PTW(PLFT)).

Reg 7 PTW(PLFT) establishes automatic unfair dismissal and detriment protections for the actions of individuals related to exercising and enforcing their Reg 5 and 6 rights (see *Unfair dismissal* and *Detriment*).

A worker may present a complaint to the tribunal that a right conferred on him or her by Reg 5 has been infringed (Reg 8(1) PTW(PLFT)).

Remedy: Where a tribunal upholds a complaint that a worker has been subject to less favourable treatment, the tribunal may take any of the following steps as it considers just and equitable (Reg 8(7) PTW(PLFT)):

- make a declaration as to the rights of the complainant and the employer in relation to the complaint;

- order the employer to pay compensation to the complainant;

- make a recommendation that the employer take certain steps to obviate or reduce any relevant adverse effect.

Where compensation is awarded the amount will be that which the tribunal considers just and equitable in all the circumstances (this phrase is used in the assessment of the compensatory award for unfair dismissal and similar principles will apply). The tribunal will have regard to the infringement and any loss which is attributable to it. Losses suffered by the complainant will be taken to include any expenses reasonably incurred as a consequence of the infringement and the loss of any benefit he would have had but for the infringement (see Regs 8(9) and (10) PTW(PLFT)). The common law principles of mitigation apply and the tribunal may reduce any award for contributory fault (Reg 8(13) PTW(PLFT)).

There is no right to compensation for injury to feelings where there has been infringement of the right not to be less favourably treated under Reg 5 PTW(PLFT) (however, an award for detriment under Reg 7 PTW(PLFT) may include such an award (see *Detriment* and *Injury to feelings*).

If an employer fails, without reasonable justification, to comply with a recommendation (see above), the tribunal may make an award of compensation if it has not already done so, or increase an award of compensation it has already made (Reg 8(14) PTW(PLFT)).

Gross or net: This will depend on whether the sums paid are treated as suppressed wages, an award for discrimination or injury to feelings (see *Tax* below within this entry). Where a sum is paid to represent a net loss it will be calculated on the net figure and grossed up where appropriate to make the final award. Where the sum is viewed as suppressed wages the award will be calculated on gross earnings, with the employer deducting tax and NI.

Any maximum or minimum: No, there is no statutory cap.

Adjustments: A percentage deduction for contributory conduct can be applied (Reg 8(13) PTW(PLFT)). Also, if the employer fails to comply with a tribunal's recommendation, any award may be increased (Reg 8(14) PTW(PLFT)).

Mitigation: The usual principles of mitigation apply.

Tax: Any payment to compensate for an employee's reduced wages or benefits would probably be classed as arrears of pay and taxed under s62 ITEPA 2003 in the normal way (see *EIM02550* and *EIM02530*, HMRC). The tax to be paid should be calculated according to the tax year in which the pay was withheld, not the tax year in which the repayment is made.

However, *EIM12965* of the Employment Income Manual states that payments of compensation for discrimination which occurs before termination is not employment income for the purposes of s401 and that they are therefore not taxable. It is arguable that the award for infringement of Reg 5 would not be subject to tax as it would be compensation for discrimination (in its broadest sense).

Statutory authorities: *PTW(PLFT) Regs 2000 Regs 5 to 8*

Paternity leave: see *Detriment; Table 16; Unfair dismissal*

Payment in lieu of notice (PILON)

(See also *Effective date of termination; Tax and termination payments*)

Where an employee's employment contract is terminated and the employee does not work a notice period, but instead receives a payment equivalent to what would have been earned during that period, this is often described as a payment in lieu of notice or a 'PILON'. It is not the same as payment during 'gardening leave', where the employee is still in employment during the notice period, even though he or she is not present at work.

There are four types of PILON:

- Contractual PILON, where the payment is made under an express contractual term (or occasionally an implied term);

- Automatic PILON, where payment is made as an automatic response by the employer to termination;

- Discretionary PILON, where payment is made

under a discretionary power provided by a contractual term; and

- PILONs paid as compensation for breach of contractual entitlement to notice.

If the contract provides that termination can be achieved by making a payment in lieu of notice, the amount to be paid is a matter of the interpretation of the contract.

The employment contract is terminated when the terms of the PILON clause have been satisfied (such as payment being received by the employee), with the EDT being the date of termination of the contract (see *Société Générale, London Branch v Geys* [2013] IRLR 122).

If there is no contractual provision for PILON, a termination of employment with PILON is likely to be a breach of the employment contract. The value of the PILON sufficient to cover an employee's right to damages will be determined by what the terms of the contract establish the employee would have been entitled to receive had they been given their proper notice.

All payments in lieu of notice, not just contractual payments in lieu of notice, are taxable earnings. All employees will pay tax and Class 1 NICs on the amount of basic pay that they would have received if they had worked their notice in full, even if they are not paid a contractual payment in lieu of notice. This means the tax and NICs consequences will no longer depend on how the employment contract is drafted or whether payments are structured in some other form, such as damages.

Penalty for leaving pension scheme early: see *Pension loss*

Pension loss

(see also *State pension: Tables 25 to 39*)

Following the withdrawal of the 2003 edition of 'Compensation for Loss of Pension Rights: Employment Tribunals', a working party of Employment Judges developed the "Principles for compensating pension loss" which were published in August 2017. The *Principles* were revised in December 2019 and again in March 2021 to take account of the 8th edition of the Ogden Tables which were published on 2020. This entry explains how the loss of state pension, pension under a defined contribution scheme and under a defined benefit scheme is calculated.

Some definitions

Deferred pension

This is the pension entitlement built up by an employee who left employment before normal retirement date.

Final salary (defined benefit) pension scheme

This is a pension scheme where the value of a person's pension on retirement is calculated by reference to their final salary. Sometimes, the pension may be calculated according to the average of the last few years' salary. The value of the pension will also be calculated according to the number of years' service - typically entitlement will increase by a particular fraction of final salary for each year of employment. Some pension fractions are more generous than others - a pension fraction of 1/60 is more generous than a pension of 1/80 for example. A person who works for 30 years with a pension fraction of 1/60 will retire on half their final salary, whereas a person with a pension fraction of 1/80 will have to work for 40 years to retire on half their salary.

Gross weekly pensionable pay

The pensionable pay is that part of the employee's salary which will be used to calculate employer and employee pension contributions and may not be the same as their gross weekly pay. If pension loss is to be calculated on the basis of loss of employer contributions according to the Principles, the employee's gross weekly pensionable pay will first have to be ascertained, usually from the pension provider or the employer.

Money purchase (defined contribution) pension scheme

In such a scheme, a private provider, usually chosen by the employer, invests the pot or fund with a view to increasing it. The usual situation is that both the employer and the employee have contributed defined amounts to the pot or fund, expressed as percentages of salary. The amount of the resulting pension will depend on the performance of that pot or fund and the size of the annuity it can purchase.

Normal retirement date

There is no longer a normal retirement age as between employers and their employees (see *Employment Equality (Repeal of Retirement Age Provisions) Regulations 2011/1069*). Any dismissal on grounds of age will be discriminatory, subject to any justification defence, and so far as unfair dismissal is concerned the usual protections, regardless of age, will apply. However, pension scheme rules may specify a normal age at which employees are able to begin to receive a pension, and some schemes may make provision for earlier receipt of benefits.

Ogden Tables

The Ogden Tables are primarily used to assess lump sum damages for personal injury awards but they can also be used to calculate pension loss in certain cases for state pension and defined benefit pension schemes. They provide *multipliers* for different *discount rates* which are then multiplied by the *multiplicand* to arrive at a lump sum figure. The latest tables, the 8th edition, were published in July 2020 where the multipliers have been calculated using the projected mortality rates underlying the 2018-based principal population projection for the United Kingdom and assuming a date of trial in 2022. Additional Tables to the 8th edition of the Ogden Tables have also been produced which provide multipliers at selected rates of discount that can be used to capitalise multiplicands payable from any age at the date of trial to any future age (up to age 125).

Essentially, the *multiplier* is the number of years for which the loss will be incurred and will depend on the sex, age at EDT, retirement age of the claimant, and the current rate of return. The multipliers have been calculated with reference to 2018 mortality rates for the population at large - these rates are not the same as for the population in DB schemes. A *2 year mortality adjustment* to both age and date of retirement will therefore need to be applied for loss of pension (but not earnings).

The *discount rate* is an adjustment to reflect the interest a claimant can expect to earn by investing a lump sum representing pension loss, as well as the effects of tax, expenses and inflation on these returns. The discount rate should ensure that people receive the full compensation that they were awarded - no more or less - by taking into account what they are likely to earn on that money before they are expected to have spent it. It is currently a negative figure, -0.25%, although in Scotland, the ET has decided to keep the previous discount rate of -0.75%. This negative discount rate effectively means that it is assumed a lump sum invested will actually lose money rather than increase in value - the rate has therefore been calculated to mitigate the claimant against this potential loss.

The *multiplicand* is the present-day value of the future loss of annual pension.

All of the Ogden Tables have been summarised at the back of this book (Tables 25 to 39) to include the multipliers for discount rates of -0.25% and -0.75%, and for all the retirement ages between 50 and 75. Tables 26 to 33 list the multipliers with and without the 2 year adjustment.

All references to the tables in the examples below refer to the number of the table at the back of this book, not to the Ogden Table number. In each example the discount rate for England and Wales has been used and the 2 year adjustment applied to loss of pension (but not earnings).

Loss of State Pension

Since 6 April 2016, the state pension has been called the new State Pension or nSP. An individual needs to accrue 10 qualifying years on their NI record to get some nSP and will be entitled to the full nSP (currently £179.60 a week, or £9,339.20 a year, (2021/22)) if they accrue 35 qualifying years.

Dismissal interrupts an individual's NI record. In most cases it will not interrupt it for long enough to result in a loss of nSP benefits. This is because it will rarely stop a person from going on to accrue the 35 qualifying years needed to receive the full amount of nSP. Nonetheless, in exceptional cases, dismissal might be said to reduce nSP benefits if NI credits were not available and dismissal means that the claimant will fail to reach 35 qualifying years (or will accrue fewer years) than if not dismissed.

If a tribunal decides it is appropriate to award a sum for loss of state pension rights, the Ogden Tables for loss of pension will be needed.

Example

- Male
- Aged 63 at date of dismissal
- State pension age of 66 and no prospect of finding alternative work
- Number of qualifying years already accrued: 32
- nSP at date of dismissal: £9,339.20 a year (using current figures).

The individual will lose 3 qualifying years resulting in a reduction by 3/35ths of his full state pension from retirement until death.

It is necessary first of all to calculate the annual loss which is 3/35 x 9,339.20 = 800.50 (this is called the multiplicand – see above for more detail).

Next, the Ogden tables should be used to obtain the number of years for which this loss is likely to be incurred (this is called the multiplier). Using Table 26, the multiplier for a man aged 63 who will retire at age 66 is 21.75.

Therefore the capital sum which represents loss of nSP = 800.50 x 21.75 = £17,410.88.

As the example above demonstrates, the loss of nSP may not be an insignificant sum especially if the claimant is close to retirement and is unlikely to secure alternative employment.

Defined Contribution (DC or money purchase) schemes

Method of calculation in simple cases

Where the claimant has lost benefits from a DC

scheme, pension loss will be calculated on the basis of lost employer contributions as follows:

- obtain details of the claimant's pay and employer contributions (the tribunal may assume auto-enrolment levels if there is no evidence);

- identify the date at which the period of loss ends;

- calculate the employer contributions to the remedy hearing (no recoupment);

- calculate the future loss of employer contributions (taking account of future pay rises);

- credit any employer contributions made by a new employer against the award (again the tribunal may assume auto-enrolment with new employer, rebuttable by evidence).

There is no loss by reason of lost facility to make Additional Voluntary Contributions.

Career long loss

The tribunal may consider that the contributions method is not appropriate if there is significant disparity between the level of employer contributions in the new job compared to the old job which will remain through to the claimant's retirement. Instead, the tribunal may add the employer contributions to net salary and use the Ogden Tables to calculate net loss of earnings. The relevant Ogden tables in these cases are Multiples for loss of Earnings (Ogden Tables 3 to 18) (Tables 34 to 37 listed at the back of this book).

Example

- Female
- Aged 54 at date of dismissal
- Pension age 70
- Pension contributions in old job = £9,750 per year
- Pension contributions in new job = £2,250 per year
- Loss each year = 9,750 − 2,250 = 7,500
- Table 35 without 2 year adjustment 15.78
- Loss of pension, before grossing up = 7,500 x 15.78 = £118,350.

Defined Benefit (DB or final salary) schemes

There are two methods of calculation depending on the complexity of the case.

Simple cases

These could include cases where it is disproportionate to engage in complex analysis (e.g. because of the compensation cap or a relatively short period of loss).

Method of calculation
There will usually be no award for loss of enhancement of accrued pension rights. The pension loss in simple

cases should be calculated according to loss of contributions as for DC schemes as follows:

- obtain details of the employer's contribution rate (which could be an average for scheme members);

- identify the date at which the period of loss ends;

- calculate the employer contributions to the remedy hearing (no recoupment) by applying the average employer contribution rate to the claimant's gross salary at EDT;

- calculate the future loss of employer contributions in the same way (taking account of future pay rises);

- credit any employer contributions made by a new employer against the award (again the tribunal may assume auto-enrolment with the new employer, rebuttable by evidence).

Complex cases

These cases are typically cases with longer periods of loss (e.g. career-long loss cases) and no compensation cap, warranting more complex analysis.

Case management
Cases which could be described as complex should be identified at an early stage and parties should include a pension loss element on the schedule of loss at the start of the process i.e. before any liability is found. The Employment Tribunal's *Agenda for Case Management for Preliminary Hearing* now contains a section to identify this at a Case Management Preliminary Hearing. Use of expressions such as "to be confirmed" are discouraged.

For complex cases, there will be a split liability and remedy hearing, the remedy hearing being in two stages:

1) The first stage will identify the non-pension losses and make findings of fact relevant to pension losses. There will then be a period for the parties to try and agree the pensions figure between themselves.

2) The second stage will identify the pension loss, either by using Ogden tables or expert actuarial evidence.

Calculation
There could be two types of loss to be considered: loss of annual pension and loss of a lump sum.

Method of calculation of loss of annual pension using Ogden tables

The Principles identity seven steps that the tribunal and the parties should follow when calculating loss of DB pension rights using the Ogden Tables.

Step 1: Identify what the claimant's net pension income

would have been at their retirement age if the dismissal had not occurred.

Step 2: Identify what the claimant's net pension income will be at their retirement age in the light of their dismissal.

Step 3: Deduct the result of Step 2 from the result of Step 1, which produces a figure for net annual loss of pension benefits. This is the *multiplicand*.

Step 4: Identify the period over which that net annual loss is to be awarded, using Tables 26 to 33 at the back of this book to identify the *multiplier* as follows:

- Choose the correct table depending on the sex of the individual, the discount rate (-0.25% for claims in England and Wales; -0.75% for claims in Scotland) and whether the 2 year adjustment applies;

- Identify the age of the claimant at the date of the remedy hearing (the numbers down the side) and the claimant's retirement age (the numbers across the top).

Step 5: Multiply the multiplicand by the multiplier to obtain the capitalised value of the lost pension, subject to any further adjustment the tribunal considers appropriate.

Step 6: Check the lump sum position and perform a separate calculation if required (see below).

Step 7: Taking account of the other sums awarded by the tribunal, gross up the compensation awarded.

Example
- Man
- Aged 59 at dismissal
- Normal retirement age: 75
- Annual pension if not been dismissed: £15,000
- Annual pension having been dismissed: £7,000
- Annual pension loss: £8,000
- Multiplier from Table 26: 13.50
- Capital sum representing pension loss = 8,000 x 13.50 = £108,000

Lump sums

At retirement, claimants could receive either (i) a commuted lump sum (i.e. a lump sum in return for giving up some of their annual pension) or (ii) a non-commuted lump sum (i.e. one where the annual pension is not reduced). It may be appropriate to apply a discount factor, using Table 38, to any lost non-commuted lump sum to reflect the fact that it is being received early (any lost commuted lump sum will be ignored as this will already have been factored in when calculating annual pension loss).

Calculation method

The calculation of loss of lump sum is as follows:

- Identify the multiplicand. This is:

  the lump sum that would have been paid at retirement if the claimant had not been dismissed

  minus

  the lump sum they will now receive, taking account of withdrawal factors.

- Identify the number of years between dismissal and retirement date. This is the number down the side of Table 38.

- Identify the discount rate (along the top, which is currently -0.25% in England and Wales and -0.75% in Scotland).

- Find the appropriate multiplier.

- Multiply the multiplicand by the multiplier to find the present capital value of that loss.

Example
- Number of years to retirement: 25
- Lump sum payable but for dismissal: £25,000
- Lump sum payable having been dismissed: £20,000
- Lump sum loss = £5,000
- Table 38 multiplier: 1.0646
- Capital value of loss = £5,000 x 1.0646 = £5,323

Perks: see *Financial losses*

Permanent employment: see *Damages for wrongful dismissal*

Physical and psychiatric injury

(see also *Discrimination; Interest*)

Claimants can claim damages for personal injury caused by unlawful discriminatory acts including detriment for whistleblowing (see *Sheriff v Klyne Tugs (Lowestoft) Ltd* [1999] IRLR 481 and *Virgo Fidelis Senior School v Boyle* [2004] IRLR 268). However, it is not always easy to identify where injury to feelings ends and physical and psychiatric injury starts and there is a risk of double counting.

Although there is no absolute requirement for medical evidence to establish a claim for personal injury in employment tribunals, obtaining such evidence is advisable where possible, especially where claims are complex and there are issues over causation or divisibility (*Hampshire County Council v Wyatt* UKEAT/0013/16).

Divisible and Indivisible Harm

In some cases, issues may arise where a claimant has suffered an injury through multiple causes. In such cases, the tribunal will need to consider whether the harm is 'divisible' or 'indivisible'.

Divisible Harm is where different acts cause *different* damage, or *quantifiable parts* of the damage. In these cases, the tribunal must establish and award compensation only for that part of the harm for which the respondent is truly responsible.

Indivisible Harm is where multiple acts result in the *same* damage, usually either:

> **Monocausally:** where all of the acts operate in the same way to cause the damage, only one act could have actually caused the damage, but it is impossible to tell which of them was the actual cause; or

> **Multicausally:** where a single condition or harm is caused by a combination of separate acts or factors. For example, where the cumulative effect of their separate acts crosses a threshold that gives rise to that damage, or distinct acts combine to produce a single form of damage.

If the harm is indivisible, any respondent whose act has been the proximate cause of the injury must compensate for the *whole* of it. That others had a part to play in the injury is a matter for *contribution*, not apportionment.

Whether an injury is divisible or indivisible will depend on evidence, but it is '*more likely that an injury will be held to be indivisible if the competing causes are closely related to the injury and it is difficult to separate out the consequences*' (*Olayemi v Athena Medical Centre & Anor* UKEAT/0140/15, paragraph 25).

The issue of divisibility of harm was considered by the Court of Appeal in *BAE Systems (Operations) Ltd v Konczak* [2017] EWCA Civ 1188. The case confirmed the following propositions:

1) Where the harm has more than one cause, a respondent should only pay for the proportion attributable to their wrongdoing unless the harm is truly indivisible.

2) The burden is on the employer to raise the issue of apportionment.

3) Tribunals should try to '*identify a rational basis on which the harm suffered can be apportioned between a part caused by the employer's wrong, and a part which is not so caused.*' The Tribunal should see if it '*can identify, however broadly, a*

particular part of the suffering which is due to the wrong'.

4) Where such a '*rational basis*' can be found, the Tribunal should apportion accordingly, even if the basis for doing so is '*rough and ready*'.

5) Any such assessment must consider any pre-existing disorder or vulnerability, and account for the chance that the claimant would have succumbed to the harm in any event, either at that point or in the future.

6) In cases of psychiatric injury, careful evidence should be obtained from experts, particularly in relation to the likelihood of suffering the harm in any event. Paragraph 93 of Irwin LJ's judgment identifies some of the matters that may be useful to put to such an expert.

Remedy: When it comes to the assessment of damages in relation to a proven psychiatric injury, tribunals are '*obliged to approach the assessment of damages for psychiatric injury on the same basis as a common law court in an ordinary action for personal injuries*' (*HM Prison Service v Salmon* [2001] IRLR 425).

The Judicial College has published guidelines for the assessment of general damages in personal injury cases. The latest 15th edition was published in November 2019. According to the College, the following factors need to be taken into account when valuing claims of psychiatric injury:

a) the injured person's ability to cope with life and work;

b) the effect on the injured person's relationships with family, friends and those with whom he comes into contact;

c) the extent to which treatment would be successful;

d) future vulnerability;

e) prognosis;

f) whether medical help has been sought;

g) whether the injury results from sexual and/or physical abuse and/or breach of trust; and if so, the nature of the relationship between victim and abuser, the nature of the abuse, its duration and the symptoms caused by it.

There are 4 categories of award (including the *Simmons v Castle* uplift):

1) Less Severe: between £1,440 and £5,500. Where the claimant has suffered temporary symptoms that have adversely affected daily activities;

2) Moderate: between £5,500 and £17,900. Where, while the claimant has suffered problems as a result of the discrimination, marked improvement

has been made by the date of the hearing and the prognosis is good;

3)   Moderately Severe: between £17,900 and £51,460. Moderately severe cases include those where there is work-related stress resulting in a permanent or long-standing disability preventing a return to comparable employment. These are cases where there are problems with factors a) to d) above, but there is a much more optimistic prognosis than Severe;

4)   Severe: between £51,460 and £108,620. Where the claimant has serious problems in relation to the factors at a) to d) above, and the prognosis is poor.

Separate criteria apply for cases of Post-Traumatic Stress Disorder, and the Guidelines should be consulted accordingly in an appropriate case.

Any maximum or minimum: Only so far as the guidelines have suggested.

Adjustments:

Causation: The award can be adjusted to allow for the extent to which the act of discrimination caused the illness. So, if it is found that the discriminatory act caused the illness to the extent of 30%, the award will be reduced by 70%.

Double counting: Injury to feelings and physical and psychiatric injury are distinct heads of loss, but care should be taken that no double counting has taken place. Either one could be reduced if this is the case.

Discount rate: Where an employee suffers a life-changing personal injury resulting in long-term loss of earnings, the discount rate is applied to reflect early receipt. As of July 2019, that rate is now -0.25% in England and Wales and -0.75% in Scotland (see also *Accelerated/decelerated receipt*).

Interest: Interest could also be awarded (see *Interest*).

Simmons v Castle uplift: The figures quoted above include the *Simmons v Castle* 10% uplift (see *De Souza v Vinci Construction (UK) Ltd* [2017] EWCA Civ 879 paragraph 26).

Scotland:

● The discount rate remains at -0.75%;

● The tribunal can choose not to apply the *Simmons v Castle* uplift, but must set out reasons for doing so.

Mitigation: N/A

Tax: Awards for injury are exempted from tax under s406 ITEPA 2003 (see *Tax and termination payments*).

Recoupment: N/A

Relevant case law: *De Souza v Vinci Construction (UK)*

Ltd [2017] EWCA Civ 879; *HM Prison Service v Salmon* [2001] IRLR 425; *Sheriff v Klyne Tugs (Lowestoft) Ltd* [1999] IRLR 481; *Virgo Fidelis Senior School v Boyle* [2004] IRLR 268

Polkey

(see also *Adjustments and order of adjustments*)

A '*Polkey*' deduction is the phrase used in unfair dismissal cases to describe the reduction in any award for future loss to reflect the chance that the individual would have been dismissed fairly in any event (*Polkey v AE Dayton Services Ltd* [1987] IRLR 50 (HL)).

This may take the form of a percentage reduction, or it may take the form of a tribunal making a finding that the individual would have been dismissed fairly after a further period of employment (for example a period in which a fair procedure would have been completed). Alternatively, a combination of the two approaches could be used, but not in the same period of loss (as confirmed in *Zebrowski v Concentric Birmingham Ltd* UKEAT/0245/16/DA). The question for the tribunal is whether the *particular employer* (as opposed to a hypothetical reasonable employer) would have dismissed the claimant in any event had the unfairness not occurred.

There are useful reviews of the case law (which is not without its difficulties) in *Software 2000 Ltd v Andrews* [2007] IRLR 568, *V v Hertfordshire County Council and another* UKEAT/0427/14/LA and *Contract Bottling Ltd v Cave & Anor* UKEAT/0100/14/DM).

The *Polkey* adjustment is only applicable to the compensatory award, not the basic award (apart from in very limited circumstances where such a (fair) dismissal might have taken place virtually contemporaneously with the unfair dismissal which actually occurred, presumably applying s122(2) ERA 1996 - see *Granchester Construction (Eastern) Ltd v Attrill* UKEAT/0327/12/LA, paragraph 19). A similar approach to a *Polkey* deduction is taken in discrimination cases where the tribunal will assess the chance that a particular future loss has been suffered (see *Loss of chance*).

The tribunal must assess any *Polkey* deduction in two respects:

1)   If a fair process had occurred, would it have affected when the claimant would have been dismissed? and

2)   What is the percentage chance that a fair process would still have resulted in the claimant's dismissal?

Where there is a significant overlap between the factors taken into account in making a *Polkey* deduction and when making a deduction for contributory conduct, the ET should consider expressly, whether in the light of that overlap, it is just and equitable to make a finding of contributory conduct, and, if so, what its amount should be. This is to avoid the risk of penalizing the claimant twice for the same conduct (see *Lenlyn UK Ltd v Kular* UKEAT/0108/16/DM).

Relevant case law: *Contract Bottling Ltd v Cave & Anor* UKEAT/0100/14/DM; *Granchester Construction (Eastern) Ltd v Attrill* UKEAT/0327/12/LA; *Lenlyn UK Ltd v Kular* UKEAT/0108/16/DM; *Polkey v AE Dayton Services Ltd* [1987] IRLR 50 (HL);*Software 2000 Ltd v Andrews* [2007] IRLR 568; *V v Hertfordshire County Council and another* UKEAT/0427/14/LA; *Zebrowski v Concentric Birmingham Ltd* UKEAT/0245/16/DA

Pregnancy: see *Discrimination; Time off for ante-natal care*

Prescribed element: see *Recoupment*

Prescribed period: see *Recoupment*

Presidential guidance on remedy

APPENDIX 1 reproduces Guidance Note 6 from the Presidential Guidance - General Case Management which was amended and re-issued in 2018. This sets out in easily readable form the tribunal's procedure and expectations for dealing with remedy. The tribunal will expect parties to comply with the guidance.

Profit related bonus: see *Financial losses; Bonuses*

Protected act: see *Discrimination*

Protected disclosure

(see also *Detriment; Unfair dismissal*)

Where an employee has suffered a detriment, or has been dismissed, for making a protected disclosure, the tribunal may award financial compensation.

The right to bring a claim for detriment is established by s47B ERA 1996, and the right to not be unfairly dismissed for the sole or principal reason of making a protected disclosure is established by s103A ERA 1996.

For detriment (not dismissal) the tribunal must award such an amount as it considers is just and equitable having regard to:

1) the infringement to which the complaint relates;

2) any loss which is attributable to the act, or failure

to act, which infringed the claimant's right (s49(2) ERA 1996).

If the employee has been dismissed, awards can be made for unfair dismissal (see *Additional award; Basic award; Compensatory award; Unfair dismissal*).

Remedy: For detriment (not dismissal) the loss to be compensated shall be taken to include: any expenses reasonably incurred by the claimant in consequence of the act, or failure to act, to which the complaint relates; and loss of any benefit which the claimant might reasonably be expected to have had but for the act or failure to act (s49(3) ERA 1996).

Such a detriment award may also include compensation for injury to feelings. Where a worker has brought the claim under s47B and the detriment is termination of the contract, which is akin to a claim for unfair dismissal of an employee, it is arguable that injury to feelings may be awarded, but only up to the amount of a basic award (see *Injury to feelings*). Compensation for injury to feelings is not available in an award for unfair dismissal.

Gross or net: If the claimant has been dismissed, see the individual awards for unfair dismissal. Otherwise, it will be a figure that the tribunal considers just and equitable (see *Detriment*).

Any maximum or minimum: The award is unlimited unless the detriment is termination of the contract of a worker when any compensation must not exceed the compensation that would be payable if the worker had been an employee and had been dismissed for making a protected disclosure (there is currently no limit to such financial losses) (s49(6) ERA 1996).

Adjustments: If the tribunal considers that the act or failure to act was caused or contributed to by action of the claimant, it may reduce the award if it thinks that it would be just and equitable to do so (ss49(4) and (5) ERA 1996).

The tribunal can also reduce the award of compensation by up to 25% if they find that any disclosure was not made in good faith.

ACAS uplift:The ACAS Code of Pratice on Disciplinary and Greivance Procedures defines a grievance as *'concerns, problems or complaints that employees raise with their employers'*. A protected disclosure is likely to satisfy this definition, and thus may justify an uplift in compensation if there is any unreasonable failure to comply with the Code's requirements for handling grievances (*Ikejiaku v British Institute of Technology Ltd* UKEAT/0243/19).

Cap: The statutory cap on unfair dismissal does not apply if the employee has been dismissed as a result of making the protected disclosure, and there is no statutory cap if the claim is for detriment.

Mitigation: The tribunal may reduce the amount if it considers that the claimant has failed to mitigate his/her loss.

Tax: The award will be taxable under s401 ITEPA 2003 if the employee has been dismissed, although the tax treatment is unclear in the case of an employee who receives a payment because of suffering detriment but is still employed (see *Detriment; Tax and termination payments*).

Recoupment: Recoupment will only apply to unfair dismissal awards.

Statutory authorities: ERA 1996 *ss49* and *103A*

Protective award

Where an employer is proposing to dismiss as redundant 20 or more employees at one establishment within a period of 90 days or less, the employer shall consult about the dismissals all the persons who are appropriate representatives of any of the employees who may be affected by the proposed dismissals or may be affected by measures taken in connection with those dismissals (s188 and s188A TULR(C)A 1992).

The consultation shall begin in good time and in any event:

a)   where the employer is proposing to dismiss 100 or more employees, at least 45 days; and

b)   otherwise, at least 30 days,

before the first of the dismissals takes effect.

Where it is alleged that an employer has failed to comply with the consultation requirements the appropriate representatives, or in some limited situations an affected employee, may bring a complaint to a tribunal who, if the complaint is well founded, shall make a declaration to that effect and may make a 'protective award' covering the employees affected by the failure.

The protective award is remuneration for the 'protected period', of up to 90 days.

If the employer is insolvent, the employees may make a claim to the National Insurance Fund for payment of some (or in some cases all) of this award (see *Insolvency*).

Remedy (1): Under TULR(C)A 1992 s189(3), (4) and s190 the tribunal may make an award of up to 90 days' pay, with the length of the period determined by what is just and equitable in all the circumstances having regard to the seriousness of the employer's failure to comply with TULR(C)A 1992 s188. The award is calculated as starting on the day the first dismissals took effect. The award will identify the description of employees to whom it applies, who will be those

employees whose representative has not been consulted properly.

The rate of remuneration payable is a week's pay for each week of the protected period; and remuneration in respect of a period less than one week shall be calculated by reducing proportionally the amount of a week's pay (s190(2)).

A day's pay is found by dividing the employee's actual gross weekly pay by 7.

The principles for determining the size of a protective award are set out in *Susie Radin Ltd v GMB & Ors* [2004] ICR 893. The award is designed to be punitive, not to compensate the employee for losses suffered, with the calculation starting at 90 days where there has been no consultation and being reduced to reflect the seriousness of the breach and any mitigating factors. It is important to remember that, even if the consultation period is only 30 days, the starting point and maximum protected period is still 90 days.

Remedy (2): If the employer fails to comply with s190 by not paying an employee within the description the amount due under the award, the employee may bring a complaint to the tribunal who may order the employer to pay the amount of remuneration due (s192(1) and (3)).

Gross or net: Gross. A week's pay is as defined in ss220 to 229 ERA 1996 (see *Week's pay*). Part weeks are to be calculated pro rata. Only the basic pay should be taken into account and not any discretionary bonus (see *Canadian Imperial Bank of Commerce v Beck* UKEAT/0141/10/RN).

Limit on a week's pay: None. The limit on a week's pay does not apply.

Limit on number of days: 90.

An employee will be entitled to payment of the protective award from the date the protected period begins but will cease being entitled at the date he is fairly dismissed, unreasonably terminates his contract of employment or unreasonably refuses an offer of employment during the protected period (see s191 TULR(C)A 1992).

Any maximum or minimum: None

Adjustments: None

Cap: There is no cap on the award.

Mitigation: N/A, as the award is a sanction for breach, not compensation for losses suffered.

Tax: The award will be taxable under s401 ITEPA 2003 if the employee is no longer in employment (EIM02550, HMRC). Also, see *Mimtec Ltd v Inland Revenue* [2001] UKSC SPC00277 (see *Tax and termination payments*).

Recoupment: Yes, the prescribed element being any amount ordered to be paid to the employee in respect of so much of the relevant protected period as falls before the date of the conclusion of the tribunal proceedings (see *Table 19*).

Statutory authorities: *ITEPA 2003 s401; The Employment Protection (Recoupment of Jobseeker's Allowance and Income Support) Regulations 1996; TULR(C)A 1992 ss189 and 190*

Relevant case law: *Canadian Imperial Bank of Commerce v Beck* UKEAT/0141/10/RN; *Mimtec Ltd v Inland Revenue* [2001] UKSC SPC00277; *Susie Radin Ltd v GMB & Ors* [2004] ICR 893

Example

The claimant's gross weekly pay is £500 (which has been calculated in accordance with ss220 to 229 ERA as above) and is awarded 80 days' protective award.

A day's pay = 500/7 = £71.43 (note: the weekly pay must be divided by 7, not the number of days per week actually worked)

Thus, the protective award = £71.43 x 80 = £5,714.40

Qualifying period

(see also *Effective date of termination*)

This is the length of continuous employment (see *s211* ERA 1996) that must have been worked by the claimant before a tribunal will consider any particular complaint. Different qualifying periods apply for different types of claim (see *Table 18*).

The employee's continuous employment begins with the day on which the employee starts work, and ends with the day by reference to which the length of the employee's period of continuous employment is to be ascertained for the purposes of the provision.

But, if an employee's period of continuous employment includes one or more periods which (by virtue of ss*215, 216* or *217* ERA 1996) while not counting in computing the length of the period do not break continuity of employment, the beginning of the period shall be treated as postponed by the number of days falling within that intervening period, or the aggregate number of days falling within those periods, calculated in accordance with the section in question.

Rate of pay: see *Week's pay*

Recoupment

(see also *Non-recoupable state benefits*)

A number of awards made by tribunals are subject to recoupment, whereby the state recovers from the respondent the value of certain state benefits paid to the claimant. This involves the tribunal identifying

a part of the award that corresponds to a period of loss during which the claimant was in receipt of job seeker's allowance, income-related employment support allowance, income support or universal credit. The respondent is required to not pay the claimant the sum the tribunal identifies, but to wait until the DWP recoups from them any benefits paid, with the remainder then being paid to the claimant by the respondent. The principles to be applied are contained in the *Employment Protection (Recoupment of Jobseeker's Allowance and Income Support) Regulations 1996* (SI 1996/2349).

The types of award which may be covered by the prescribed element (see below) are listed in *Table 19*, the most common awards being for unfair dismissal, failure to make a guarantee payment, failure to pay during a period of maternity or medical suspension and protective awards (see Column 1 of the Schedule to the regulations, and Reg 3(1)(a)).

The recoupment regulations do not apply if the claimant has not claimed the relevant benefits, or if the award is compensation for discrimination statutes or for dismissal by reason of redundancy.

The recoupment regulations do not apply to settlements - this may create an incentive to settle where, because the Secretary of State will not recoup the benefits paid, a smaller sum paid by the respondent than that which would be awarded by the tribunal may well result in a higher sum being received by the claimant.

Required information

The tribunal must in its judgment identify four items of information that will then be provided to the DWP: the amount of any 'prescribed element', the prescribed period, the total amount of the award and the balance. In essence, this will define the sum within any award from which the state may seek recoupment. No greater sum will be recouped, and the respondent will be ordered by the tribunal to pay the remainder to the claimant.

Prescribed element

The prescribed element is that part of the award which is held back from the claimant until the value of any state benefits subject to the recoupment procedures is known. It is defined in Reg 3(1)(a) and Column 3 of the Schedule, and is that part of the monetary award attributable to loss of wages or arrears of pay or losses due to the claimant (including a protective award) for the period before the conclusion of the tribunal proceedings, or if it covers a protective award or award for failure to inform or consult under TUPE, up to the final day of the period covered by that protective award. The prescribed element does not include the figure that may have been awarded for loss of statutory rights, right to written particulars or the loss of benefits or pension.

The prescribed element will be reduced in line with any deduction for contributory fault that may have been made to the compensatory award. Further, the prescribed element will be reduced by the same proportion as the compensatory award when applying the statutory cap. For example, if the compensatory award has been reduced from £99,437 to the cap of £89,493 (that is, by 10%), the prescribed element will also be reduced by 10% (see Reg 4(2)).

Prescribed period

The prescribed period is identified in column 3 of the Schedule to the regulations. For straightforward unfair dismissal claims the prescribed period is the period between the EDT and the date of the remedy hearing (or the date at which the tribunal sent the remedy judgment to the parties). For concurrent wrongful and unfair dismissal claims, since recoupment does not apply to the award for breach of contract, the prescribed period is the period between the end of the period over which damages have been awarded and the date of the hearing (or the date at which the parties were sent the remedy judgment).

Total award

This is the total of all the awards that have been made by the tribunal.

Balance

This is the difference between the total and the prescribed element and must be paid to the claimant.

Once the actual state benefits that are subject to recoupment are known, the DWP will claim this figure from the prescribed element retained by the respondent and any remaining monies must be paid by the employer to the employee.

Statutory authorities: *Employment Protection (Recoupment of Jobseeker's Allowance and Income Support) Regulations 1996*

Example 1 (where the statutory cap is not applicable)

Basic award = £500

Immediate loss of earnings = £2,000

Future loss of earnings = £700

Loss of statutory rights = £200

Contributory conduct of 20% applies to compensatory award only

Calculation

Prescribed element applies only to the immediate loss of earnings, i.e. £2,000

But this amount has been reduced by 20% and is now 2,000 x 0.8 = £1,600

Total award = 500 + 1,600 + 700 + 200 = £3,000

Prescribed element is therefore £1,600 which should be held back from the claimant. Balance payable immediately to claimant = 500 + 700 + 200 = £1,400, the other £1,600 being payable if the DWP does not serve a recoupment notice on the employer. If the DWP does serve a recoupment notice, and the value of the state benefits received by the claimant is, say, £500, the employer must pay £500 to the DWP and the remaining £1,100 to the claimant.

Example 2 (where adjustments have to be made for the statutory cap)

Basic award = £11,000

Compensatory award = £100,000, of which immediate loss = £30,000 and future loss is £70,000

Loss of statutory rights = £200

Contributory conduct of 20% applies to compensatory award only

Calculation

First, the basic award remains intact.

Secondly, the compensatory award AND the loss of statutory rights should be reduced for contributory conduct = (£100,000 + £200) x 0.8 = £80,160

Thirdly, a grossing up calculation needs to be performed:

Gross up £11,000 + £80,160 - £30,000 = £61,160

Grossing up £61,160 at, say, 20% = 61,160 ÷ 0.8 = £76,450

The compensatory award is now the remainder of £30,000 - £11,000 = £19,000 plus the grossed up figure of £76,450 which comes to £95,450. This will be capped at £89,493.

Before the contributory conduct and the cap, the compensatory award was £100,200, and after these adjustments the award was £89,493 so we need to calculate the proportion by which the compensatory award has been reduced as a result. The calculation is (100,200 – 89,493) x 100/100,200 = 10.7% approximately.

So, the prescribed element of £30,000 (i.e. the immediate loss) should be reduced by 10.7%. Therefore, the prescribed element = 30,000 (immediate loss) x 0.893 = £26,790.

Redundancy

An employee with 2 years' service is entitled to be paid a redundancy payment if he or she is dismissed by reason of redundancy, or eligible by reason of being laid off or kept on short-time (see s135 ERA 1996). An employee may also be entitled to an enhanced redundancy payment by virtue of an express, incorporated or implied term of their contract of employment.

Statutory redundancy pay (see also *Basic award*)

If an employee has been dismissed by reason of redundancy and has not been paid the statutory redundancy pay to which they are entitled, s163 ERA 1996 permits the employee to bring a claim to the tribunal, which may order the employer to pay such amount as it thinks appropriate to compensate the worker for any financial loss arising from this non-payment (s163(5)). However, the claimant is not entitled to receive both a redundancy payment and a basic award, and any redundancy pay already paid will reduce the basic award accordingly. If redundancy was not the real reason for dismissal, the redundancy payment will not be set off against any basic award (*Boorman v Allmakes Ltd* [1995] IRLR 553).

Calculation: The redundancy payment is calculated according to the employee's length of service, age and gross weekly pay (up to the specified limit) (s162 ERA 1996). The calculation is identical to that for working out the basic award.

The employee will receive 1 ½ weeks' gross pay for each year of employment in which they were not below the age of 41, 1 week's gross pay for each year of employment in which they were at some point below the age of 41 but not below the age of 22 and ½ a week's gross pay for each year of employment in which they were at any point below the age of 22. The maximum number of reckonable years is 20.

Limit on a week's pay: £544. A week's pay as defined in ss220 to 229 ERA 1996 applies (see *Week's pay* and *Table 1* for historical rates).

Limit on the number of weeks: 30

Adjustments: The ACAS uplift does not apply. The 2015 ACAS Code of Practice states that the Code does not apply to redundancy dismissals, and therefore nor does the ACAS adjustment. *Holmes v Qinetiq Ltd* UKEAT/0206/15 confirms that the Code only applies to dismissals involving some form of *'culpable conduct'*.

The redundancy payment can be reduced or in certain circumstances withheld completely, for example if the employee commits an act of misconduct, leaves before the redundancy notice period has expired or the employee had taken part in a strike and refused to comply with a notice of extension served by the employer (see ss140 to 143 ERA 1996).

Mitigation: N/A

Tax: Any redundancy pay will be taxed under s401 ITEPA 2003 and therefore be counted towards the £30,000 tax free allowance.

Recoupment: N/A

Enhanced redundancy payment (awarded at tribunal)

An employee entitled to an enhanced redundancy payment may claim this from the tribunal.

Remedy: Any amount that the employee would have been entitled to over and above the statutory redundancy payment can be claimed.

Adjustments: Any enhanced redundancy payment will be part of the compensatory award and adjusted accordingly.

Cap: The statutory cap will apply to the whole of the compensatory award which includes any enhanced redundancy payment.

Tax: The enhanced redundancy payment, if awarded, will form part of the compensatory award and will be taxed under s401 ITEPA 2003 and therefore be counted towards the £30,000, tax free allowance.

Recoupment: Recoupment does not apply to any enhanced redundancy pay awarded.

Statutory authorities: ERA 1996 *ss155, 162* and *163*

Enhanced redundancy payment (paid on termination of employment)

The employee is not permitted to receive both a statutory redundancy payment and a basic award. The basic award will be reduced by the equivalent of the statutory redundancy payment made (s122(4) ERA 1996), and any enhanced redundancy payment that has been paid in excess of the statutory redundancy figure will go towards reducing the compensatory award (s123(7) ERA 1996). Note that the employer will enjoy the full benefit of any enhanced redundancy paid. In other words, any adjustments, such as contributory conduct, are made before the enhanced redundancy payment is taken off the compensatory award but interest will apply after the enhanced redundancy payment. The statutory cap is applied after the enhanced redundancy payment has been taken into account. It is important that the order is complied with, as in the following example:

Example

Compensatory award before adjustments = £50,000

After contributory conduct of 10% has been applied, compensatory award = £45,000

Enhanced redundancy payment of £25,000 reduces the compensatory award to £20,000

Example (where the redundancy pay received reduces the tax free sum available for other awards)

Redundancy payment received (tax free) = £5,000

The tax free sum available after the redundancy payment has been made is £30,000 - £5,000 = £25,000

Basic award = £11,000

Compensatory award = £40,000

The amount that should be grossed up = £11,000 + £40,000 - £25,000 = £26,000.

Statutory and contractual redundancy payments (awarded at tribunal)

If a contractual claim is brought under the Employment Tribunal's Extension of Jurisdiction (England and Wales) Order 1994, the jurisdiction of the ET under that Order is subject to a cap of £25,000 on contractual claims: see Article 10 of the Order. But if a claim for a statutory redundancy payment is made in addition to the contractual redundancy payment, the EAT has ruled that there are two causes of action; a contractual cause of action and a statutory cause of action, and the claimant would be entitled to both payments. The respondent is entitled to set off the statutory redundancy payment against the contractual redundancy payment but the set off should be against the uncapped amount, not against the capped amount (see *Ugradar v Lancashire Care NHS Foundation Trust* UKEAT/0301/18/BA).

Example

Statutory redundancy entitlement = £10,000

Contractual redundancy entitlement = £60,000 of which £10,000 can be set off because of the statutory redundancy payment, leaving £50,000

Payment to claimant = £35,000, consisting of:

- £10,000 Statutory redundancy pay; and
- £25,000 Contractual redundancy pay (the remaining £50,000 capped)

Statutory authorities: ERA 1996 *ss122(4)* and *123(7)*

Re-engagement and reinstatement

(see also *Additional award; Unfair dismissal*)

When a claimant succeeds in an unfair dismissal claim the three remedies available are reinstatement, re-engagement and compensation (ss112 to 126 ERA 1996).

The tribunal is obliged to explain to a successful claimant the availability of these three orders (s112(2) ERA 1996) and ask them whether they wish the tribunal to make such an order. Although reinstatement and re-engagement are sometimes stated as the primary remedies for unfair dismissal, this is only true in the sense that they must be considered before any claim for compensation (*Park Chinois Ltd v Ozkara* [2019] UKEAT/0017/19). In practice such orders are rarely granted, with most cases resulting in an award of compensation only.

If the claimant has expressed a wish to be reinstated or re-engaged, and communicated that to the respondent not fewer than 7 days before the final hearing, the respondent is obliged to adduce reasonable evidence about the availability of the job from which the claimant was dismissed, or of comparable or suitable employment. If the respondent fails to do so without special reason, and this results in the postponement or adjournment of the final hearing, the tribunal is obliged to order that the respondent pay the costs incurred as a result of that postponement or adjournment (Employment Tribunals (Constitution and Rules of Procedure) Regulations 2013, r76(3)).

Reinstatement

This is an order that the employer shall treat the claimant in all respects as if they had not been dismissed (s114(1) ERA 1996)).

The claimant is to be reinstated to the same contractual rights, terms and conditions as they had before they were dismissed, and the tribunal has no right to order reinstatement that alters the terms of the claimant's employment (although there is a limited right to change job duties insofar as this is not a change to the contract of employment) (*McBride v Scottish Police Authority* [2016] UKSC 27).

In making such an order the tribunal shall:

- Specify an amount payable in respect of any benefit the claimant might reasonably have expected to have had between the Effective Date of Termination and his reinstatement, including back pay.

  In calculating this figure, the tribunal must reduce the respondent's liability by the amount of any payment in lieu of notice or *ex gratia* payments by the employer, and any remuneration by another employer in the period between the EDT and the date of reinstatement, as well as any such other benefits as the tribunal thinks appropriate in the circumstances;

- State any rights and privileges to be restored to the employee;

- Specify the date by which the order must be complied with; and

- Require that the claimant be treated as if they had benefited from any improvement to their terms and conditions of employment that they would have obtained had they not been dismissed.

Re-engagement

This is an order that the claimant be engaged by the employer, a successor or associated employer, 'in employment comparable to that from which he was dismissed or other suitable employment' (s115(1) ERA 1996)). There is an exception where the employee caused or contributed to their dismissal, in which case the tribunal can order re-engagement on less favourable terms.

Any such order must specify: the identity of the employer; the nature of the employment; remuneration; back pay (as with reinstatement above); any rights and privileges to be restored to the employee; and the date to comply with the order. There are identical provisions for reducing back pay liability for re-engaged employees as there are for reinstatement.

The terms of an order for re-engagement 'must be specified with a degree of precision'. It is not sufficient to simply order that the employer employ the claimant in a comparable role (*Lincolnshire County Council v Lupton* UKEAT/0328/15/DM).

Procedure

The tribunal must first consider reinstatement and, if it decides against it, then move on to consider re-engagement.

In assessing the suitability of each order, the tribunal must consider:

- the claimant's wishes;
- the practicability of compliance by the employer;
- if the claimant caused or contributed to his dismissal, whether it is just to order reinstatement or re-engagement.

Practicability

This is considered in two stages: first on a provisional basis at the time of making the order; second on a conclusive basis if the employer fails to comply with the order. At this second stage the burden is on the employer to prove impracticability.

Practicability is a question of fact for the tribunal, not a matter of whether the employer's views fall within a band of reasonable responses. However, where the barrier to practicability is said to be a lack of trust and confidence in an employee (for example because of the employee's dishonesty), the tribunal need only consider whether that belief is genuinely held and based on rational grounds (*Kelly v PGA European Tour*

[2021] EWCA Civ 559). The cause of the loss of trust and confidence need not be conduct that resulted in dismissal, and extend to matters of which the employer was unaware during the individual's employment.

The matter is to be judged in a broad common-sense fashion and is to be assessed at the time an order would take effect. It is a question of possibility bearing in mind the circumstances of the employer's business and industrial relations realities. It means more than merely possible, but '*capable of being carried into effect with success*' (*Coleman v Magnet Joinery Ltd* [1985] ICR 46). It is also based on the specific employer rather than a hypothetical reasonable employer (*Kelly*, above). Relevant factors include matters such as:

- whether the parties are able to trust each other;
- whether the nature of the allegations makes it impossible for the employee and the subjects of those allegations to work together;
- whether the industrial atmosphere has been poisoned against the employee or their reinstatement or re-engagement is otherwise likely to lead to strife; or
- (Re-engagement only) whether the employee meets the essential requirements of a particular post (*Kelly*, above).

In reaching such a decision, however, the tribunal is not to take into account the fact that the employer has engaged a permanent replacement for the claimant unless the employer shows that it is not practicable to arrange for the work to be done without engaging a permanent replacement. This principle does not extend to '*comparable or suitable alternative posts [that] had become vacant, but had been filled before the remedies hearing*' (*Kelly*, above).

A tribunal is also not bound to conclude reinstatement is impracticable '*just because reinstatement may require the employer to make some adjustments to the business to accommodate the returning employee*' (*Ozkara*, above).

Non-Compliance

If an employer fails to comply with an order for reinstatement or re-engagement the tribunal will, as noted above, consider practicability on a conclusive basis with the burden of proof on the employer. If the employer fails to establish impracticability, the tribunal will make an Additional Award (see *Additional award*). Where an employer declines to re-engage (or, probably, reinstate) an employee, no interest accrues on any sum awarded under it (*Fotheringhame v Barclays Services Ltd* UKEAT/0208/19/BA).

Statutory authorities: ERA 1996 ss112 to 126

Retirement: see *Pension loss; Table 20; Table 21*

Schedule of loss

The schedule of loss is an integral part of the claim and needs to be devised with care. The sum being claimed must reflect the claimant's reasonable losses, and several versions of the schedule of loss might need to be designed to illustrate the effect of any adjustments that could be made for contributory fault for example.

In particular, future loss is notoriously difficult to calculate due the high degree of speculation involved, but the period needs to be justified, for example by taking into account the health and age of the claimant, their particular expertise and the state of the job market. Any representative should ask very direct questions of their client and check carefully all the information that has been given to them before serving a schedule of loss on the other parties and the tribunal.

See *APPENDIX 2* for an example schedule of loss.

Settlement agreements

(see also *Tax and termination payments*)

Employment may be terminated by mutual agreement, as may tribunal proceedings. Tribunal claims may be settled through early conciliation through ACAS, after the proceedings have begun through a COT3 by ACAS, by agreement between the parties or in the form of a tribunal order dismissing the proceedings upon agreement having been reached between the parties. Agreement between the parties may be reached by a number of routes both informal and formal including mediation, with some cases being mediated by tribunal judges under the official judicial mediation schemes.

Formalities

Where the agreement between the parties is reached other than by use of the COT3 procedure, any agreement by an individual that they will not bring any of a number of employment rights will be ineffective unless certain formalities have been undertaken (see for example s203 ERA 1996 and ss144 and 147 EA 2010). For the compromise of a claim to be valid:

- The contract must be in writing;

- The contract must relate to a particular complaint;

- The individual must, before entering into the contract, have received advice from a relevant independent legal advisor about its terms and effect;

- On the date of giving the advice there must have

been in force insurance or an indemnity against losses arising from giving the advice;

- The contract must identify the advisor;

- The contract must state that bullet points 3 and 4 above have been complied with.

A settlement agreement or COT3 can be set aside by an Employment Tribunal on the same common law grounds as any other agreement (e.g. misrepresentation, duress, undue influence): *Cole v Elders' Voice* UKEAT/0251/19.

Non-Disclosure Agreements (NDAs)

It is common for settlement agreements to contain clauses requiring parties to keep the nature and terms of the agreement, and/or the circumstances giving rise to it, confidential. These clauses are the subject of ongoing public, political and regulatory scrutiny and controversy.

It is beyond the scope of this work to address the matter in detail, but representatives are advised to keep an eye on the potential for ongoing regulatory and legal developments in this area, and to have particular regard to the Law Society's practice note: *Non-disclosure agreements and confidentiality clauses in an employment law context*.

Contractual entitlements

Where a settlement agreement makes payment for contractual payments that have already crystallised, it may well be that such sums would be taxable as earnings rather than under s401 ITEPA 2003 (see *EIM12856*).

Legal expenses

The employer may agree to pay legal costs incurred by the employee. Such a payment may be within s401 ITEPA 2003 since it is made in connection with the termination (see *EIM13010*), but there is a potential tax exemption where the fees are paid directly to the employee's lawyers (see *Tax and termination payments*).

What tax rate should be used when deducting tax?

PAYE74015 explains the different rules when deducting tax.

Termination payment made on or before date of P45

If the termination payment is paid on or before the P45 is issued, tax and NI will be deducted from any taxable termination payment through the normal payroll using the employee's tax code at that date.

Termination payment made after the date of P45

Any taxable termination payments made after the P45 is issued should have tax deducted using the tax code 0T (effectively ignoring any personal tax allowance) and on a non-cumulative basis (which treats each pay period as a separate tax period). This can mean that the employee pays too much tax initially and would have to claim it back from HMRC on their self-assessment.

Sometimes payments paid in instalments may benefit the cash flow for both parties. Each tranche of the termination payment will be taxable independently on the above 0T basis, on the date of entitlement.

For monthly paid employees (using 2021/2022 tax bands)

Only the first £3,142 (i.e. 1/12 x £37,700) of the settlement payment will be charged at the basic rate of 20%;

The next £9,358 (i.e. 1/12 x (£150,000 - £37,700) = 1/12 x £112,300) will be charged to tax at the higher rate of 40%; and

Any remaining balance of the termination payment will be taxed at the additional rate of 45%.

Example

A termination payment of £75,000 is paid to an employee on 01/05/2021 after his P45 has been issued. £55,000 of this payment is taxable. He will pay:

20% of £3,142 = £628.40, plus

40% of £9,358 = £3,743.20, plus

45% of (£55,000 − £3,142 − £9,358) = 45% of £42,500 = £19,125

So his total tax liability, which is payable immediately by the employer, is £23,496.60.

Sex discrimination: see *Discrimination*

Sex Equality Clause

A 'sex equality clause' is implied into every contract of employment, if one is not already present (s66 EA 2010). The effect of a sex equality clause is that any term of an individual's contract of employment, if it is less favourable to him or her than the same term is to a comparable employee of the opposite sex, will be modified so as to not be less favourable. A comparable employee will be of the opposite sex, and the work they are employed to do will be equal (s64 and 65 EA 2010).

This applies to all the parts of the contract including:

- wages and salaries;
- non-discretionary bonuses;
- holiday pay;
- sick pay;
- overtime;

- shift payments;
- occupational pension benefits; and
- non-monetary terms such as holiday or other leave entitlements or access to sports and social benefits.

An employee may bring a claim to the tribunal for breach of his/her sex equality clause under s132 EA 2010.

Remedy: If a tribunal finds that there has been a breach of the sex equality clause it may make a declaration as to the rights of the parties (for example, stating what pay or rate of pay the individual is entitled to). The tribunal may also order an award of arrears of pay or damages (s132 EA 2010).

A limit is imposed on the period over which arrears of pay may be claimed (see s132(4)). In the standard case arrears over the preceding 6 years may be awarded, but where the breach of the clause has been concealed or the individual had an incapacity at the date of the breach, and the claim was presented within 6 years of the date the claimant knew of the claim or was capable of bringing the claim, arrears may be claimed from the date the arrears first occurred (s132(3) EA 2010).

Gross or net: Gross (but then taxed by the employer in the normal way through the payroll).

Limit on a week's pay: None

Limit on number of years: Normally 6

Adjustments: Interest can be awarded for arrears of pay and will be calculated according to the mid-point rule (see *Interest*).

Any maximum or minimum: None

Tax: Awards (or settlements) in respect of claims under the Equal Pay Act 1970 (now EA 2010 Part V, Ch 3) are arrears of pay and therefore should be taxed under s62 ITEPA 2003 (see *EIM02530* HMRC). The tax liability arises in the year of entitlement not in the year of eventual payment. It is unclear whether any interest would also be taxed.

Statutory authorities: EA 2010 *ss66* and *132*; *Employment Tribunals (Interest on Awards in Discrimination Cases) Regulations 1996*

Share options: see *Financial losses*

Shared parental leave (SPL): see *Parental leave*

Short time working: see *Guarantee payment; Week's pay*

Sickness: see *Holiday pay*

Social security benefits: see *Income support; Job seekers allowance; Non-recoupable state benefits; Recoupment*

State pension

This is the pension based on previous NI contributions paid. Women born after 5 April 1953 and men born after 5 April 1951 will claim the new State Pension (nSP) and will need a certain number of NI qualifying years to receive any nSP. See *Table 20* and *Table 21* for state pension ages for men and women and *Table 22* for the current weekly state pension and the number of qualifying years required.

Claimants are not expected to give credit for any state pension benefits received when a tribunal assesses losses suffered by a claimant.

Loss of state pension on termination of employment can be claimed in some circumstances - see *Pension loss* for more information.

Statutory cap

(see also *Additional award; Arrears of pay (reinstatement/re-engagement); Compensatory award; Discrimination; Recoupment; Table 1*)

A statutory cap applies to a compensatory award under s117(1) and (2) ERA and s123. The applicable statutory cap is the lower of the current figure of £89,493 or 52 weeks' gross pay (as defined in ss220 to 229 ERA 1996) (see s124 ERA 1996). *Table 1* lists the historical statutory caps.

Because the definition of a week's pay does not cover all pay or valuable benefits received, an employee may not be compensated for an entire year's losses. However, the cap applies to 52 weeks' gross pay, which effectively means that a claimant could be awarded up to 15 to 16 months' net pay, assuming a combined tax/NI rate of 30%.

There are three situations in which the cap does not apply:

- If the reason for dismissal was discriminatory, the financial losses will be awarded under the discrimination legislation where there is no cap;

- If the employee is regarded as unfairly dismissed by virtue of s100 or 105(3) (Health and Safety cases), 103A or 105(6A) (Whistleblowing);

- If an award under s117 would otherwise not fully reflect the amount of arrears payable to the employee (see also *Arrears of pay (reinstatement/re-engagement)*).

The cap is applied after all the adjustments such as contributory conduct and *Polkey* have been applied. It is also applied **after** any grossing up calculation has been done.

Example

Basic award = £11,000

Compensatory award after all adjustments (see *Adjustments and order of adjustments*) = £90,000

Grossing up calculation (assuming marginal tax rate of 25%)

Gross up £11,000 + £90,000 - £30,000 = £71,000

Grossed up compensatory award of £71,000 = 71,000 ÷ 0.75 = £94,666.67

Compensatory award now = £19,000 + £94,666.67 = £113,666.67

Statutory cap = £89,493

Total award = £11,000 + £89,493 = £100,493

Note: the grossing up should be done **before** the cap is applied.

Statutory authorities: ERA 1996 *ss117(1) & (2), 100, 103A, 105(3), 105(6A), 123* and *124*

Statutory notice period

(see also *Contractual notice period; Effective date of termination; Table 14*)

Section 86 ERA 1996) provides for minimum notice of termination to be given by the parties to the contract of employment. Under normal circumstances, an employee with more than 1 month's continuous service is entitled to 1 week's notice, and having completed 2 years' service is entitled to 2 weeks, with the number of weeks increasing by one each year until a maximum of 12 weeks' notice. The notice an employee must give an employer, having completed 1 month's service, is 1 week (see *Table 14*).

By s86(6) no notice need be given by either party where the other has so seriously breached the contract as to be regarded as having repudiated the contract, in which case the other party may accept the breach and terminate the contract without notice, for example where an employee has committed gross misconduct.

The parties to an employment contract may agree to a longer, contractual notice period. The parties may also waive their right to notice on any occasion or accept payment in lieu of notice (see s86(3)).

Statutory redundancy: see *Redundancy; Table 13; Table 14*

Statutory rights

One of the heads of loss for which a tribunal may award compensation is the value of accrued statutory rights that have been lost: where an employee begins a new job following the termination of their employment, they will need to accrue 2 years' continuous service before they will have acquired the right to claim unfair dismissal or a statutory redundancy payment, and may have lost the right to a lengthy statutory notice period if they have been employed for several years. The sum awarded is usually between £250 and £500, and is not generally governed by the personal circumstances of the employee such as would increase or decrease the actual value of the loss.

Remedy: There is no particular figure that should be awarded, but it is usually around £250 to £500. In *Countrywide Estate Agents & Ors v Turner* UKEAT/0208/13/LA, the EAT held that the ET was entitled to award 2 weeks' gross pay (limited to the weekly pay in force) for loss of statutory rights, as the claimant would take another 2 years to accrue those rights.

No award should be made where there is a finding that the claimant would have been fairly dismissed in any event (*Puglia v C James and Sons* [1996] IRLR 70).

Any maximum or minimum: None

Adjustments: The award is part of the compensatory award and will be adjusted accordingly (see *Hope v Jordan Engineering Ltd* [2008] UKEAT/0545/07). This includes *Polkey* deductions (*Gardner v The Coopers Company & Coborn School* UKEAT/0235/19/BA).

Cap: The award is part of the compensatory award (see *Statutory cap*).

Tax: The award is part of the compensatory award and will be subject to the grossing up calculation, if appropriate, in the normal way.

Recoupment: Recoupment will not apply to this head of loss.

Relevant case law: *Countrywide Estate Agents & Ors v Turner* UKEAT/0208/13/LA; *Gardner v The Coopers Company & Coborn School* UKEAT/0235/19/BA; *Hope v Jordan Engineering Ltd* [2008] UKEAT/0545/07; *Puglia v C James and Sons* [1996] IRLR 70

Summary dismissal: see *Effective date of termination; Notice pay*

Suspension

Part VII ERA 1996 provides the express right for an employee to be paid whilst suspended for particular reasons:

1) An employee who is suspended from work by his employer on medical grounds is entitled to be paid by his employer remuneration while he is so suspended for a period not exceeding 26 weeks (s64(1) ERA 1996);

2) An employee who is suspended from work on maternity grounds is entitled to be paid remuneration by her employer while she is so suspended (s68(1) ERA 1996). Suspension on maternity grounds in effect means suspension on grounds that a woman is pregnant, has recently given birth or is breastfeeding;

3) However, the employee has a right to be offered suitable alternative work, where it exists, before being suspended from work on maternity grounds (s67(1) ERA 1996);

4) Related rights to remuneration or alternative work apply to agency workers, see ss68A to 68D ERA 1996.

A common thread between these rights is that the suspension must be required by other legislative provisions, generally regarding the health and safety of workers (see ss64(2) to (4) and s66 ERA 1996).

An employee may bring a claim that his or her employer has not paid them the remuneration to which they are entitled (see s70 ERA 1996). A similar right exists for agency workers, regarding their maternity suspension rights (see s70A ERA 1996).

Remedy: Where the tribunal finds that the employee or agency worker has not been paid the remuneration to which he or she was entitled, the tribunal will order the employer (or agency) to pay the individual the amount of remuneration which it finds is due to him or her (ss70(3) and 70A(3) ERA 1996). Remuneration is calculated according to the definition of a week's pay (see *Week's pay*) in s220 to s229 (see s69), save that the limit on a week's pay does not apply.

Where a tribunal finds that suitable alternative work has not been provided to an employee or agency worker, the tribunal may make an award of compensation (see s70(6) and (7) and s70A(6) and (7) ERA 1996). The amount of the compensation is that which the tribunal considers just and equitable in all the circumstances having regard to:

a) the infringement of the employee's right under s67 by the failure on the part of the employer to which the complaint relates; and

b) any loss sustained by the employee which is attributable to that failure.

It is likely that an award for injury to feelings can be made where there has been a failure to provide suitable alternative work, since the statutory wording for calculating the loss is that used in the detriment provisions (s49 ERA 1996) and the protection of a woman who may be suspended on maternity grounds may be seen to be akin to the protection provided by discrimination legislation.

Gross or net: The award for lost remuneration will be calculated gross, as the definition of a week's pay in ss220 to 229 ERA 1996 applies (see *Week's pay*).

The award for a failure to provide suitable alternative work will be based on net losses, and also any injury to feelings award.

Limit on a week's pay: None

Limit on number of weeks: 26 weeks' remuneration for suspension on medical grounds (see s64(1)); otherwise unlimited

Any maximum or minimum: None, other than the maximum award will be 26 weeks' actual gross pay where the award is for remuneration for suspension on medical grounds (see s64(1)).

Adjustments: None

Tax: To the extent that the sum awarded is compensation for lost earnings, it is likely to be taxed under s62 ITEPA 2003 (see *Tax and termination payments* and EIM02550).

Recoupment: Recoupment applies to awards made in respect of a failure to pay remuneration (see Schedule to *The Employment Protection (Recoupment of Jobseeker's Allowance and Income Support) Regulations 1996*).

Statutory authorities: ERA 1996 *ss64(1)*, *67(1)* and *s68(1)*; Schedule to *The Employment Protection (Recoupment of Jobseeker's Allowance and Income Support) Regulations 1996*

Tax and termination payments

(see also *Gourley principle; Grossing up; Injury to feelings*)

Specific tax regimes apply to income and benefits derived from employment (*s62* ITEPA 2003), and to payments made in connection with employment (*ss401 to 416* ITEPA 2003). Where a tribunal makes a monetary award it will take into account how that sum will be treated for tax: the award may amount to an order that the employer pay salary; the award may be for a sum

due in connection with employment; an award may fall outside the tax regimes or fall within an exception or allowance. Where tax will be paid by the claimant on the sum he receives, the tribunal will gross up the award to ensure that the sum received after tax is appropriate.

The tax regimes apply to a variety of sums including earnings, *ex gratia* payments, sums paid under settlement agreements and tribunal awards. The tax treatment of any sum will depend on the nature of the underlying sum, and the circumstances of its payment. Essentially, any sum will be taxed under the applicable employment provisions (see further below) - if none of them apply then the sum may be taxed as being paid in connection with termination. If none of the foregoing regimes apply, the payment will not be subject to tax.

By way of example:

- Earnings and benefits will be taxed (and have NIC deducted) by the employer under the applicable tax code;

- An award by a tribunal that an employer pay unlawfully deducted wages will be calculated gross, and the employer will pay the sum (and deduct tax on it) as he does wages;

- Sums paid under a termination agreement between employer and employee, providing for sums owing under the contract that are earnings, will be taxed by the employer under the applicable tax code;

- Sums paid under a termination agreement between employer and employee, which do not amount to sums owing under the contract that are earnings, such as an enhanced redundancy payment, may fall within the regime for payments made in connection with termination. A £30,000 allowance applies to such sums;

- An award by a tribunal for losses arising from unfair dismissal, including the failure to pay an enhanced redundancy payment, will be treated as a payment made in connection with termination, where the £30,000 allowance applies.

Some sums do not fall within easily identifiable categories, for example, punitive awards such as a protective award, injury to feelings and an award for discrimination occurring independently of termination.

The applicable principles are dealt with below.

Identifying the applicable tax regime

The starting point is to ascertain whether the payment could be classed as earnings, in which case tax and employee and employer NI will be payable under s62 ITEPA 2003, or as a taxable benefit under Part 3 Chapters 2 to 11 ITEPA 2003.

If the payment does not fall under the category of earnings, the next consideration is whether it is a payment in consideration of a restrictive covenant, in which case it is fully taxable (*s225* ITEPA 2003).

If neither of the first two conditions apply, the next question is whether the payment is in respect of an employer-financed retirement benefit, taxable under Part 6 Chapter 2 of ITEPA 2003.

If the answer to all the previous questions is in the negative, and the payment is *'received directly or indirectly in consideration of or in consequence of or otherwise in connection with the termination of employment'*, it will be taxed under Part 6 Chapter 3 of ITEPA. A tax free allowance of £30,000 applies to such payments.

From 6 April 2020, in respect of any payments which fall under s401 ITEPA 2003, employer (but not employee) National Insurance is payable on any amount exceeding £30,000.

If none of the above apply, the compensation is unconnected with the employment or its termination and is therefore outside the scope of income tax and NIC. For example, payments or awards for damages for breach of contract prior to termination do not fall within the above provisions, neither do awards for injury to feelings from discrimination unconnected with termination.

Fully taxable and subject to NI deductions

- Earnings from employment;
- Arrears of pay (but see 'Reinstatement or re-engagement' later in this entry);
- Accrued holiday pay;
- Payments made in consideration of restrictive covenants (s225 ITEPA 2003), unless the specific consideration is attached to the restatement of existing covenants or an agreement to discontinue proceedings (see *Appellant v Inspector of Taxes* [2001] STC (SCD) 21);
- Payment in respect of a non-approved retirement benefit;
- Contractual and non-contractual PILONs;
- Implied contractual right to a PILON;
- Termination payments/'post employment notice pay';
- Contractual benefits in kind;
- Payments during garden leave;
- Payments to an employee suspended from work on medical grounds under Sections *64* and *70(3)* ERA 1996 (EIM02550, HMRC);

- Maternity suspension payments under Sections 68 and 70(3) ERA 1996 (EIM02550, HMRC);
- Payments under Sections 51(3)(b) or 63(4) ERA 1996 for infringing the employee's rights to time off for public duties under s50 or Trade Union duties or activities under ss61 and 62 respectively (EIM02550, HMRC);
- Payments under the Sex Discrimination Acts, the Equal Pay Act 1970 (see *EIM02530*), the Wages Act 1986, the Trade Union and Labour Relations (Consolidation) Act 1992 and the National Minimum Wage Act 1998 for wrongfully depressing the employee's remuneration in the employment (*EIM02550*, HMRC).

Payments which are fully taxable by the employer before payment to the individual should not be grossed up by the tribunal.

Payments in lieu of notice (PILONS)

From 6 April 2018, payments in lieu of notice, whether contractual or otherwise, are taxable as earnings and are not taxed under, or qualify for, any exemptions in ss401 to 416 ITEPA 2003. The taxable component is defined as "post employment notice pay" and calculated In line with the formula in s402D ITEPA 2003. This is fully subject to income tax and Class 1 NICs. Any element that exceeds this, however, is subject to the £30,000 threshold under ITEPA 2003. Previously, only payments where there was an express or implied contractual right to a PILON, or where there was a discretion to make a PILON, were fully taxable (see *EMI Group Electronics Ltd v Coldicott* [1999] IRLR 630).

Subject to the above, where a payment made on termination, in a settlement agreement or in the form of a tribunal award, falls within Part 6 Chapter 3 of ITEPA, that particular regime will apply. This includes a £30,000 allowance, so for example in a straightforward unfair dismissal award made by a tribunal the first £30,000 will be exempt from tax, and any award above this will be grossed up by the tribunal to ensure the individual retains the value of his net loss. However, note *Hill v Revenue & Customs* [2015] UKFTT 295 (TC) where the claimant was transferred under TUPE and the tribunal did not accept his argument that a payment of £30,000 in settlement of his grievance was not taxable because his employment was ongoing.

Payments and other benefits that fall within this regime include:

- Non-contractual benefits in kind;
- Statutory, non-contractual and contractual redundancy payments, provided that they are genuinely on account of redundancy (see *Mairs v Haughey* [1994] 1 AC 303);
- Basic award;

- Awards for financial loss whether for unfair dismissal or as a result of discrimination;

- Damages for wrongful dismissal;

- An additional award;

- An award for employer failing to provide a statement of written particulars (see *EIM12960*);

- Protective awards;

- Payment by the employer of the employee's legal expenses (but see 'Specific categories of award' below).

Any part of the total award in excess of the £30,000 tax free allowance and which has been calculated on a net basis should be grossed up to ensure the employee receives the sum that has been awarded. This means that any of the compensatory award or award of damages which forms part or all of the excess figure should be grossed up.

Exempt from taxation

Certain payments are exempted from taxation under s401 ITEPA 2003 and will therefore not be taxed at all. Payments include:

- Payment made by reason of the death of an employee or on account of an injury to, or disability of, the employee (but **not** for injured feelings – see *Injury to feelings*);

- Payment of legal expenses where the sum is either awarded by the tribunal or paid under a settlement agreement directly to the individual's lawyer (*Enactment of Extra-Statutory Concessions Order 2011 SI 2011/1037*, Article 10);

- Certain costs in connection with counselling, outplacement and retraining courses (ss310 and 311 ITEPA 2003).

Payments which are exempt from tax should not be grossed up.

Foreign service exemption

Prior to 6 April 2018, full and partial exemptions applied to payments made in respect of foreign service, where an employee was both non-resident and non-ordinarily resident in the UK (s413 ITEPA 2003). From 6 April 2018, employees who are UK resident in the tax year their employment is terminated will not be eligible for foreign service relief on their termination payment.

Specific categories of award

Unlawful deduction from wages

A tribunal ought to award payment for unlawful deduction from wages under s13 ERA 1996 gross, with the employer deducting tax and NIC at source, as such payments fall within s62 ITEPA 2003.

Reinstatement or re-engagement

Where a tribunal has made an award for lost salary between the date of dismissal and the reinstatement or re-engagement, that sum is not taxed as earnings under s62 ITEPA 2003 but will fall within s401 (*Wilson v Clayton* [2005] IRLR 108). Such sums will be calculated on a net basis and grossed up where appropriate (see *EIM12960*).

Discrimination not involving termination

According to HMRC in EIM12965 and *Yorkshire Housing Ltd v Cuerden* UKEAT/0397/09, compensation payments made for discrimination that does not cause termination will not be subject to tax. See also *Mr A v Revenue & Customs (Income tax/Corporation tax: Employment income)* [2015] UKFTT 189 where the claimant accepted £600,000 in settlement of his threatened claim for discrimination. The first tier tribunal ruled that the reason the payment was made by the employer was (rightly or wrongly on their part) to settle a discrimination claim and not to pay back money which they thought the appellant was entitled to in respect of underpaid salary and bonus.

Compensation payments would include any financial and non-financial losses such as an award for injury to feelings. Such an award should be calculated on a net basis, and there will not be a need to gross up.

Discrimination involving termination

Awards made in connection with termination arising from discrimination will be taxable under s401 ITEPA 2003 (*Walker v Adams* [2001] STC 101, *Orthet v Vince Cain* [2004] IRLR 857 and *Oti-Obihara v Commissioners for HM Revenue & Customs* [2011] IRLR 386 and *Moorthy v The Commissioners for Her Majesty's Revenue & Customs* [2014] UKFTT 834 (TC), and *Moorthy v Revenue & Customs* [2016] UKUT 13 (TC).

Equality clauses

Where an award is made for breach of an equality clause, the award will be subject to tax on the basis of the tax due in the year the sum ought to have been paid (EIM02530). The award should be calculated on a gross basis, with the employer operating an appropriate special PAYE procedure.

Injury to feelings

Awards for injury to feelings unrelated to termination of employment are tax-free, as are such awards related to the termination of employment prior to 6 April 2018 (*Moorthy v HMRC* [2018] EWCA Civ 847). However, from 6 April 2018, any compensation for injury to feelings in a termination payment will be taxable to the extent that the £30,000 'allowance' has been exceeded, following an amendment to s406 ITEPA 2003, except where the compensation is for a psychiatric injury.

Protective awards and TUPE consultation

Though protective awards are calculated by reference to pay over a protected period, such sums are not paid by reference to the individual acting as an employee, but under statute (and as punishment for breach of a statutory obligation) (see *Mimtec Ltd v Inland Revenue* [2001] UKSC SPC00277). They therefore fall under s401 rather than s62 ITEPA 2003.

The logic applied in *Mimtec* might suggest that where an award has been made for failure to inform and consult under TUPE, which is unconnected to any termination, the award would not be subject to tax at all. Where an individual in receipt of such an award has been subject to a transfer, it might be argued that the transfer, for the purposes of the tax regime, did amount to a termination (see *Kuehne & Nagel Drinks Logistics Ltd, Scott & Joyce v HMRC* [2009] UKFTT 379 (TC)). That argument would not however apply to an individual affected by the transfer, whose representatives were not appropriately consulted, but who did not themselves transfer.

Payments unrelated to termination

Where an award is made for breach of a statutory right, for example if the employer has not complied with the right of an employee to be accompanied at a disciplinary hearing, this is unrelated to the individual's termination and may well not be earnings. There is no official guidance on how such sums should be treated. However, the logic in *Mimtec Ltd v Inland Revenue* [2001] UKSC SPC00277, that such sums are not paid by reference to the individual acting as an employee but under statute (and as punishment for breach of a statutory obligation), could apply. Such payments may well not be subject to tax and should not be grossed up.

Payment of employee's legal expenses by the employer

An employer may agree to pay legal costs incurred by an employee in relation to a claim against the employer after the contract of employment has been terminated. Such a payment falls within s401 ITEPA 2003 since it is made in connection with the termination (see EIM13010), but as a concession the sum will not be charged where:

1) the dispute is settled without recourse to the courts and three conditions are met:

   a) the payment is made direct to the employee's solicitor rather than to the employee himself or herself; and

   b) the payment is applied to discharge the bill for solicitor's costs that the employee has incurred only in connection with the termination of the employment; and

   c) the payment is made under a specific term in the agreement that settles the dispute;

or

2) the payment of costs by the employer is made in accordance with a court order. This applies even if the payment is made directly to the employee.

Note that the concession:

- applies only to legal costs, not to any other professional costs (such as accountancy fees). However, it does include the expenses of expert professional witnesses incurred by the employee's legal advisor;

- does not allow an employee to claim a deduction for his or her own legal costs in any way.

Interim relief

Payments made under a continuation order are taxable as payments in connection with termination under s401, not in full as earnings under s62 ITEPA (see also *Interim relief*). See *Turullols v HMRC* [2014] UKFTT 672 (TC) where the First Tier Tribunal held that the claimant, who was found to have been unfairly dismissed, could claim back the tax that had been paid on the salary payments made under the interim relief order because they were payments in connection with the termination of her employment and therefore should have been tax-free up to £30,000. This would also have been the case even if the ET had not upheld the unfair dismissal claim.

From April 2020

From 6 April 2020, Employer National Insurance, but not employee NI, is payable at 13.8% on any amount above £30,000.

Time off to accompany to ante-natal appointment

(see also *Time off for ante-natal care*)

An expectant father, or the partner of a pregnant woman, and other employees who have a qualifying relationship with a pregnant woman or her expected child are entitled to be permitted by his or her employer to take time off during the employee's working hours in order that he or she may accompany the woman when she attends by appointment at any place for the purpose of receiving ante-natal care (s57ZE ERA 1996).

An employee may present a complaint to an employment tribunal that his or her employer has unreasonably refused to let him or her take time off as required by s57ZE.

Equivalent rights to time off and remuneration for the period of absence are given to agency workers, with the remuneration to be paid by the agency (see s57ZH).

Remedy: Where a tribunal finds a complaint well founded, it will make a declaration to that effect (s57ZF(4a)).

Further, if the tribunal has found that the employer has unreasonably refused to permit the employee to take time off, the tribunal will also order the employer to pay compensation to the employee according to the following formula (s57ZF(5)):

> Amount to be paid = Appropriate hourly rate for the employee x Number of working hours for which the employee would have been entitled under s57ZE to be absent if the time off had not been refused x 2

Unless the employee works a varying number of working hours, the appropriate hourly rate is one week's pay divided by the normal working hours in a week when the time off would have been taken. For employees whose hours of work vary over a week or longer period, the appropriate hourly rate is obtained by dividing one week's pay by the average number of hours worked over the previous 12 weeks, or where the employee has not been employed for 12 weeks, a number which fairly represents the number of normal working hours in a week (see s57ZF(7)).

A week's pay will be calculated in accordance with s220 to s229 ERA 1996 (see *Week's pay*).

Gross or net: The sum for unpaid earnings will be calculated gross and paid through payroll as with ordinary remuneration.

Any maximum or minimum: None

Adjustments: The claimant will have to give credit for any amount paid towards the entitlement under the contract.

Mitigation: N/A

Tax: The tax treatment is not clear. To the extent that the sum awarded is compensation for lost earnings for work done, it is likely to be taxed under s62 ITEPA 2003 (see *Tax and termination payments*).

Recoupment: N/A

Statutory authorities: ERA 1996 ss57ZE and 57ZF

Time off to attend adoption appointments

Employees proposing to adopt a child may take time off to attend up to 5 adoption appointments. The time off must be paid where the employee is adopting the child on their own (ss57ZJ to ZL ERA 1996).

If the employee is adopting jointly, then one of the parents may elect to receive the time off as paid and the other will be entitled to take unpaid leave for up to 2 appointments.

A maximum of 6 ½ hours is allowed for each appointment in all cases.

An employee may present a complaint to an employment tribunal that his or her employer has unreasonably refused to let him or her take time off as required by s57ZJ to L. Equivalent rights to time off and remuneration for the period of absence are given to agency workers, with the remuneration to be paid by the agency (see s57ZN).

Remedy: Where a tribunal finds a complaint well founded, it will make a declaration to that effect (s57ZM(4)).

If the complaint is that the employer has failed to pay the employee the whole or part of any amount to which the employee is entitled under s57ZK (paid time off), the tribunal must order the employer to pay compensation to the employee the amount which it finds due to the employee.

Further, if the tribunal has found that the employer has unreasonably refused to permit the employee to take time off, the tribunal will also order the employer to pay to the employee according to the following formula (s57ZM(7)):

> Amount to be paid = Appropriate hourly rate for the employee x Number of working hours for which the employee would have been entitled under s57Z to be absent if the time off had not been refused x 2

Unless the employee works a varying number of working hours, the appropriate hourly rate is one week's pay divided by the normal working hours in a week when the time off would have been taken. For employees whose hours of work vary over a week or longer period, the appropriate hourly rate is obtained by dividing one week's pay by the average number of hours worked over the previous 12 weeks, or where the employee has not been employed for 12 weeks, a number which fairly represents the number of normal working hours in a week (see s57ZK).

A week's pay will be calculated in accordance with s220 to s229 ERA 1996 (see *Week's pay*).

Gross or net: The sum for unpaid earnings will be calculated gross and paid through payroll as with ordinary remuneration.

Any maximum or minimum: None

Adjustments: The claimant will have to give credit for any amount paid towards the entitlement under the contract.

Mitigation: N/A

Tax: The tax treatment is not clear. To the extent that the sum awarded is compensation for lost earnings for work done, it is likely to be taxed under s62 ITEPA 2003 (see *Tax and termination payments*).

Recoupment: N/A

Statutory authorities: ERA 1996 ss57ZJ to 57ZN

Time off for ante-natal care

(see also *Time off to accompany to ante-natal appointment*)

An employee who has an appointment for the purpose of receiving ante-natal care is entitled to be permitted by her employer to take time off during the employee's working hours in order to enable her to keep the appointment (s55 ERA 1996).

The employee is entitled to be paid at their 'appropriate hourly rate' for their period of absence. Unless the employee works a varying number of working hours, the appropriate hourly rate is one week's pay divided by the normal working hours in a week when the time off was taken. For employees whose hours of work vary over a week or longer period, the appropriate hourly rate is obtained by dividing one week's pay by the average number of hours worked over the previous 12 weeks, or where the employee has not been employed for 12 weeks, a number which fairly represents the number of normal working hours in a week (see s56(2), (3) and (4) ERA 1996).

A week's pay will be calculated in accordance with ss220 to 229 ERA 1996 (see *Week's pay*).

Any contractual remuneration paid to an employee in respect of such a period of time off goes towards discharging the liability under s56 (see s56(5) and (6) ERA 1996).

An employee may bring a complaint to a tribunal that her employer has unreasonably refused to permit her to take the time off under s55, or has failed to pay the sums due under s56 (see s57(1) ERA 1996).

Equivalent rights to time off and remuneration for the period of absence are given to agency workers, with the remuneration to be paid by the agency (see ss57ZA to 57ZD).

Remedy: Where a tribunal finds a complaint well founded, it will make a declaration to that effect (s57(3)).

Further, if the tribunal has found that the employer has unreasonably refused to permit the employee to take time off, the tribunal will also order the employer to pay to the employee an amount equal to the remuneration to which she would have been entitled under s56 if the employer had not refused (s57(4)). Also, if the tribunal finds that the employer has failed to pay the employee the whole or part of any amount to which she is entitled under s56, the tribunal will also order the employer to pay to the employee the amount she is owed (s57(5)).

For employees working fixed number of hours per week

Sum to which the employee is entitled = (gross weekly pay) x 1/(number of normal working hours in a week) x (number of hours absent) (s56(2) ERA 1996)

For employees with varying number of hours worked per week

Sum to which the employee is entitled = gross weekly pay x 12/(number of normal hours worked in the last 12 weeks ending with the last complete week before the day on which the time off is taken) x (number of hours absent) (s56(3) ERA 1996)

For employees with varying number of hours worked per week and who have worked for less than 12 weeks

Sum to which the employee is entitled = (gross weekly pay) x 1/(number of normal hours which fairly represents the number of normal working hours in a week) x (number of hours absent) (s56(3) and (4) ERA 1996)

Gross or net: The sum for unpaid earnings will be calculated gross and paid through payroll as with ordinary remuneration.

Any maximum or minimum: None

Adjustments: The claimant will have to give credit for any amount paid towards the entitlement under the contract.

Mitigation: N/A

Tax: The tax treatment is not clear. To the extent that the sum awarded is compensation for lost earnings for work done, it is likely to be taxed under s62 ITEPA 2003 (see *Tax and termination payments*).

Recoupment: N/A

Statutory authorities: ERA 1996 *ss55, 56* and *ss57ZA to 57ZD*

Time off for dependants

An employee is entitled to be permitted by his employer to take a reasonable amount of time off during the employee's working hours in order to care for or sort out issues in relation to a dependant (s57A ERA 1996). The definition of a dependant includes amongst others a spouse, a civil partner, a child and a parent.

An employee may bring a complaint to a tribunal that his employer has unreasonably refused to permit him to take this time off (s57B ERA 1996).

Remedy: Where the tribunal finds such a complaint well founded it will make a declaration to that effect (s57B(3)(a)).

It may also make an award of compensation to be paid by the employer (s57B(3)(b) and (4)).

The amount of compensation will be that which it considers just and equitable in all the circumstances having regard to:

a)   the employer's default in refusing to permit time off to be taken by the employee; and

b)   any loss sustained by the employee as a result.

Any maximum or minimum: There is no statutory limit to the compensation.

Adjustments: N/A

Mitigation: It is likely that the principle of mitigation would be applied in an appropriate case. However, this would most likely operate to restrict the losses that would be compensated for where it would have been reasonable for the employee to have incurred a lower level of losses than were in fact incurred, for example where the alternative care was unreasonably expensive and reasonably avoidable.

Tax: The tax treatment is not clear. To the extent that the sum awarded is compensation for lost earnings for work done, it is likely to be taxed under s62 ITEPA 2003 (see *Tax and termination payments* and EIM02550).

Recoupment: N/A

Statutory authorities: ERA 1996 *s57A and 57B*

Time off for employee representatives

An employee representative for the purposes of collective consultation or TUPE consultation is entitled to take reasonable time off during the employee's working hours to perform his functions as such an employee representative, or candidate in an election for such a role, or in order to undergo training to perform such functions (s61 ERA 1996).

The employee is entitled to be paid at their 'appropriate hourly rate' for their period of absence. Unless the employee works a varying number of working hours, the appropriate hourly rate is one week's pay divided by the normal working hours in a week when the time off was taken.

For employees whose hours of work vary over a week or longer period, the appropriate hourly rate is obtained by dividing one week's pay by the average number of hours worked over the previous 12 weeks, or where the employee has not been employed for 12 weeks, a number which fairly represents the number of normal working hours in a week (s62 ERA 1996).

A week's pay will be calculated in accordance with ss220 to 229 ERA 1996 (see *Week's pay*).

Any contractual remuneration paid to an employee in respect of such a period of time off goes towards discharging the liability under s62 (see s62(5) and (6)).

An employee may bring a complaint to a tribunal that his or her employer has unreasonably refused to permit him or her to take the time off under s61, or has failed to pay the sums due under s62 (see s63(1) ERA 1996).

Remedy: Where a tribunal finds a complaint well founded, it will make a declaration to that effect (s63(3) ERA 1996).

Further, if the tribunal has found that the employer has unreasonably refused to permit the employee to take time off, the tribunal will also order the employer to pay to the employee an amount equal to the remuneration to which he or she would have been entitled under s62 if the employer had not refused (s63(4) ERA 1996).

Also, if the tribunal finds that the employer has failed to pay the employee the whole or part of any amount to which he or she is entitled under s62, the tribunal will also order the employer to pay to the employee the amount he or she is owed (s63(5) ERA 1996).

For employees working fixed number of hours per week

Sum to which the employee is entitled = (gross weekly pay) x 1/(number of normal working hours in a week) x (number of hours absent) (s62(2) ERA 1996)

For employees with varying number of hours worked per week

Sum to which the employee is entitled = gross weekly pay x 12/(number of normal hours worked in the last 12 weeks ending with the last complete week before the day on which the time off is taken) x (number of hours absent) (s62(3)(a) ERA 1996)

For employees with varying number of hours worked per week and who have worked for less than 12 weeks

Sum to which the employee is entitled = (gross weekly pay) x 1/(number of normal hours which fairly represents the number of normal working hours in a week) x (number of hours absent) (s62(3) and (4) ERA 1996)

Gross or net: The sum will be calculated gross and paid through payroll as with ordinary remuneration.

Any maximum or minimum: None

Adjustments: The claimant will have to give credit for any amount paid towards the entitlement under the contract.

Mitigation: N/A

Tax: Taxable under s62 ITEPA 2003 (see *EIM02550*).

Recoupment: N/A

Statutory authorities: ERA 1996 *ss61 to 63*

Time off for employee representatives (ICE)

An employee representative who is a negotiating representative or an information and consultation representative within the Information and Consultation of Employees Regulations 2004 is entitled to take reasonable time off during the employee's working hours to perform his functions as such a representative (Reg 27 ICE Regs 2004).

The employee is entitled to be paid at their 'appropriate hourly rate' for their period of absence. Unless the employee works a varying number of working hours, the appropriate hourly rate is one week's pay divided by the normal working hours in a week when the time off was taken. For employees whose hours of work vary over a week or longer period, the appropriate hourly rate is obtained by dividing one week's pay by the average number of hours worked over the previous 12 weeks, or where the employee has not been employed for 12 weeks, a number which fairly represents the number of normal working hours in a week (see Reg 28(3), (4) and (5)).

A week's pay will be calculated in accordance with ss220 to 229 ERA 1996 (see *Week's pay*) (Reg 28(2)).

Any contractual remuneration paid to an employee in respect of such a period of time off goes towards discharging the liability under Reg 28 (see Reg 28(6) and (7)).

An employee may bring a complaint to a tribunal that his or her employer has unreasonably refused to permit him or her to take the time off under Reg 27, or has failed to pay the sums due under Reg 28 (see Reg 29).

Remedy: Where a tribunal finds a complaint well founded, it will make a declaration to that effect (Reg 29(3)).

Further, if the tribunal has found that the employer has unreasonably refused to permit the employee to take time off, the tribunal will also order the employer to pay to the employee an amount equal to the remuneration to which he or she would have been entitled under Reg 28 if the employer had not refused (Reg 29(4)).

Also, if the tribunal finds that the employer has failed to pay the employee the whole or part of any amount to which he or she is entitled under Reg 28, the tribunal will also order the employer to pay to the employee the amount he or she is owed (Reg 29(5)).

For employees working fixed number of hours per week

Sum to which the employee is entitled = (gross weekly pay) x 1/(number of normal working hours in a week) x (number of hours absent) (Reg 28(3))

For employees with varying number of hours worked per week

Sum to which the employee is entitled = gross weekly pay x 12/(number of normal hours worked in the last 12 weeks ending with the last complete week before the day on which the time off is taken) x (number of hours absent)

For employees with varying number of hours worked per week and who have worked for less than 12 weeks

Sum to which the employee is entitled = (gross weekly pay) x 1/(number of normal hours which fairly represents the number of normal working hours in a week) x (number of hours absent) (Reg 28(4) and (5) ICE 2004)

Gross or net: Gross. A week's pay as defined in ss220 to 229 ERA 1996 applies (see *Week's pay*) (Reg 28(2)).

Limit on a week's pay: None. The calculation is based on actual gross weekly pay.

Limit on number of weeks: None

Any maximum or minimum: None

Adjustments: None

Mitigation: N/A

Tax: The tax treatment is not clear. To the extent that the sum awarded is compensation for lost earnings for work done, it is likely to be taxed under s62 ITEPA 2003 (see *Tax and termination payments* and EIM02550).

Recoupment: N/A

Statutory authorities: ICE 2004 (SI 2004/3426) Regs *27* and *29*

Time off for employee representatives (OPPS)

A 'consulted representative' within the Occupational and Personal Pension Schemes (Consultation by Employers and Miscellaneous Amendment) Regulations 2006 (OPPS Regs 2006) is entitled to take reasonable time off during the employee's working hours to perform his functions as such a representative (Sch para 2 OPPS 2006). A 'consulted representative' is an employee who is a trade union representative, appointed representative, elected representative or one identified in an appropriate agreement (Reg 12(2)(a) and (3) and Reg 13(2) of OPPS Regs 2006).

The employee is entitled to be paid at their 'appropriate hourly rate' for their period of absence. Unless the employee works a varying number of working hours, the appropriate hourly rate is one week's pay divided by the normal working hours in a week when the time off was taken. For employees whose hours of work vary over a week or longer period, the appropriate hourly rate is obtained by dividing one week's pay by the average number of hours worked over the previous 12 weeks, or where the employee has not been employed for 12 weeks, a number which fairly represents the number of normal working hours in a week (see Sch para 3(3), (4) and (5)).

A week's pay will be calculated in accordance with ss220 to 229 ERA 1996 (see *Week's pay*) (Sch para 3(2)).

Any contractual remuneration paid to an employee in respect of such a period of time off goes towards discharging the liability under Sch para 3 (see Sch para 3(6) and (7)).

An employee may bring a complaint to a tribunal that his or her employer has unreasonably refused to permit him or her to take the time off under Sch para 2, or has failed to pay the sums due under Sch para 3 (see Sch para 4 OPPS 2006).

Remedy: Where a tribunal finds a complaint well founded, it will make a declaration to that effect (Sch para 4(3) OPPS 2006).

Further, if the tribunal has found that the employer has unreasonably refused to permit the employee to take time off, the tribunal will also order the employer to pay to the employee an amount equal to the remuneration to which he or she would have been entitled under Sch para 3 if the employer had not refused (Sch para 4(4)).

Also, if the tribunal finds that the employer has failed to pay the employee the whole or part of any amount to which he or she is entitled under Reg 28, the tribunal will also order the employer to pay to the employee the amount he or she is owed (Sch para 4(5)).

For employees working fixed number of hours per week

Sum to which the employee is entitled = (gross weekly pay) x 1/(number of normal working hours in a week) x (number of hours absent) (Sch para 3(3) OPPS Regs 2006)

For employees with varying number of hours worked per week

Sum to which the employee is entitled = gross weekly pay x 12/(number of normal hours worked in the last 12 weeks ending with the last complete week before the day on which the time off is taken) x (number of hours absent) (Sch para 3(4) OPPS Regs 2006)

For employees with varying number of hours worked per week and who have worked for less than 12 weeks

Sum to which the employee is entitled = (gross weekly pay) x 1/(number of normal hours which fairly represents the number of normal working hours in a week) x (number of hours absent) (Sch para 3(4) and (5) OPPS Regs 2006)

Gross or net: Gross. A week's pay as defined in ss220 to 229 ERA 1996 applies (see *Week's pay*).

Limit on a week's pay: None. The calculation is based on actual gross weekly pay.

Limit on number of weeks: None

Any maximum or minimum: None

Adjustments: None

Mitigation: N/A

Tax: The tax treatment is not clear. To the extent that the sum awarded is compensation for lost earnings for work done, it is likely to be taxed under s62 ITEPA 2003 (see *Tax and termination payments* and EIM02550).

Recoupment: N/A

Statutory authorities: OPPS Regs 2006 (SI 2006/349) Regs *12*, *13* and *Schedule paragraphs 2 to 4*

Time off for members of a European Works Council

An employee who is:

a)   a member of a special negotiating body;

b)   a member of a European Works Council;

c)   an information and consultation representative; or

d)   a candidate in an election in which any person elected will, on being elected, be such a member or representative,

is entitled to take reasonable time off during the employee's working hours to perform his functions as such a representative (Reg 25 Transnational Information and Consultation of Employees Regulations 1999 (SI 1999/3323) (TICE 1999)).

An employee who is:

a)   a member of a special negotiating body;

b)   a member of a European Works Council,

is entitled to take reasonable time off during the employee's working hours to undertake the training permitted by Reg 19B (Reg 25(1A) TICE Regs 1999).

The employee is entitled to be paid at their 'appropriate hourly rate' for their period of absence. Unless the employee works a varying number of working hours, the appropriate hourly rate is one week's pay divided by the normal working hours in a week when the time off was taken. For employees whose hours of work vary over a week or longer period, the appropriate hourly rate is obtained by dividing one week's pay by the average number of hours worked over the previous 12 weeks, or where the employee has not been employed for 12 weeks, a number which fairly represents the number of normal working hours in a week (see Reg 26(3), (4) and (5)).

A week's pay will be calculated in accordance with ss220 to 229 ERA 1996 (see *Week's pay*) (Reg 26(2)).

Any contractual remuneration paid to an employee in respect of such a period of time off goes towards discharging the liability under Reg 26 (see Reg 26(6) and (7)).

An employee may bring a complaint to a tribunal that his or her employer has unreasonably refused to permit him or her to take the time off under Reg 25, or has failed to pay the sums due under Reg 26 (see Reg 27 TICE 1999).

Remedy: Where a tribunal finds a complaint well founded, it will make a declaration to that effect (Reg 27(3)).

Further, if the tribunal has found that the employer has unreasonably refused to permit the employee to take time off, the tribunal will also order the employer to pay to the employee an amount equal to the remuneration to which he or she would have been entitled under Reg 26 if the employer had not refused (Reg 27(4)).

Also, if the tribunal finds that the employer has failed to pay the employee the whole or part of any amount to which he or she is entitled under Reg 26, the tribunal will also order the employer to pay to the employee the amount he or she is owed (Reg 27(5)).

For employees working a fixed number of hours per week

Sum to which the employee is entitled = (gross weekly pay) x 1/(number of normal working hours in a week) x (number of hours absent) (Reg 26(3) TICE 1999)

For employees with varying number of hours worked per week

Sum to which the employee is entitled = gross weekly pay x 12/(number of normal hours worked in the last 12 weeks ending with the last complete week before the day on which the time off is taken) x (number of hours absent) (Reg 26(4) TICE 1999)

For employees with varying number of hours worked per week and who have worked for less than 12 weeks

Sum to which the employee is entitled = (gross weekly pay) x 1/(number of normal hours which fairly represents the number of normal working hours in a week) x (number of hours absent) (Reg 26(4) and (5) TICE 1999)

Gross or net: Gross. A week's pay as defined in ss220 to 229 ERA 1996 applies (see *Week's pay*).

Limit on a week's pay: None. The calculation is based on actual gross weekly pay.

Limit on number of weeks: None

Any maximum or minimum: None

Adjustments: None

Mitigation: N/A

Tax: The tax treatment is not clear. To the extent that the sum awarded is compensation for lost earnings for work done, it is likely to be taxed under s62 ITEPA 2003 (see *Tax and termination payments* and *EIM02550*).

Recoupment: N/A

Statutory authorities: TICE 1999 (SI 1999/3323) Regs 19B, 25 to 27

Time off for pension scheme trustees

An employee who is the trustee of his employer's pension scheme is permitted to take time off to perform the duties of a trustee and undergo relevant training. The amount of time off is that which is reasonable in all the circumstances having regard to how much time is required to be taken off and the effect of the employee's absence on the running of the employer's business (s58 ERA 1996).

The employee must be paid by his or her employer for the time taken off under s58 (s59). Where the employee's remuneration would not have varied with the amount of work done during the period of absence, the employee should be paid as if he or she had worked for the whole of that time (s59(2)). However, where the employee's remuneration would have varied with the amount of work done, he or she should be paid their average hourly earnings for the period (s59(3) and (4)).

Any contractual remuneration paid to an employee in respect of such a period of time off goes towards discharging the liability under s59 (see s59(5) and (6)).

An employee may bring a complaint to a tribunal that his or her employer has unreasonably refused to permit him or her to take the time off under s58, or has failed to pay the sums due under s59 (see s60 ERA 1996).

Remedy: Where the tribunal finds such a complaint well founded it will make a declaration to that effect (s60(3)(a)). It may also make an award of compensation to be paid by the employer (s60(3)(b) and (4) ERA 1996).

The amount of compensation will be that which it

considers just and equitable in all the circumstances having regard to:

a) the employer's default in refusing to permit the employee to take time off; and

b) any loss sustained by the employee as a result.

Gross or net: Payment under s60(5): gross but taxable as normal under PAYE; Payment under s60(4): N/A

Limit on a week's pay: None. For payment under s60(5) the calculation is based on actual weekly pay.

Any maximum or minimum: There is no statutory limit to the award.

Mitigation: It is likely that the principle of mitigation would be applied in an appropriate case. However, this would most likely operate to restrict the losses that would be compensated for where it would have been reasonable for the employee to have incurred a lower level of losses than were in fact incurred, for example where the expenses incurred in making alternative arrangements were unreasonably expensive and reasonably avoidable.

Tax: The tax treatment is not clear. To the extent that the sum awarded is compensation for lost earnings for work done, it is likely to be taxed under s62 ITEPA 2003 (see *Tax and termination payments* and EIM02550).

Statutory authorities: ERA 1996 *ss58 to 60*

Time off for public duties

An employee who holds any of a number of specified public offices is entitled to take time off during his or her working hours for the purpose of performing specified duties. The duties that fall within the right depend on the office held. Offices include Justices of the Peace, and members of statutory tribunals, independent monitoring boards and visiting committees of a prison, volunteers in the criminal justice system, a relevant health or education body, the Environment Agency, the Scottish Environment Protection Agency and Scottish Water. Duties for which an individual is entitled to time off include meetings and discharging the functions of the body (see ss50(1) to (3) and (5) to 9B ERA 1996).

The amount of time off permitted is that which is reasonable in all the circumstances having regard to how much time is required to be taken off, how much time off the individual has taken off for trade union duties and activities and the effect of the employee's absence on the running of the employer's business (s50(4) ERA 1996).

An employee may bring a complaint to a tribunal that his or her employer has unreasonably refused to permit him or her to take the time off under s50 (s51 ERA 1996).

Remedy: Where the tribunal finds such a complaint well founded it will make a declaration to that effect (s51(3)(a)). It may also make an award of compensation to be paid by the employer (s51(3)(b) and (4)).

The amount of the compensation shall be such as the tribunal considers just and equitable in all the circumstances having regard to:

a) the employer's default in refusing to permit the employee to take time off; and

b) any loss sustained by the employee as a result.

Any maximum or minimum: There is no statutory limit to the compensation.

Mitigation: It is likely that the principle of mitigation would be applied in an appropriate case. However, this would most likely operate to restrict the losses that would be compensated for where it would have been reasonable for the employee to have incurred a lower level of losses than were in fact incurred, for example where the expenses incurred in making alternative arrangements were unreasonably expensive and reasonably avoidable.

Tax: See EIM02550. To the extent that the sum awarded is compensation for lost earnings for work done, it is likely to be taxed under s62 ITEPA 2003 (see *Tax and termination payments* and EIM02550).

Statutory authorities: ERA 1996 *ss50 and 51*

Time off for study or training

Section 63D ERA 1996 creates the right to make a request for time off in relation to study or training where the purpose of the study or training is to improve the employee's effectiveness or performance in the employer's business. The procedure for making the application and for the employer's consideration of it are set out at s63D to 63H ERA 1996.

An employee may bring a complaint to an employment tribunal that his or her employer has failed to follow the required procedure, reached its decision on impermissible basis or based its decision on incorrect facts (s63I(1) ERA 1996). There are various procedural hurdles to bringing such a claim (s63I(2) to (6) ERA 1996).

Remedy: If an employment tribunal finds the complaint well founded it must make a declaration to that effect and may make an order for:

a) reconsideration of the application; and/or

b) an award of compensation.

The amount of any compensation will be that which the tribunal considers just and equitable in all the circumstances, limited to 8 weeks' pay (see s63J ERA 1996 and EST(ECR) Regs 2010).

Gross or net: Gross. The definition of a week's pay as defined in ss220 to 229 ERA 1996 will apply (see *Week's pay*).

Limit on a week's pay: Currently £544 (see *Table 1* for historical rates).

Limit on number of weeks: 8 (see the Employee Study and Training (Eligibility, Complaints and Remedies) Regulations 2010 SI No. 156)

Any maximum or minimum: Currently the maximum is £4,352

Adjustments: None

Mitigation: N/A

Tax: The tax treatment is not clear. To the extent that the sum awarded is compensation for lost earnings for work done, it is likely to be taxed under s62 ITEPA 2003 (see *Tax and termination payments* and *EIM02550*).

Statutory authorities: ERA 1996 *ss63D to K, The Employee Study and Training (Eligibility, Complaints and Remedies) Regulations 2010* (SI 2010/156)

Time off for union duties, activities and union learning reps

An employee who is an official of an independent trade union recognised by his or her employer is entitled to take time off during working hours to carry out various official union duties (s168 TULR(C)A 1992)

An employee who is a member of a recognised trade union and a learning representative of that trade union is entitled to take time off during his working hours for a number of training related activities (s168A).

An employee who is a member of a recognised trade union is entitled to take time off during his working hours to take part in activities of the union, and activities in relation to which the employee is acting as a representative of the union (s170).

The amount of time off which must be permitted is that which is reasonable in all the circumstances having regard to any relevant provisions of a code of practice issued by ACAS (s168(3), s168A(8) and s170(3)).

The employee must be paid by his or her employer for the time taken off under s168 or s168A, but not s170 (s169). Where the employee's remuneration would not have varied with the amount of work done during the period of absence, the employee should be paid as if he or she had worked for the whole of that time (s169(2)). However, where the employee's remuneration would

have varied with the amount of work done, he or she should be paid their average hourly earnings for the period (s169(3) and (4)).

Any contractual remuneration paid to an employee in respect of such a period of time off goes towards discharging the liability under s169 (see s169(4)).

An employee may bring a complaint to a tribunal that his employer has unreasonably refused to permit him to take time off (s168(4), s168A(9) and s170(4)). An employee may bring a complaint to a tribunal that his or her employer has failed to pay them during their time off under s169 (s169(5)).

Remedy: Where the tribunal upholds a complaint for failure to permit time off it will make a declaration to that effect and may also make an award of compensation to be paid by the employer (s172(1) and (2) TULR(C)A 1992).

The amount of compensation will be that which it considers just and equitable in all the circumstances having regard to:

a) the employer's default in refusing to permit the employee to take time off; and

b) any loss sustained by the employee as a result.

Where a tribunal finds that an employer has failed to pay the employee during their time off, the tribunal will order that the employer pay the amount found to be due (s172(3)).

Gross or net: Net loss, or gross where taxable under s62 ITEPA 2003.

Adjustments: None

Mitigation: It is likely that the principle of mitigation would be applied in an appropriate case. However, this would most likely operate to restrict the losses that would be compensated for where it would have been reasonable for the employee to have incurred a lower level of losses than were in fact incurred, for example where the expenses incurred in making alternative arrangements were unreasonably expensive and reasonably avoidable.

Tax: The tax treatment is not clear. To the extent that the sum awarded is compensation for lost earnings for work done, it is likely to be taxed under s62 ITEPA 2003 (see *Tax and termination payments* and EIM02550).

Recoupment: N/A

Statutory authorities: TULR(C)A 1992 *ss168 to 173*

Time off for young person for study or training

An employee who is aged 16 or 17, is not receiving full-time secondary or further education, and has not attained such standard of achievement as is prescribed by regulations made by the Secretary of State, is entitled to take time off during his or her working hours to undertake study or training leading to a relevant qualification (s63A(1) and (2) ERA 1996). The right extends to such employees who are supplied by their employer to another 'principal' (s63A(3) ERA 1996). The right also extends to employees who have begun their study or training but have turned 18 (s63A(4) ERA 1996).

The amount of time off permitted is that which is reasonable in all the circumstances having regard to the requirements of the employee's study or training and the effect of the employee's absence on the running of the employer's business (s63A(5) ERA 1996).

The employee is entitled to be paid at their 'appropriate hourly rate' for their period of absence. Unless the employee works a varying number of working hours, the appropriate hourly rate is one week's pay divided by the normal working hours in a week when the time off was taken. For employees whose hours of work vary over a week or longer period, the appropriate hourly rate is obtained by dividing one week's pay by the average number of hours worked over the previous 12 weeks, or where the employee has not been employed for 12 weeks, a number which fairly represents the number of normal working hours in a week (see s63B(1) to (4) ERA 1996).

A week's pay will be calculated in accordance with ss220 to 229 ERA 1996 (see *Week's pay*). Any contractual remuneration paid to an employee in respect of such a period of time off goes towards discharging the liability under s63B (see s63B(5) and (6) ERA 1996).

An employee may bring a complaint to a tribunal that his or her employer has unreasonably refused to permit him or her to take the time off under s63A, or has failed to pay the sums due under s63B (see s63C ERA 1996).

Remedy: Where a tribunal finds a complaint well founded, it will make a declaration to that effect (s65C(3) ERA 1996).

Further, if the tribunal has found that the employer has unreasonably refused to permit the employee to take time off, the tribunal will also order the employer to pay to the employee an amount equal to the remuneration to which he or she would have been entitled under s63B if the employer had not refused (s63C(4) ERA 1996).

Also, if the tribunal finds that the employer has failed to pay the employee the whole or part of any amount to which he or she is entitled under s63B, the tribunal will also order the employer to pay to the employee the amount he or she is owed (s63C(5) ERA 1996).

For employees working fixed number of hours per week

Sum to which the employee is entitled = (gross weekly pay) x 1/(number of normal working hours in a week) x (number of hours absent) (s63B(2) ERA 1996)

For employees with varying number of hours worked per week

Sum to which the employee is entitled = gross weekly pay x 12/(number of normal hours worked in the last 12 weeks ending with the last complete week before the day on which the time off is taken) x (number of hours absent) (s63B(3) ERA 1996)

For employees with varying number of hours worked per week and who have worked for less than 12 weeks

Sum to which the employee is entitled = (gross weekly pay) x 1/(number of normal hours which fairly represents the number of normal working hours in a week) x (number of hours absent) (s63B(3) and (4) ERA 1996)

Gross or net: Gross. The definition of a week's pay as defined in ss220 to 229 ERA 1996 will apply (see *Week's pay*).

Limit on a week's pay: None. The calculation is based on actual gross weekly pay.

Limit on number of weeks: None

Any maximum or minimum: None

Adjustments: None

Mitigation: N/A

Tax: The tax treatment is not clear. To the extent that the sum awarded is compensation for lost earnings for work done, it is likely to be taxed under s62 ITEPA 2003 (see *Tax and termination payments* and EIM02550).

Recoupment: N/A

Statutory authorities: ERA 1996 *ss63A to 63C*

Time off to look for work or arrange training after being made redundant

An employee who is given notice of dismissal by reason of redundancy and who has sufficient continuity of service to receive a statutory redundancy payment, is entitled to take reasonable time off during his or her working hours before the end of his notice in order to look for new employment, or make arrangements for training for future employment (s52 ERA 1996).

The employee is entitled to be paid at their 'appropriate hourly rate' for their period of absence. Unless the employee works a varying number of working hours, the appropriate hourly rate is one week's pay divided by the normal working hours in a week when the time off was taken. For employees whose hours of work vary over a week or longer period, the appropriate hourly rate is obtained by dividing one week's pay by the average number of hours per week worked over the previous 12 weeks (s53(1) to (3) ERA 1996).

If an employer unreasonably refuses to permit an employee to take the time permitted by s52, the employee is entitled to be paid the amount of remuneration he would have been entitled to if he had been given the time off (s53(4) ERA 1996). A week's pay will be calculated in accordance with ss220 to 229 ERA 1996 (see *Week's pay*). Any contractual remuneration paid to an employee in respect of such a period of time off goes towards discharging the liability under s53 (see s53(6) and (7) ERA 1996).

The total liability to pay remuneration for an employee's time off is limited to 40% of a week's pay for that employee (s53(5) ERA 1996).

An employee may bring a complaint to a tribunal that his or her employer has unreasonably refused to permit him or her to take the time off under s52, or has failed to pay the sums due under s53 (see s54 ERA 1996).

Remedy: Where a tribunal finds a complaint well founded, it will make a declaration to that effect (s54(3)(a) ERA 1996) and will order the employer to pay the employee the amount which it finds due to him (s54(3)(b) ERA 1996).

For employees working fixed number of hours per week

Sum to which the employee is entitled = (gross weekly pay) x 1/(number of normal working hours in a week) x (number of hours absent) (s53(2) ERA 1996)

For employees with varying number of hours worked per week

Sum to which the employee is entitled = gross weekly pay x 12/(number of normal hours worked in the last 12 weeks ending with the last complete week before the day on which the time off is taken) x (number of hours absent) (s53(3) ERA 1996)

Gross or net: Gross. The definition of a week's pay as defined in ss220 to 229 ERA 1996 will apply (see *Week's pay*).

Limit on a week's pay: None. The calculation is based on actual gross weekly pay.

Limit on number of weeks: None

Any maximum or minimum: The maximum payable is 40% of an actual week's gross pay (s53(5) ERA 1996).

Tax: The tax treatment is not clear. To the extent that the sum awarded is compensation for lost earnings for work done, it is likely to be taxed under s62 ITEPA 2003 (see EIM02550). The sum may also be paid in connection with termination and be taxable under s401 (see *Tax and termination payments*).

Statutory authorities: ERA 1996 *ss52 to 54*

Trade unions: see *Union activities or collective bargaining (inducements); Union member (deduction of contributions to political fund); Union member (deduction of unauthorised or excessive subscriptions); Union member (expelled or excluded); Union member (refusal of employment); Union member (unjustifiably disciplined)*

TUPE (information and consultation)

The employer of any employees affected by a TUPE transfer must inform and consult their appropriate representatives before the transfer to enable consultation with any affected employees. The information must include: the fact that the transfer is to take place, the date or proposed date of the transfer and the reasons for it; the legal, economic and social implications of the transfer for any affected employees; the measures which he envisages he will take in relation to any affected employees; and if the employer is the transferor, the measures, in connection with the transfer, which he envisages the transferee will take in relation to any affected employees who will become employees of the transferee after the transfer by virtue of regulation 4. The employer is under a duty to consult where they envisage that they will be taking measures in relation to any affected employee. Consultation must be with a view to seeking the agreement of the representatives to the intended measures (Reg 13 TUPE 2006).

Appropriate employee representatives will be the representatives of a recognised trade union, or if none exist, representatives appointed or elected with the authority to be informed and consulted (Regs 13(3) and 14). There is an exception for employers with fewer than 10 employees who, if certain conditions are met, may inform and consult the affected employees directly (Reg 13A).

Generally speaking, it is the representatives who may bring a claim to a tribunal for failure to inform and/ or consult (Reg 15(1)). Once a tribunal has made an award, any employee who falls within the description of employees covered by that award may bring a complaint to a tribunal that the particular award to which he is entitled has not been paid to him (Reg 15(10)). However, where the claim is brought by affected employees rather than their representatives, then the award is only payable to those employees who have actually brought claims (*Ferguson and ors v Astrea Asset Management Ltd* [2020] UKEAT/0139/19).

Remedy: Where the tribunal finds a complaint under Reg 15(1) well founded it will make a declaration to that effect and can award such compensation as the tribunal considers just and equitable having regard to the seriousness of the failure of the employer to comply with the duty, of up to 13 weeks' pay. The compensation will be ordered to be paid to '*such descriptions of affected employees as may be specified*', which will reflect the employees in respect of whom there has been a failure (Reg 15(7) and (8)).

The award is punitive, not compensatory. Its purpose is to provide a sanction for breach of the obligation to inform and consult. The tribunal has a wide discretion but it will focus on the seriousness of the default, which may vary from the merely technical to a complete failure to comply with the duties, and it may consider the deliberateness of the failure.

The proper approach where there has been no consultation is to start at the maximum and reduce it if there are mitigating circumstances justifying a reduction (see *Susie Radin Ltd v GMB & Ors* [2004] ICR 893). This approach has recently been doubted by the EAT in *Ferguson and others v Astrea Asset Management Limited* [2020] UKEAT/0139/19. However, the reasoning for this is brief and it is unclear to what extent it truly changes the approach taken by tribunals given that it goes on to accept that there exists a '*paradigm "really serious" case where, for example, a transferor employer had wholly failed to inform or consult its employees and the first they had heard about a transfer was on the very day it was to take effect, causing serious alarm and distress*' (paragraph 54).

However, the tribunal should not take this approach where there has been some information given and/ or some consultation (see *Todd v Strain & Ors* [2011] IRLR 11 and *London Borough of Barnet v Unison & Ors* UKEAT/0191/13).

Gross or net: Gross. A week's pay as defined in ss220 to 229 ERA 1996 applies (see *Week's pay*).

Limit on a week's pay: None. The calculation is based on actual gross weekly pay (see *Zaman & Ors v Kozee*

Sleep Products Ltd t/a Dorlux Beds UK UKEAT/0312/10/ CEA).

Limit on number of weeks: 13

Adjustments: None

Mitigation: N/A

Tax: The tax treatment is unclear but it is likely that HMRC would regard any payment made under TUPE to fall under s401 ITEPA 2003 (see *Tax and termination payments*).

Recoupment: N/A

Statutory authorities: TUPE 2006 *Regs 13 to 16*

Relevant case law: *Cable Realisations Ltd v GMB Northern* [2010] IRLR 42; *Ferguson and ors v Astrea Asset Management Ltd* [2020] UKEAT/0139/19; *London Borough of Barnet v Unison & Ors* UKEAT/0191/13; *Susie Radin Ltd v GMB & Ors* [2004] ICR 893; *Sweeting v Coral Racing* [2006] IRLR 252; *Todd v Strain & Ors* [2011] IRLR 11; *Zaman & Ors v Kozee Sleep Products Ltd t/a Dorlux Beds UK* UKEAT/0312/10/CEA

TUPE (failure to notify employee liability information)

The transferor is obliged to provide specified employee liability information to the transferee for any employees who will be transferred, at least 14 days before the relevant transfer (Reg 11 TUPE 2006). For any transfer occurring on or after 1 May 2014, the information must be provided at least 28 days before the relevant transfer (Reg 10 CRATU(PE) Regs 2014).

A transferee may present a complaint to a tribunal that the transferor has failed to comply with any provisions of Reg 11 (Reg 12(1)).

Remedy: Where a tribunal finds a complaint well founded it must make a declaration to that effect and may make an award of compensation to be paid by the transferor to the transferee (Reg 12(3)). The amount of compensation will be that which the tribunal considers just and equitable in all the circumstances having particular regard to the losses sustained by the transferee as a result of the failure to provide information, and any relevant terms of any contract between the transferor and transferee dealing with payment for such a failure (Reg 12(4)).

There are two further provisions that may influence the amount of any award:

- By Reg 12(5) the amount of compensation must be a minimum of £500 per employee whose liability information has not been provided, subject to the discretion of the tribunal to award a lesser sum if in all the circumstances it considers it just and equitable.

- By Reg 12(6) the tribunal must apply the common law rules as to mitigation in assessing the loss suffered by the transferee.

Gross or net: Loss will likely be calculated net of any tax that may be payable.

Any maximum or minimum: Minimum is £500 per employee whose liability information has not been provided, unless the tribunal considers it is just and equitable to award a lesser sum.

Adjustments: N/A

Mitigation: The transferee is under a duty to mitigate their loss.

Tax: The tax treatment is unclear.

Statutory authorities: TUPE 2006 *Regs 11 and 12*; *CRATU(PE) Regs 2014 Reg 10*

Unauthorised deductions: see *Unlawful deductions from wages*

Unfair dismissal

(see also *Additional award; Adjustments and order of adjustments; Basic award; Compensatory award; Damages for wrongful dismissal; Mitigation*)

The right not to be unfairly dismissed is established by *s94* ERA 1996. An individual may bring a complaint to a tribunal that he or she has been unfairly dismissed (*s111* ERA 1996).

The definition of a dismissal is set out at *s95*, and includes dismissal with or without notice, the termination of a fixed term contract and dismissal where the employer or employee has committed a repudiatory breach of contract entitling the other to terminate the contract immediately (constructive dismissal).

Whether a dismissal is fair or unfair will be determined by a tribunal applying the tests set out in *s98*, which include that the employer's reason for the dismissal must be one of a number of specified reasons (including misconduct and redundancy), and require the tribunal to assess whether the employer acted reasonably or unreasonably in treating its reason as a sufficient reason for dismissing the employee. This second stage is itself the subject of extensive further guideline cases, which are outside the scope of this work.

Automatic unfair dismissal

Where the reason, or if more than one reason the principal reason for the dismissal is one of a number of protected reasons, the dismissal will be automatically unfair. The protected reasons are:

- Being summoned to attend for jury service or being absent for attending jury service (*s98B* ERA 1996);

- Exercising rights to family leave (*s99* ERA 1996);

- Exercising various health and safety functions (*s100* ERA 1996);

- Refusing to work on a Sunday (if a specified shop or betting worker) (*s101* ERA 1996) or refusing to work additional hours on a Sunday (s101ZA ERA 1996);

- Taking various actions under the Working Time Regulations 1998 (*s101A* ERA 1996);

- Exercising various rights to participate in education or training (*s101B* ERA 1996);

- Performing various functions of the trustee of an occupational pension scheme (*s102* ERA 1996);

- Performing various functions related to being an employee representative (*s103* ERA 1996);

- Making a protected disclosure (whistleblowing) (*s103A* ERA 1996);

- Asserting one of a number of statutory rights (*s104* ERA 1996);

- Reasons related to action taken under the National Minimum Wage Act 1998 (*s104A* ERA 1996);

- Reasons related to actions taken under the Tax Credits Act 2002 (*s104B* ERA 1996);

- Exercising various rights to flexible working (*s104C* ERA 1996);

- Reasons related to actions taken relating to pension enrolment (*s104D* ERA 1996);

- Exercising various rights to study and training (*s104E* ERA 1996);

- Reasons related to the existence of trade union blacklist (*s104F* ERA 1996);

- Refusing to accept an offer of employee shareholder status (*s104G* ERA 1996);

- Reasons relating to actions taken related to trade union recognition (*para 161 Sch A1* TULR(C)A 1992);

- Reasons related to trade union membership or activities (*s152* TULR(C)A 1992); and

- Redundancy, but the reason or principal reason for selection for redundancy was one of a long list of protected reasons (*ss105(3) to (7N)*, *s153* TULR(C) A 1992 and *paragraph 162* Sch 1A TULR(C)A 1992).

The right to not be dismissed unfairly generally accrues to an employee after the completion of 2 years' service (see *s108(1)* ERA 1996). However, where the dismissal relates to a number of protected reasons, the period of continuous service required is either reduced or removed entirely (s108(2) to (4)). Most of the automatically unfair dismissal provisions can be relied upon by a dismissed employee who has not completed 2 years' continuous service.

Industrial action

Where the reason for a dismissal is related to industrial action, specific provisions apply (see *ss237 to 239* TULR(C)A 1992).

Interim relief

An individual may also bring a complaint to a tribunal that he or she has been unfairly dismissed and seek an order for continuation of the contract of employment under the interim relief provisions (ss128 to 132 ERA 1996 and ss161 to 167 TULR(C)A 1992). This remedy is limited to allegations of unfair dismissal where the alleged reason or principal reason for the dismissal falls within the automatically unfair dismissal provisions relating to representative roles, the existence of a blacklist, trade union membership and activities and making a protected disclosure.

Remedy: Where a tribunal has found a dismissal to be unfair the remedies available are reinstatement, re-engagement and compensation (ss112 to 126 ERA 1996). See *Re-engagement and reinstatement*.

The tribunal must explain to a successful claimant the three orders available to it (s112(2) ERA 1996). Though the primary remedies are reinstatement or re-engagement, this is rarely granted in practice and it is most often the case that claimants seek only an award of compensation.

Where an order for reinstatement or re-engagement is not fully complied with (and the respondent fails to establish that such reinstatement or re-engagement was not practicable), the tribunal will award compensation under s117(2) (s117(1) ERA 1996).

Where the tribunal is not asked to order reinstatement or re-engagement, or where a claimant has not been reinstated or re-engaged, the tribunal will make an award of compensation under ss118 to 126 ERA 1996 (s117(3) and (4) and s112(4) ERA 1996) (see also *Additional award*).

The award of compensation under ss118 to 126 ERA 1996 consists of a basic award and compensatory award (see *Basic award, Compensatory award*).

The basic award is calculated on the basis of (capped) gross weekly pay and the number of years' continuous service (the longer the service the higher the award).

The compensatory award compensates the individual

for the financial losses suffered as a result of the dismissal and is based on actual net weekly pay. Except where the dismissal is for one of a limited number of protected reasons, the compensatory award is capped at the lesser of one year's gross pay and currently £89,493 (see *Statutory cap* and *Table 1*). Compensation for non-pecuniary losses, such as injury to feelings, is not available within a compensatory award (see *Dunnachie v Kingston upon Hull City Council* [2004] UKHL 36).

Awards of compensation for unfair dismissal may be adjusted for failure to comply with a relevant code of practice (see *Adjustments and order of adjustments*).

The specific interim remedy of a continuation order is available in limited circumstances where a claimant has sought interim relief under ss128 to 132 ERA 1996 and ss161 to 167 TULR(C)A 1992 (see *Interim relief*).

Statutory authorities: ERA 1996 s94, s95, ss98 to 104, s108, s111, ss112 to 126, s117, ss128 to 132; TULR(C)A 1992 Schedule 1A, Schedule A1, s105, s152, s153, ss161 to 167, ss237 to 239

Union activities or collective bargaining (inducements)

A worker has the right not to have an offer made to him by his employer to induce the worker: not to be or seek to become a member of a trade union; not to take part in the activities of a trade union; not to make use of trade union services; or to be or become a member of any trade union (s145A of TULR(C)A 1992).

A worker who is a member of a trade union which is recognised, or seeking to be recognised, by his employer has the right not to have an offer made to him by his employer if: acceptance of the offer, together with other workers' acceptance of offers which the employer also makes to them, would have 'the prohibited result', and the employer's sole or main purpose in making the offers is to achieve that result. The 'prohibited result' is that the workers' terms will not or will not continue to be determined by collective bargaining (s145B of TULR(C)A 1992).

A worker or former worker may bring a complaint to a tribunal that the employer has made an offer in contravention of s145A or 145B (s145A(5) and s145B(5)).

Remedy: Where a tribunal finds such a complaint well founded, it will make a declaration to that effect and will make an award of £4,341 (s145E(1) to (3) TULR(C)A 1992).

Section 145E prescribes certain other consequences

where an unlawful offer has been made, which exist without a claim having been brought to a tribunal. By s145E(4) any agreement to vary the terms of employment between the worker and employer will not be enforceable by the employer, however if merely as a result of the acceptance (e.g. because collectively agreed terms would have been different in those circumstances) nothing in s145A or s145B makes the variation unenforceable by either party.

Adjustments: s38 EA 2002 adjustment for failure to give statement of employment particulars applies. ACAS uplift applies (Schedule A2 TULR(C)A).

Mitigation: N/A

Tax: The tax treatment of this award is unclear.

Recoupment: N/A

Statutory authorities: TULR(C)A 1992 *ss145A, B & E*

Union member (deduction of contributions to political fund)

Trade unions may maintain political funds, and seek contributions to that fund from members. A member may object to contributing to the political fund. If a member of a trade union which has a political fund informs his employer in writing that he is exempt from the obligation to contribute to the fund, or he has notified the union in writing of his objection to contributing to the fund, the employer is obliged to ensure that no amount representing a contribution to the political fund is deducted by him from emoluments payable to that individual (see s84 and s86 TULR(C)A 1992).

A member may bring a claim to the tribunal alleging that his employer has made a deduction contrary to s86 (s87(1) TULR(C)A 1992).

A member may bring a further complaint in circumstances where an order granted under the first complaint to prevent a repetition of the failure has not been complied with (s87(5) TULR(C)A 1992).

Remedy: Where a tribunal finds a complaint under s87(1) well founded, it will make a declaration to that effect and may order the employer to pay to the complainant the amount deducted less any part of that amount already paid to him by the employer (s87(4)(a) TULR(C)A) The tribunal may also order the employer to take steps to prevent a repetition of the failure (s87(4)(b)).

A complainant may bring a complaint alleging that his or her employer has not complied with the order under s87(4)(b) (s87(5)). If the tribunal finds that the

employer has without reasonable excuse failed to comply with the order, it will order the employer to pay the complainant 2 weeks' pay (s87(7)).

Gross or net:

Deductions under s87(4)(a): the actual amount of the deducted owing must be paid.

Non-compliance with s87(4)(b): gross weekly pay according to ss220 to 229 ERA 1996 (s87(8) TULR(C)A 1992).

Limit on a week's pay: None

Limit on number of weeks: For a complaint under s87(7) ERA 1996 the limit is 2 weeks' pay.

Any maximum or minimum: None

Adjustments: None

Mitigation: N/A

Tax: The actual deductions should be repaid, and there should be no impact on tax calculations. It is unclear whether the 2 weeks' pay will be subject to tax.

Recoupment: N/A

Statutory authorities: TULR(C)A 1992 *ss84 to 87*

Union member (deduction of unauthorised or excessive subscriptions)

Where arrangements exist between an employer and a trade union for the deduction of membership subscriptions from an employee, the employer must ensure that no subscription deductions are made for any worker if he or she has not authorised the deduction or has withdrawn authorisation (see s68 TULR(C)A 1992).

A worker may bring a complaint to a tribunal that that his employer has made such a deduction (s68A(1) TULR(C)A 1992).

Remedy: Where a tribunal finds that the complaint is well founded, it will make a declaration to that effect and will order the employer to pay to the worker the amount of the deduction owing to the employee (s68A(3)). s68A(4) makes provision to ensure there is no double recovery where the sum deducted might also be claimed under another jurisdiction, such as s13 ERA 1996 (unlawful deductions from wages).

Gross or net: The actual amount of any deductions owing should be paid.

Any maximum or minimum: None

Statutory authorities: TULR(C)A 1992 *ss68 and 68A*

Union member (expelled or excluded)

An individual is protected from being excluded or expelled from a trade union unless the exclusion or expulsion is permitted by s174(2) TULR(C)A. The legitimate reasons for exclusion or expulsion include that the individual no longer satisfies enforceable membership criteria or has committed misconduct.

This right gives rise to two circumstances in which a claim may be brought to a tribunal. First, a member may bring a claim alleging that he or she has been excluded or expelled from a trade union (s174(5)). Second, where such a claim has been declared well founded it is envisaged the parties may reach agreement to deal with the issue between them, but the individual is may bring a claim under s176(2) to enforce such an agreement or seek compensation.

Remedy: The primary remedy, following a complaint under s174(5), is a declaration from the tribunal that the claim is well founded (s176(1)). The tribunal must also make a declaration, stating that effect, where the exclusion or expulsion was mainly attributable to a reason relating to the individual being a member of a political party (s176(1A)) and (if it applies) that the exclusion or expulsion was otherwise wholly or mainly attributable to conduct of the individual contrary to a rule of the union or an objective of the union (s176(1B)).

Where the individual has succeeded under a s176(1) claim, the individual may bring a claim under s176(2) to seek compensation. The amount of compensation awarded will be that which the employment tribunal considers just and equitable in all the circumstances (s176(4)). The tribunal may reduce any award for contributory fault (s176(5)).

Gross or net: It is likely that this will be paid gross.

Any maximum or minimum:

Minimum: The amount of compensation will not be less than £10,132 where on the date the s176(1) application was made the union has not admitted or readmitted the member (TULR(C)A 1992 s67(8A) and s176(6A)), unless the tribunal also made declarations under s176(1A) and (1B) (see s176(6B)).

Maximum: The total award will not exceed the aggregate of 30 times the limit on a week's pay under s227(1)(a) ERA 1996 (£16,320) and the maximum compensatory award (£89,493) i.e. £105,813 (TULR(C)A 1992 s176(7) and ERA 1996 s227(1)(a) and s124(1)).

Adjustments: Yes, for contributory conduct.

Cap: A cap applies (see above).

Mitigation: The member is likely to be under a duty to mitigate any losses for which he or she seeks compensation

Tax: It is likely that this will be treated as a punishment or fine, and not taxed.

Recoupment: N/A

Statutory authorities: ERA 1996 *ss113, 124(1)* and *227(1)*; TULR(C)A 1992 *ss174 to 176*

Union member (refusal of employment)

It is unlawful to refuse a person employment because he is or is not a member of a trade union, or because he is unwilling to accept a requirement that he take steps to cease to be or to remain or to become a member of a trade union, or a requirement to make payments or suffer deductions in the event of him not being a member of a trade union (s137 TULR(C)A 1992).

An equivalent right applies where an employment agency refuses such a person any of its services (s138 TULR(C)A 1992).

An individual may bring a complaint to a tribunal that this right has been infringed (s137(2) and s138(2) TULR(C)A 1992).

Remedy: Where a tribunal finds such a complaint well founded, it will make a declaration to that effect and may make an order of compensation (s140(1)(a)) and/or a recommendation (s140(1)(b)).

Compensation will be assessed on the same basis as damages for breach of statutory duty (as are discrimination claims) and may include compensation for injury to feelings (s140(1)(a) and s140(2) TULR(C)A). The total compensation is limited to the maximum sum available under a compensatory award (s140(4)).

Any recommendation will require the respondent to take action to obviate or reduce the adverse effect on the complainant of the conduct that forms the basis of the complaint (s140(1)(b)).

Where the respondent fails without reasonable justification to comply with a recommendation, the tribunal may make an award of compensation, or increase it if it has already made an award (s140(3)).

Gross or net: The award of compensation will be made on the basis of net loss.

Limit on a week's pay: None

Limit on number of weeks: None

Any maximum or minimum: The maximum award is that of the statutory cap on unfair dismissal in force at the date of the breach under s124(1) ERA 1996, currently the lesser of £89,493 and 52 weeks' gross pay. There is no minimum.

Adjustments: None

Compensation cap: See maximum above.

Mitigation: The usual rules as to mitigation in discrimination claims will apply.

Tax: The tax treatment of this award is unclear.

Recoupment: N/A

Statutory authorities: ERA 1996 *s124(1)*; TULR(C)A 1992 *ss137 to 143*

Union member (unjustifiably disciplined)

An individual who is or has been a member of a trade union has the right not to be unjustifiably disciplined by the union (s64(1) TULR(C)A 1992). Section 64(2) identifies what actions of the union amount to 'discipline', whilst s65 identifies those reasons for the discipline which render the discipline 'unjustified'.

This right gives rise to two circumstances in which a claim may be brought to a tribunal. First, a member may bring a claim alleging that he or she has been unjustifiably disciplined (s66(1)). Second, where such a claim has been declared well founded it is envisaged the parties may reach agreement to deal with the issue between them, but the individual may bring a claim under s67(1) to enforce such an agreement or seek compensation.

Remedy: The primary remedy, following a complaint under s66(1), is a declaration from the tribunal that the individual has been unjustifiably disciplined (s66(3)).

Where the individual has succeeded under a s66(1) claim, it is envisaged the parties may reach agreement to deal with the issue between them, but the individual may bring a claim under s67(1) to enforce such an agreement or seek compensation.

The amount of compensation awarded will be that which the employment tribunal considers just and equitable in all the circumstances (s67(3)). The tribunal will apply the common law principles of mitigation (s67(4)) and may reduce any award for contributory fault (s67(5)).

Gross or net: It is likely that this will be paid gross.

Any maximum or minimum:

Minimum: The amount of compensation will not be less than £10,132 where on the date the s67(1) application was made the union has not revoked the decision to discipline the member or taken all necessary steps to secure the reversal of anything done to give effect to

the disciplinary sanction (TULR(C)A 1992 s67(8A) and s176(6A)).

Maximum: The total award will not exceed the aggregate of the maximum basic award (£16,320) and the maximum compensatory award (£89,493) i.e. £105,813 (TULR(C)A 1992 s67(7) and ERA 1996 s227(1) (a) and s124(1)).

Adjustments: Yes, for contributory conduct.

Cap: A cap applies (see above).

Mitigation: Yes, the member is under a duty to mitigate any losses.

Tax: It is likely that this will be treated as a punishment or fine, and not taxed.

Recoupment: N/A

Statutory authorities: ERA 1996 *s227(1)(a) and s124(1)*; TULR(C)A 1992 *ss64 to 67*

Union membership (blacklists, unfair dismissal/redundancy): see *Basic award, minimum; Unfair dismissal*

Union membership or activities (detriment): see *Detriment*

Unlawful deductions from wages

(see also *Holiday pay*; *National Minimum Wage***)**

A worker has the right not to suffer deductions from wages except under prescribed circumstances, which are as follows:

- Deductions required or authorised by statute (such as PAYE) or by a provision in the worker's contract (s13(1)(a) ERA 1996);

- Deductions previously agreed to and signified in writing by the worker (s13(1)(b) ERA 1996);

- Deductions for reimbursement of an overpayment of wages or expenses (s14(1) ERA 1996);

- Payment to third parties for which the individual has given written consent (s14(4) ERA 1996);

- Deductions on account of the worker's participation in industrial action (s14(5) ERA 1996);

- Deductions made in respect of an attachment of earnings order made by a court, where the individual has given written consent (s14(6) ERA 1996);

- Deductions made to a public authority as required under statute (s14(3) ERA 1996).

Wages is broadly interpreted, including salaries, fees, bonuses, commissions and holiday pay (both contractual and under the WTR 1998 (see *HMRC v Stringer* [2009] IRLR 677). The definition of wages does not usually include pay in lieu of notice (see *Delaney v Staples* [1992] ICR 483). Also, where the sum claimed is dependent on the exercise of a discretion by the employer that has yet to be determined, such as a discretionary bonus, no identifiable sum exists and the claim must be brought as a breach of contract claim in the tribunal or the civil courts, rather than as an unlawful deduction claim (see *Adcock v Coors Brewers Ltd* [2007] IRLR 440).

Workers in the retail industry have special protection, whereby deductions to compensate for cash or stock shortages within a period may not exceed 10% of the worker's gross wages in that period (see ss17 to 22 ERA 1996).

A worker may bring a claim to a tribunal that his employer has made unlawful deductions from his wages (s23(1) ERA 1996).

The Court of Appeal in *Agarwal v Cardiff University & Anor* [2018] EWCA Civ 1434 has confirmed that employment tribunals have the power to interpret the relevant provisions of a contract of employment to determine the amount properly payable to an employee.

Remedy: Where a tribunal finds a complaint under s23 well founded, it will make a declaration to that effect and will order the employer to pay the worker the sum found to have been deducted unlawfully (s24(1)). The tribunal may also make such award as it considers appropriate in all the circumstances to compensate the worker for any financial loss sustained by him which is attributable to the unlawful deduction (s24(2)).

Gross or net: The sums awarded ought to be calculated on a gross basis, since they will be taxable under s62 ITEPA 2003.

Adjustments: The ACAS uplift applies (Schedule A2 TULR(C)A).

Cap: There is no statutory cap on the sums that may be awarded by the tribunal but sums can only be claimed for the previous 2 years before the claim was made (*Deductions from Wages (Limitation) Regulations* 2014 SI 2014/3322, effective 1 July 2015). This includes holiday pay as well as any other deduction. For claims before this period there is no such limit, and the Limitation Act 1980 does not apply (*Bath Hill Court (Bournemouth) Management Co Ltd v Coletta* [2019] EWCA Civ 1707).

Mitigation: The usual principles of mitigation will likely apply to any award under s24(2), but the award for repayment of deductions does not need to be mitigated.

Tax: Taxable under s62 ITEPA 2003

Recoupment: N/A

Statutory authorities: ERA 1996 ss13 to 26; *Deductions from Wages (Limitation) Regulations* 2014 SI 2014/3322

Relevant case law: Adcock v Coors Brewers Ltd [2007] IRLR 440; *Agarwal v Cardiff University & Anor* [2018] EWCA Civ 1434; *Bath Hill Court (Bournemouth) Management Co Ltd v Coletta* [2019] EWCA Civ 1707; *HMRC v Stringer* [2009] IRLR 677

Unreasonable refusal to be reinstated: see *Additional award*

Variable hours: see *Holiday pay; Week's pay*

Varying pay with output: see *Holiday pay; Week's pay*

Victimisation: see *Discrimination*

Week's pay

The concept of a week's pay is defined by ss220 to 229 and s234 ERA 1996. It is used for calculating a remedy in each of the following employment rights (see *Table 5* for a list of claims, the relevant calculation date and whether a limit on a week's pay applies):

- Additional award (s117(1) ERA 1996);
- Basic award/Redundancy pay (s119(2), s121 and s162(2) ERA 1996);
- Guarantee pay (s30(2) ERA 1996);
- Payments on the insolvency of an employer (s182 ERA 1996);
- Protective award (s190(2) TULR(C)A 1992);
- Remuneration whilst suspended on medical or maternity grounds (s69(1) ERA 1996);
- Right for union member not to be unjustifiably disciplined/expelled and blacklisting claims (ss67(8)(a) and 176(6)(a) TULR(C)A 1992);
- Failure to inform and consult union on training for workers (s70C(4) TULR(C)A 1992);
- Time off to look for work or arrange training after being made redundant (s54(4) ERA 1996);
- Time off for antenatal care (s56(2) ERA 1996);
- Absence during statutory notice period (ss88(1) to 89(1) ERA 1996);
- Time off for employee representatives (including ICE and OPPS) (s62(2) ERA 1996, Reg 28(2) ICE Regs 2004, Sch para 3(2) OPPS Regs 2006);

- Time off for study or training (s63J(3) ERA 1996);

- Time off for young person for study or training (s63B(2) ERA 1996);

- Time off for members of a European Works Council (Reg 26(2) TICE 1999);

- Failure to inform and consult under TUPE (Reg 16(3) TUPE Regs 2006);

- Right to be accompanied at a disciplinary or grievance meeting (s11(3) ERelA 1999);

- Infringement of right to be accompanied at flexible working meeting (Reg 15(3) FW(PR) Regs 2002);

- Rejection of flexible working application (Reg 7 FW(ECR) Regs 2002);

- Written reasons for dismissal (s93(2) ERA 1996);

- Written statement of particulars (s38 EA 2002); and

- Paid annual leave under the Working Time Regulations (Reg 16(1) WTR 1998).

What is a week's pay?

In essence, a week's pay is the gross contractual remuneration an employee is entitled to be paid when working their normal hours each week. Difficulties emerge in the calculation where an individual typically receives pay in addition to their contractual salary (such as voluntary overtime), or where they do not have normal working hours each week, such as when working irregular shift patterns.

For the purpose of calculating maximum compensation, a week's pay can include employer pension contributions (see *University of Sunderland v Drossou* UKEAT/0341/16/RN).

Since pay will vary over the period of employment of an individual, for each remedy that uses the definition of a week's pay, a calculation date is specified (see *Table 5*). For a number of remedies, a week's pay is capped, currently at £544 (again, see *Table 5* for a full list).

Working hours

An employee's normal working hours will often be identified in their written particulars (s221(1)) or other contractual documentation. Failing this, it may be clear from the hours actually worked.

Matters are complicated where a contract specifies a minimum number of hours to be worked each week and also provides for an increased overtime wage to be paid beyond a certain number of hours. By s234, in that situation the normal working hours will be the minimum number of hours specified, even if overtime is paid for a smaller number of hours, and even if the minimum number of hours can be reduced in certain circumstances.

- Where overtime is obligatory for the employee, but is not guaranteed by the employer, the normal working hours will not include those additional hours - they will only amount to normal working hours if the obligation to work and provide work for that period is mutual (see *Tarmac Roadstone Holdings Ltd v Peacock* [1973] ICR 273). Further, where employees are paid on the basis of a pre-estimate of the number of hours a task will take, though the time taken may vary, the pre-estimate will not amount to normal working hours (see *Sanderson v Exel Management Services Ltd* [2006] ICR 1337).

- Remuneration where an employee has normal working hours is calculated as the contractual payments made to the employee for the work they have done.

- Contractual bonuses are usually included, such as a regular shift bonus (see *Mole Mining Ltd v Jenkins* [1972] ICR 282). It may be possible to infer a contractual term that a regular bonus, such as a site bonus in the construction industry, will be paid unless certain conditions are met, such that it falls within remuneration (see *Donelan v Kerrby Constructions* [1983] ICR 237).

- Discretionary bonuses will not form part of the remuneration, unless deemed a contractual payment (see *Canadian Imperial Bank of Commerce v Beck* EAT/0141/10/RN and *Hoyland v Asda Stores Ltd* [2006] IRLR 468).

- Tips paid by the employer (but not by customers to the employee in cash) will count as remuneration (see *Palmanor Ltd v Cedron* [1978] ICR 1008 and *Nerva v RL&G Ltd* [1997] ICR 11). However, it may be that non-cash tips distributed through a tronc system set up by the employer do not count as remuneration, as they do not count towards the minimum wage (see *Revenue and Customs Commissioners v Annabel's (Berkeley Square) Ltd* [2009] ICR 1123).

- Commission which is a regular part of an employee's earnings will amount to remuneration, and can be apportioned as the tribunal deems appropriate (see *Weevsmay Ltd v Kings* [1977] ICR 244 and *J and S Bickley Ltd v Washer* [1977] ICR 425).

- Benefits in kind, such as free lodging, will not count as remuneration.

- Where an individual has been paid less than the minimum wage, the calculation of a week's pay should be based on the pay the individual ought to have received, but at the rate applicable at the date of the hearing (see *Paggetti v Cobb* [2002] IRLR 861).

- A profitability bonus, where completion of normal working hours is a necessary but not sufficient condition for payment, does not fall to be included in the calculation of a week's pay under section 221(2) ERA 1996 (*Econ Engineering Ltd v Dixon* UKEAT/0285/19).

Where an employee has normal working hours

There are three alternative routes to calculating a week's pay:

- **'time workers'**, where the remuneration does not vary with the amount of work done, which includes work where commission is awarded for success achieved, as opposed to being awarded for the work actually done (see *Evans v Malley Organisation Ltd t/a First Business Support* [2003] ICR 432). A week's pay is the amount payable by the employer to the employee under the contract in force at the calculation date if the individual works the normal working hours in a week (s221(2));

- **'piece workers'**, where the remuneration varies according to the amount of work done during normal working hours but does not vary according to the times or days when the work is done. A week's pay is the average hourly rate for the normal working hours calculated over the previous 12 weeks (s221(3)). For these purposes remuneration will include commission which is awarded for success achieved, as opposed to being awarded for the work actually done (see *Evans v Malley Organisation Ltd t/a First Business Support* [2003] ICR 432);

- **'shift workers'**, where normal working hours are worked at times of the day or days of the week that vary from week to week and where remuneration also varies from week to week. A week's pay is calculated over a period of 12 weeks by reference to the average hourly rate multiplied by the average number of normal weekly hours (s222).

Where an employee has no normal working hours

A week's pay is calculated by reference to average weekly remuneration over a 12 week period (s224). In this situation, any overtime payments received will count towards remuneration, whether or not there is a mutual obligation to work and provide overtime (see above re normal working hours).

The 12 week period is based on complete weeks worked (s221(3) and (4) and s235(1)). Any week in which the individual was not working or was not paid remuneration will not count, and an earlier week will be brought in to make up the 12 weeks (s223(2) and s224(3)).

Is the calculation of a week's pay in compliance with EU law?

The concept of a week's pay is used in the working time regulations to calculate holiday pay entitlement. However, the particular means to calculate a week's pay frequently leads to individuals receiving less money than they would have received had they not taken the holiday, for example where regular overtime is required but there is no obligation on the employer to offer it. Please see the section on *Holiday pay* for a more detailed discussion of this issue.

The following examples demonstrate the calculation of a week's pay.

Normal working hours

Straightforward number of hours and constant pay per hour/week/month

1. Weekly pay for hourly paid employees
Weekly pay for hourly paid employees = Number of normal hours worked per week x (hourly rate + hourly commission/bonus if they are constant).

If the commission is not constant, this calculation does not apply (see below). If the period of commission does not coincide with the period of payment, the weekly pay should be calculated in a manner which is just, over the whole period (s229(2)).

2. Weekly pay for monthly, annual or other period paid employees
The tribunal must apportion the payment in the manner that is considers just (ERA 1996 s229(2)).

One way in which this could be done is as follows:

Weekly pay = Monthly salary ÷ 4.3 (or alternatively, monthly salary x 12 ÷ 365 x 7 which produces a slightly different answer because of rounding errors)

Weekly pay = Annual salary ÷ 52

Weekly pay = Other period salary ÷ number of days in which it was earned x 7

3. Weekly pay with differing commission
Weekly pay with differing commission = Number of hours worked in a week x hourly rate + (total commission earned ÷ number of weeks in which it was earned)

Straightforward but pay and/or commission/bonus varying with output (piece workers)

Weekly pay = Average hourly rate x hours in a normal working week = (Total remuneration, including overtime, in the previous 12 week period ÷ total hours worked in the 12 week period) x hours in a normal working week

However, note that overtime hours are rated as basic hours - overtime premiums are ignored.

Variable hours (shift workers)

Weekly pay = Average hourly rate x average hours in a normal working week = (Total remuneration in previous 12 weeks ÷ Total hours worked in previous 12 weeks, including overtime hours if they form part of the normal working hours) x (number of hours worked in the 12 week period ÷12)

Note: the 12 weeks needs to be taken prior to the pay date or the calculation date, whichever is the earlier.

Also, if in any week no remuneration or guaranteed pay was paid, those weeks are ignored and an earlier week is used in the calculation.

No normal working hours (casual workers)

Weekly pay = Total remuneration, including overtime and overtime rates, in 12 weeks immediately before calculation date (or the pay day immediately before the calculation date if calculation date is not the same as the pay date) ÷ 12

Statutory authorities: Chapter II ERA 1996

COVID-19: The coronavirus pandemic has resulted in large numbers of employees being placed on furlough under the Coronavirus Job Retention Scheme. The Employment Rights Act 1996 (Coronavirus, Calculation of a Week's Pay) Regulations SI 2020/814 (as amended) provide, in effect, that the calculation of an employee's week's pay should be calculated as if their furloughed hours were normal working hours and disregarding any reduction in pay as a result of being furloughed.

Relevant case law: *BA v Williams* [2011] IRLR 948; *Bear Scotland & Ors v Fulton & Ors* UKEATS/0047/13/BI; *Canadian Imperial Bank of Commerce v Beck* EAT 0141/10; *Donelan v Kerrby Constructions* [1983] ICR 237; *Econ Engineering Ltd v Dixon* UKEAT/0285/19; *Evans v Malley Organisation Ltd t/a First Business Support* [2003] ICR 432; *Fox v C Wright (Farmers) Ltd* [1978] ICR 98; *Hoyland v Asda Stores Ltd* [2006] IRLR 468; *J and S Bickley Ltd v Washer* [1977] ICR 425; *Mole Mining Ltd v Jenkins* [1972] ICR 282; *Nerva v RL&G Ltd* [1997] ICR 11; *Paggetti v Cobb* [2002] IRLR 861; *Palmanor Ltd v Cedron* [1978] ICR 1008; *Revenue and Customs Commissioners v Annabel's (Berkeley Square) Ltd* [2009] ICR 1123; *Sanderson v Exel Management Services Ltd* [2006] ICR 1337; *Tarmac Roadstone Holdings Ltd v Peacock* [1973] ICR 273; *Toni & Guys (St Pauls) Ltd v Georgiou* UKEAT/0085/13/DM; *Weevsmay Ltd v Kings* [1977] ICR 244; *Z.J.R. Lock v British Gas Trading Ltd and Others* [2014] ICR 813 (CJEU)

Working Time Regulations

An adult worker is entitled to various periods of rest as detailed in the *WTR 1998.* A breach of these regulations could entitle the worker to bring a claim at the ET.

By Reg 30(1)(a) a worker may bring a claim to the tribunal that his employer has denied him the following rights:

- Sufficient daily rest under Reg 10(1) or (2);
- Sufficient weekly rest under Reg 11(1), (2) or (3);
- Sufficient rest breaks within a working day under Reg 12(1) or (4);
- Sufficient annual leave under Reg 13;
- Entitlement to additional annual leave under Reg 13A;
- Compensatory rest under Reg 24;
- Adequate rest (if a mobile worker) under Reg 24A;
- Compensatory rest (if a young worker in the armed forces) under Reg 25(3);
- Compensatory rest (during night work if a young worker) under Reg 27A(4)(b); or
- Compensatory rest (if a young worker and certain exceptional circumstances apply) under Reg 27(3).

By Reg 30(1)(b) a worker may bring a bring a claim to the tribunal that his employer has failed to pay him the whole or any part of his or her entitlement to paid leave or payment in lieu of leave untaken at termination (Reg 30(1)(b)). Such a claim may also be brought as a deduction from wages claim under s13 ERA 1996 (see *Stringer v HM Revenue and Customs* [2009] IRLR 677).

Remedy: Where a tribunal finds a complaint under Reg 30(1)(a) well founded, it will make a declaration to that effect and may make an award of compensation.

Compensation will be determined as that which the tribunal considers to be just and equitable in all the circumstances having regard to the employer's default in refusing to permit the worker to exercise his right and any loss sustained by the worker as a result. Such an award does not include injury to feelings, as these claims are akin to breach of contract rather than discrimination (*Gomes v Higher Level Care Ltd* [2018] EWCA Civ 418). They can, however, include a claim for injury to health (*Grange v Abellio London Limited* UKEAT/0304/17/JOJ).

Where a tribunal finds a complaint under Reg 30(1)(b) that certain pay for leave entitlement has not been paid, it will order the employer to pay the worker the sums owing (Reg 30(5)).

Gross or net: N/A for Regs 10, 11, 12, 13, 24 or 24A; Gross for Regs 14 and 16

Tax: The tax treatments is unclear for payments under Regs 10, 11, 12, 13, 24 or 24A. However, tax should be paid under s62 ITEPA 2003 for payments under Regs 14 and 16.

Statutory authorities: WTR 1998 Regs 10 to 13, Reg 24, Reg 24A, Reg 25, Reg 27, Reg 27A, Reg 30(1)(a)

Relevant case law: Gomes v Higher Level Care Ltd [2018] EWCA Civ 418; *Grange v Abellio London Limited* UKEAT/0304/17/JOJ; *Stringer v HM Revenue and Customs* [2009] IRLR 677

Written reasons for dismissal

An employee is entitled to a written statement of reasons for dismissal from his or her employer where the dismissal arises from either: a) the employer giving notice; b) the employer terminating without notice; or c) if a limited term contract terminates by virtue of its limiting event (s92(1) ERA 1996). Generally, the employee must have made a request for the written reasons and must have been continuously employed for 2 years (s92(2) and (3)). The exception is where someone is dismissed when she is pregnant or on maternity leave until dismissed (s92(4)), or he or she is on adoption leave until dismissed (s92(4A)).

An employee may make a complaint to a tribunal that his or her employer has unreasonably failed to provide the statement or that the particulars of the statement given are inadequate or untrue (s93(1)).

Remedy: Where a tribunal finds such a complaint well founded, it may make a declaration as to what it finds the employer's reasons were for dismissing the employee and will make an award of 2 weeks' pay.

Gross or net: Gross. A week's pay as defined in ss220 to 229 ERA 1996 applies (see *Week's pay*).

Limit on a week's pay: None

Limit on number of weeks: 2

Any maximum or minimum: The award is simply 2 weeks' pay.

Adjustments: None

Cap: The award will form part of the compensatory award and the cap will apply in non-discriminatory unfair dismissal cases.

Mitigation: N/A

Tax: Any payment made in connection with the termination of employment will be taxed under s401 ITEPA 2003, of which this award will form a part.

Recoupment: The award should not form part of the prescribed element.

Statutory authorities: ERA 1996 *ss92 and 93*

Written statement of particulars

The *Employment Rights (Employment Particulars and Paid Annual Leave) (Amendment) Regulations 2018* amended sections 1 to 7B of Part I of the Employment Rights Act 1996. The amendments, which came into force on 6 April 2020, have the effect of making the right to a written statement of employment particulars a 'day 1' right for all workers (not just employees) and adding additional contents to the written statement. This means:

1) They are entitled to receive the 'principal statement' of the written statement no later than the first day of their new job (before 6 April 2020 the employer had a period of two months in which to provide the statement).

2) There is no qualifying period of employment (prior to 6 April 2020 employees were entitled to a written statement only if their employment had continued for at least one month).

An employee may bring a claim to a tribunal alleging that his or her employer has not complied with these obligations (s11(1)), and either party may bring a reference to a tribunal to determine what particulars ought to have been supplied (s11(2)).

Remedy (1): The tribunal has the power to determine the particulars of employment between the parties (s12(1) and (2)). Where an itemised pay statement has not been provided, or where deductions have been made which were not itemised on such a statement, the tribunal will make a declaration to that effect and may order the employer to pay the employee the value of the deductions (s12(3) and (4)).

Remedy (2): There is an additional right to a remedy from a tribunal where a claim has been brought within the list of jurisdictions in Sch 5 to EA 2002 (the list is extensive and includes many of the common, and not so common, claims). Where under such a claim the tribunal finds for the employee, whether or not it makes an award in respect of that claim, and where when the proceedings were brought the employer was in breach of the duty to give written particulars, the tribunal will make an award of 2 weeks' pay unless it would be unjust and inequitable to do so, and may if it considers it just and equitable in all the circumstances make an award of 4 weeks' pay (see ss38(1) to (5) EA 2002). For such an award to be made, the employer must be in breach of the obligation at the time the proceedings have begun. Where the employer has complied with its obligations under section 1, even belatedly, before the proceedings have begun, the tribunal has no power to make such an award (*Govdata Ltd v Denton* UKEAT/0237/18/BA).

Gross or net: Gross. A week's pay as defined in ss220 to 229 ERA 1996 applies (see *Week's pay*).

Limit on a week's pay: The current weekly limit is £544 (see *Table 1* for historical rates).

Limit on number of weeks: Minimum is 2; Maximum is 4 (s38(4) EA 2002).

Any maximum or minimum: Minimum is 2 weeks' pay, capped; Maximum is 4 weeks' pay, capped.

Adjustments: Contributory conduct applies. See *Adjustments and order of adjustments* for information about the order in which they apply when this head of loss is being claimed.

Cap: The award or increase of any award will fall within any applicable statutory cap for that award.

Mitigation: The usual rules of mitigation apply to the compensatory award.

Tax: The tax rules applicable to the particular award that has been made or increased will apply.

Recoupment: The award should not be included in the prescribed element.

Statutory authorities: EA 2002 *s38*; ERA 1996 *ss1 to 12,* and *ss220 to 229*; *Employment Rights (Employment Particulars and Paid Annual Leave) (Amendment) Regulations 2018* (SI 2018/1378)

Relevant case law: *Govdata Ltd v Denton* UKEAT/0237/18/BA

Wrongful dismissal: see *Damages for wrongful dismissal*

Zero-hours contracts

A zero-hours contract is one in which the employer does not guarantee the individual any hours of work. The employer offers the individual work when it arises, and the individual can either accept or decline the work offered on that occasion. Individuals on a zero-hours contract may have the employment status of a 'worker' or an 'employee'.

The term is a political rather than a legal concept, potentially covering a range of different contracts and working arrangements.

Regardless of how many hours are actually offered, the employer must pay at least the National Minimum Wage.

Section 27A(3) of the ERA 1996 (as inserted by the Small Business, Enterprise and Employment Act, s153(1) and (2)) provides that, from 26 May 2015, a provision in a zero hours contract which prohibits the worker from doing work under any other arrangement is unenforceable.

Regulation 2 of the Exclusivity Terms in Zero Hours Contracts (Redress) Regulations 2015) (ETZHC (R) Regs 2015) makes provision in relation to the right for individuals on a zero hours contract not to be unfairly dismissed or subjected to a detriment (see *Detriment*) for a reason relating to a breach of a provision of a zero hours contract to which s27A(3) of the 1996 Act applies.

There is no qualifying period for an employee bringing such an unfair dismissal or detriment claim to the ET.

Remedy

Where an employment tribunal finds that a complaint is well founded, it must take such of the following steps as it considers just and equitable:

a) making a declaration as to the rights of the complainant and the employer in relation to the matters to which the complaint relates; and

b) ordering the employer to pay compensation to the complainant (Reg 4(1) ETZHC (R) Regs 2015).

The amount of the compensation awarded must be such as the tribunal considers just and equitable in all the circumstances having regard to:

a) the infringement to which the complaint relates; and

b) any loss which is attributable to the act, or failure to act, which infringed the complainant's right (Reg 4(2) ETZHC (R) Regs 2015).

The loss must be taken to include:

a) any expenses reasonably incurred by the complainant in consequence of the act, or failure to act, to which the complaint relates; and

b) loss of any benefit which the complainant might reasonably be expected to have had but for that act or failure to act (Reg 4(3) ETZHC (R) Regs 2015).

Gross or net: The basic award will be calculated gross and the compensatory award will be calculated on the basis of net loss.

Limit on a week's pay: £544 for the basic award element.

Any maximum or minimum: If the detriment to which the worker is subjected is the termination of the worker's contract, but that contract is not a contract of employment, the total award will not exceed the aggregate of the maximum basic award (£16,320) and the maximum compensatory award (£89,493) i.e. £105,813 (Reg 4(6) ETZHC (R) Regs 2015).

Adjustments: The award can be reduced for contributory fault (Reg 4(7) ETZHC (R) Regs 2015).

Mitigation: The individual is expected to mitigate their loss (Reg 4(4) ETZHC (R) Regs 2015).

Tax: If the combined sum of any basic and compensatory award is greater than £30,000 then the excess figure will be subject to tax (see *Grossing up*).

Recoupment: It is assumed that recoupment will be apply to immediate loss of earnings.

Statutory authorities: Exclusivity Terms in Zero Hours Contracts (Redress) Regulations 2015 Regs 2,3 and 4; Small Business, Enterprise and Employment Act 2015 s153; ERA 1996 s27A

Caps and limits

Table 1: Statutory cap, maximum basic award and the limit on gross weekly pay

Date	Maximum Compensatory Award	Maximum Basic Award	Maximum Total	Gross Weekly Pay Limit
06/04/2015 to 05/04/2016	£78,335 or gross annual pay, whichever is the smaller	£14,250	£92,585	£475
06/04/2016 to 05/04/2017	£78,962 or gross annual pay, whichever is the smaller	£14,370	£93,332	£479
06/04/2017 to 05/04/2018	£80,541 or gross annual pay, whichever is the smaller	£14,670	£95,211	£489
06/04/2018 to 05/04/2019	£83,682 or gross annual pay, whichever is the smaller	£15,240	£98,922	£508
06/04/2019 to 05/04/2020	£86,444 or gross annual pay, whichever is the smaller	£15,750	£102,194	£525
06/04/2020 to 05/04/2021	£88,519 or gross annual pay, whichever is the smaller	£16,140	£104,659	£538
06/04/2021 to 05/04/2022	£89,493 or gross annual pay, whichever is the smaller	£16,320	£105,813	£544

Notes

1. The cap on gross weekly pay is only applicable to claims of Statutory redundancy pay, Basic award; Right to written particulars of employment; Right to be accompanied at a disciplinary hearing; Right to request flexible working; Insolvency provisions; Additional award

2. The Employment Rights (Increase of Limits) Order 2021 increased the limits to take effect from 06/04/2021. Limits are increased in line with inflation every 6th April.

Table 2: Limits on awards (other)

See Employment Rights (Increase of limits) Orders

	Award	06/04/2018 to 05/04/2019	06/04/2019 to 05/04/2020	06/04/2020 to 05/04/2021	06/04/2021 to 05/04/2022
s145E(3) TULR(C)A 1992	Amount of award for unlawful inducement relating to trade union membership or activities or for unlawful inducement relating to collective bargaining.	£4,059	£4,193	£4,294	£4,341
s156(1) TULR(C)A 1992	Minimum amount of basic award of compensation where dismissal is unfair by virtue of section 152(1) or 153 of the 1992 Act.	£6,203	£6,408	£6,562	£6,634
s176(6A) TULR(C)A 1992	Minimum amount of compensation where individual excluded or expelled from union in contravention of section 174 of the 1992 Act and not admitted or re-admitted by date of tribunal application.	£9,474	£9,787	£10,022	£10,132
s31(1) ERA 1996	Limit on amount of guarantee payment payable to an employee in respect of any day.	£28	£29	£30	£30
s120(1) ERA 1996	Minimum amount of basic award of compensation where dismissal is unfair by virtue of section 100(1)(a) and (b), 101A(d), 102(1) or 103 of the 1996 Act.	£6,203	£6,408	£6,562	£6,634

Table 3: Guarantee Payments

Date	Daily limit	Maximum amount in any 3 month period (5 days)
06/04/2017 to 05/04/2018	£27.00	£135.00
06/04/2018 to 05/04/2019	£28.00	£140.00
06/04/2019 to 05/04/2020	£29.00	£145.00
06/04/2020 to 05/04/2021	£30.00	£150.00
06/04/2021 to 05/04/2022	£30.00	£150.00

Table 4: Time limits for appeals

Review of ET decision	14 days
Appeal to EAT from ET	42 days
Review of EAT decision	14 days
Appeal to Court of Appeal from EAT	14 days

Table 5: Gross weekly pay: claims for which gross weekly pay is used in the calculation and the related calculation dates

Claim	Calculation date	Limit on a week's pay
Additional award	Date on which employee is given notice or the EDT.	£544
Basic award	If the employee is summarily dismissed or dismissed with less than the statutory notice, the calculation date is the date on which the employment ended. If the employee was dismissed with notice equal to or more than the statutory notice, the calculation date is found by subtracting the statutory notice period from the actual notice given. This means that if statutory notice is given, the calculation date is the date that notice was given. If statutory notice is 3 weeks and actual notice given is 4 weeks, the calculation date is the day after the end of the first week of notice.	£544
Guarantee pay	The day when the guarantee pay is due.	See separate limits
Insolvency	For arrears of pay and holiday, the date on which the employer became insolvent. For the Basic award the latest of (i) the date on which the employer became insolvent, (ii) the date of the termination of the employee's employment, and (iii) the date on which the award was made. In relation to any other debt whichever is the later of (i) the date on which the employer became insolvent, and (ii) the date of the termination of the employee's employment.	£544
Protective award	The date on which the protective award was made or, in the case of an employee who was dismissed before the date on which the protective award was made, the calculation date for the purpose of computing the amount of a redundancy payment.	Unlimited
Remuneration whilst suspended on medical grounds	The day before suspension began.	Unlimited
Right for union member not to be unjustifiably disciplined/expelled and blacklisting claims	N/A	£544 for the Basic award element
Time off to look for work or arrange training after being made redundant	The day on which the employer's notice was given.	Actual gross weekly pay is used but limited to 40% of a week's pay

Table 5: Gross weekly pay: claims for which gross weekly pay is used in the calculation and the related calculation dates

Claim	Calculation date	Limit on a week's pay
Time off for antenatal care	The day of ante-natal appointment.	Unlimited
Time off for employee representatives (including ICE and OPPS); pension trustees; union duties, activities and union learning reps; study or training; young person for study or training; members of a European Works Council	Date on which time off was taken or should have been permitted.	No limit apart from for Study or training (not Young person study or training) where the limit is £544
TUPE claims	In the case of an employee who is dismissed by reason of redundancy the date which is the calculation date for the purposes of any entitlement of his to a redundancy payment. In the case of an employee who is dismissed for any other reason, the effective date of termination. In any other case, the date of the relevant transfer.	Unlimited
Right to be accompanied at a disciplinary or grievance meeting	Date of dismissal/EDT or if no dismissal the date of the hearing.	£544
Right to request flexible working	Date on which the application was made.	£544
Written reasons for dismissal	Date notice was given or if no notice the EDT.	Unlimited
Written statement of particulars	If the employee was employed by the employer on the date the proceedings were begun, that date. If he was not, the effective date of termination.	£544
Paid annual leave under the Working Time Regulations	Payment based on a normal week's pay on the first day of the period of leave in question.	Unlimited
Redundancy payments	Depends on the circumstances.	£544

Holiday

Table 6: Holiday Pay crib sheet

Reproduced from Holidays and holiday pay leaflet – ACAS

Working Pattern	Before 1 April 2009	After 1 April 2009
Full-time (5 day week)	4.8 weeks (24 days)	5.6 weeks (28 days)
Part-time (4 day week)	4.8 weeks (19.2 days)	5.6 weeks (22.4 days)
Part-time (3 day week)	4.8 weeks (14.4 days)	5.6 weeks (16.8 days)
6 day week	4.8 weeks (28 days – the maximum statutory entitlement)	5.6 weeks (28 days – the maximum statutory entitlement)
Compressed hours e.g. 36 hours in 4 days	36 hours x 4.8 weeks = 172.8 hours per year	36 hours x 5.6 weeks = 201.6 hours per year
Annualised hours e.g. 1,600 hours at an average of 33.5 hours week	33.5 hours x 4.8 weeks = 160.8 hours per year	33.5 hours x 5.6 weeks = 187.6 hours per year
Bank Holidays	Can be included in the 4.8 weeks leave – check the contract	Can be included in the 5.6 weeks leave – check the contract

Income Tax and National Insurance

Table 7: Income Tax Rates and Taxable Bands (England & Wales)			
Rate	2019-2020	2020-2021	2021-2022
Zero rate: 0% (Personal allowance)	£0 - £12,500	£0 - £12,500	£0 - £12,570
Basic rate: 20%	The next £37,500	The next £37,500	The next £37,700
Higher rate: 40%	The next £100,000 [1]	The next £100,000	The next £99,730
Additional rate: 45%	Over £150,000	Over £150,000	Over £150,000
Starting rate for savings	£0 - £5,000	£0 - £5,000	£0 - £5,000
Savings allowance (basic rate tax payers)	£1,000	£1,000	£1,000
Savings allowance (higher rate tax payers)	£500	£500	£500
Savings allowance (additional rate tax payers)	NIL	NIL	NIL

[1] But remember that the personal allowance will decrease by £1 for every £2 of earnings over £100,000 so this will need to be taken into account.

Table 8: Income Tax Rates and Taxable Bands (Scotland)			
Rate	2019-2020	2020-2021	2021-2022
Zero rate: 0% (Personal allowance)	£0 - £12,500	£0 - £12,500	£0 - £12,570
Starter rate: 19%	The next £2,050	The next £2,085	The next £2,097
Basic rate: 20%	The next £10,395	The next £10,573	The next £10,629
Intermediate rate: 21%	The next £18,485	The next £18,272	The next £18,366
Higher rate: 41%	The next £106,570 [1]	The next £106,570	The next £106,338
Top/Additional rate: 46%	Over £150,000	Over £150,000	Over £150,000

[1] But remember that the personal allowance will decrease by £1 for every £2 of earnings over £100,000 so this will need to be taken into account.

Table 9: Income Tax Allowances (England, Wales & Scotland)			
Income Tax allowances	2019-2020	2020-2021	2021-22
Personal Allowance	£12,500	£12,500	£12,570
Income limit for Personal Allowance [1]	£100,000	£100,000	£100,000
Maximum amount of Married Couple's Allowance [2] [3]	£8,915	£9,075	£9,125
Minimum amount of Married Couple's Allowance [2] [4]	£3,450	£3,510	£3,530
Blind Person's Allowance	£2,450	£2,500	£2,520
Transferable Tax Allowance for married couples and civil partners [5]	£1,250	£1,250	£1,260
Dividend allowance	£2,000	£2,000	£2,000

[1] The personal allowance reduces where the individual's income is above this limit by £1 for every £2 above the limit. This applies regardless of the individual's date of birth.

[2] Available to people born before 6 April 1935. Tax relief for this allowance is restricted to 10%.

[3] This allowance is reduced when the individual's income is above the income limit. This is at a rate of £1 for every £2 above the income limit until it reaches the minimum amount. Any reduction in the married couple's allowance applies after any reduction to the individual's personal allowance.

[4] This is also the maximum relief for maintenance payments where at least one of the parties is born before 6 April 1935.

[5] Available to spouses/civil partners born after 5 April 1935. This allowance is 10% of the personal allowance for those born after 5 April 1938. It allows a spouse or civil partner who is not liable to income tax above the basic rate to transfer this amount of their personal allowance to their spouse/civil partner. The recipient must not be liable to tax above the basic rate. The recipient is eligible to a tax reduction of 20% of the transferred amount.

Table 10: National Insurance Contributions: Rates and Allowances (England, Wales & Scotland)

	2019-2020	2020-2021	2021-22
Lower earnings limit, primary Class 1	£118	£120	£120
Upper earnings limit, primary Class 1	£962	£962	£967
Primary threshold (employee contribution)	£166	£183	£184
Secondary threshold (employer contribution)	£166	£169	£170
Employees' primary Class 1 rate between primary threshold and upper earnings limit (not contracted out)	12%	12%	12%
Employees' primary Class 1 rate above upper earnings limit	2%	2%	2%
Class 1A rate on employer provided benefits [1]	13.8%	13.8%	13.8%
Employers' secondary Class 1 rate above secondary threshold – no limit (not contracted out)	13.8%	13.8%	13.8%
Employment Allowance	£3,000 per year, per employer	£4,000 per year, per employer	£4,000 per year, per employer
Apprentice Upper Secondary Threshold (AUST) for under 25s[2]	£962	£962	£967
Class 2 Rate	£3.00 per week	£3.05 per week	£3.05 per week
Class 2 small earnings exception/Small Profits Threshold	£6,365 per year	£6,475 per year	£6,515 per year
Special Class 2 rate for share fishermen	£3.65 per week	£3.70 per week	£3.70 per week
Special Class 2 rate for volunteer development workers	£5.90 per week	£6.00 per week	£6.00 per week
Class 3 rate	£15.00 per week	£15.30 per week	£15.40 per week
Class 4 lower profits limit	£8,632 per year	£9,500 per year	£9,568 per year
Class 4 upper profits limit	£50,000 per year	£50,000 per year	£50,270 per year
Class 4 rate between lower profits limit and upper profits limit	9%	9%	9%
Class 4 rate above upper profits limit	2%	2%	2%

[1] Class 1A NICs are payable in July and are calculated on the value of taxable benefits provided in the previous tax year, using the secondary Class 1 percentage rate appropriate to that tax year.

[2] Came into force 6 April 2016.

Table 11: Income Tax and National Insurance: Gross to Net Salaries 2021 - 2022

Gross Annual Salary	Tax (England & Wales)	Tax (Scotland)	Employee National Insurance (England, Wales and Scotland)	Net Annual Salary (England & Wales)	Net Annual Salary (Scotland)
9,000	0.00	0.00	0.00	9,000.00	9,000.00
10,000	0.00	0.00	51.84	9,948.16	9,948.16
11,000	0.00	0.00	171.84	10,828.16	10,828.16
12,000	0.00	0.00	291.84	11,708.16	11,708.16
13,000	86.00	81.70	411.84	12,502.16	12,506.46
14,000	286.00	271.70	531.84	13,182.16	13,196.46
15,000	486.00	465.03	651.84	13,862.16	13,883.13
16,000	686.00	665.03	771.84	14,542.16	14,563.13
17,000	886.00	865.03	891.84	15,222.16	15,243.13
18,000	1,086.00	1,065.03	1,011.84	15,894.00	15,923.13
19,000	1,286.00	1,265.03	1,131.84	16,582.16	16,603.13
20,000	1,486.00	1,465.03	1,251.84	17,262.16	17,283.13
21,000	1,686.00	1,665.03	1,371.84	17,942.16	17,963.13
22,000	1,886.00	1,865.03	1,491.84	18,622.16	18,643.13
23,000	2,086.00	2,065.03	1,611.84	19,302.16	19,323.13

Table 11: Income Tax and National Insurance: Gross to Net Salaries 2021 - 2022

Gross Annual Salary	Tax (England & Wales)	Tax (Scotland)	Employee National Insurance (England, Wales and Scotland)	Net Annual Salary (England & Wales)	Net Annual Salary (Scotland)
24,000	2,286.00	2,265.03	1,731.84	19,982.16	20,003.13
25,000	2,486.00	2,465.03	1,851.84	20,662.16	20,683.13
26,000	2,686.00	2,672.07	1,971.84	21,342.16	21,356.09
27,000	2,886.00	2,882.07	2,091.84	22,022.16	22,026.09
28,000	3,086.00	3,092.07	2,211.84	22,702.16	22,696.09
29,000	3,286.00	3,302.07	2,331.84	23,382.16	23,366.09
30,000	3,486.00	3,512.07	2,451.84	24,062.16	24,036.09
35,000	4,486.00	4,562.07	3,051.84	27,462.16	27,386.09
40,000	5,486.00	5,612.07	3,651.84	30,862.16	30,736.09
45,000	6,486.00	6,929.67	4,251.84	34,262.16	33,818.49
50,000	7,486.00	8,979.67	4,851.84	37,662.16	36,168.49
55,000	9,432.00	11,029.67	4,978.84	40,589.16	38,991.49
60,000	11,432.00	13,079.67	5,078.84	43,489.16	41,841.49
65,000	13,432.00	15,129.67	5,178.84	46,389.16	44,691.49
70,000	15,432.00	17,179.67	5,278.84	49,289.16	47,541.49
75,000	17,432.00	19,229.67	5,378.84	52,189.16	50,391.49
80,000	19,432.00	21,279.67	5,478.84	55,089.16	53,241.49
85,000	21,432.00	23,329.67	5,578.84	57,989.16	56,091.49
90,000	23,432.00	25,379.67	5,678.84	60,889.16	58,941.49
95,000	25,432.00	27,429.67	5,778.84	63,789.16	61,791.49
100,000	27,432.00	29,479.67	5,878.84	66,689.16	64,641.49
125,000	42,432.00	44,854.67	6,378.84	76,189.16	73,766.49
150,000	52,460.00	55,133.37	6,878.84	90,661.16	87,987.79
175,000	63,710.00	66,633.37	7,378.84	103,911.16	100,987.79
200,000	74,960.00	78,133.37	7,878.84	117,161.16	113,987.79

Assumption: the above figures are based on a tax code of 1257L (the personal allowance for 2021-22 is £12,570). For any net earnings above £100,000 the standard personal allowance has been reduced by £1 for every £2 above £100,000 and the tax calculated accordingly.

Interest

Table 12: Interest Rates

Date	Interest rate
From 01/08/1999	7%
From 01/02/2002	6%
From 01/02/2009	3%
From 01/06/2009	1.5%
From 01/07/2009	0.5%
From 29/07/2013	8%

Redundancy and Statutory Notice

Table 13: Statutory Redundancy - number of weeks redundancy pay

Age	Number of years' continuous service																		
---	2	3	4	5	6	7	8	9	10	11	12	13	14	15	16	17	18	19	20
17	1	-	-	-	-	-	-	-	-	-	-	-	-	-	-	-	-	-	-
18	1	1½	-	-	-	-	-	-	-	-	-	-	-	-	-	-	-	-	-
19	1	1½	2	-	-	-	-	-	-	-	-	-	-	-	-	-	-	-	-
20	1	1½	2	2½	-	-	-	-	-	-	-	-	-	-	-	-	-	-	-
21	1	1½	2	2½	3	-	-	-	-	-	-	-	-	-	-	-	-	-	-
22	1	1½	2	2½	3	3½	-	-	-	-	-	-	-	-	-	-	-	-	-
23	1½	2	2½	3	3½	4	4½	-	-	-	-	-	-	-	-	-	-	-	-
24	2	2½	3	3½	4	4½	5	5½	-	-	-	-	-	-	-	-	-	-	-
25	2	3	3½	4	4½	5	5½	6	6½	-	-	-	-	-	-	-	-	-	-
26	2	3	4	4½	5	5½	6	6½	7	7½	-	-	-	-	-	-	-	-	-
27	2	3	4	5	5½	6	6½	7	7½	8	8½	-	-	-	-	-	-	-	-
28	2	3	4	5	6	6½	7	7½	8	8½	9	9½	-	-	-	-	-	-	-
29	2	3	4	5	6	7	7½	8	8½	9	9½	10	10½	-	-	-	-	-	-
30	2	3	4	5	6	7	8	8½	9	9½	10	10½	11	11½	-	-	-	-	-
31	2	3	4	5	6	7	8	9	9½	10	10½	11	11½	12	12½	-	-	-	-
32	2	3	4	5	6	7	8	9	10	10½	11	11½	12	12½	13	13½	-	-	-
33	2	3	4	5	6	7	8	9	10	11	11½	12	12½	13	13½	14	14½	-	-
34	2	3	4	5	6	7	8	9	10	11	12	12½	13	13½	14	14½	15	15½	-
35	2	3	4	5	6	7	8	9	10	11	12	13	13½	14	14½	15	15½	16	16½
36	2	3	4	5	6	7	8	9	10	11	12	13	14	14½	15	15½	16	16½	17
37	2	3	4	5	6	7	8	9	10	11	12	13	14	15	15½	16	16½	17	17½
38	2	3	4	5	6	7	8	9	10	11	12	13	14	15	16	16½	17	17½	18
39	2	3	4	5	6	7	8	9	10	11	12	13	14	15	16	17	17½	18	18½
40	2	3	4	5	6	7	8	9	10	11	12	13	14	15	16	17	18	18½	19
41	2	3	4	5	6	7	8	9	10	11	12	13	14	15	16	17	18	19	19½
42	2½	3½	4½	5½	6½	7½	8½	9½	10½	11½	12½	13½	14½	15½	16½	17½	18½	19½	20½
43	3	4	5	6	7	8	9	10	11	12	13	14	15	16	17	18	19	20	21
44	3	4½	5½	6½	7½	8½	9½	10½	11½	12½	13½	14½	15½	16½	17½	18½	19½	20½	21½
45	3	4½	6	7	8	9	10	11	12	13	14	15	16	17	18	19	20	21	22
46	3	4½	6	7½	8½	9½	10½	11½	12½	13½	14½	15½	16½	17½	18½	19½	20½	21½	22½
47	3	4½	6	7½	9	10	11	12	13	14	15	16	17	18	19	20	21	22	23
48	3	4½	6	7½	9	10½	11½	12½	13½	14½	15½	16½	17½	18½	19½	20½	21½	22½	23½
49	3	4½	6	7½	9	10½	12	13	14	15	16	17	18	19	20	21	22	23	24
50	3	4½	6	7½	9	10½	12	13½	14½	15½	16½	17½	18½	19½	20½	21½	22½	23½	24½
51	3	4½	6	7½	9	10½	12	13½	15	16	17	18	19	20	21	22	23	24	25
52	3	4½	6	7½	9	10½	12	13½	15	16½	17½	18½	19½	20½	21½	22½	23½	24½	25½
53	3	4½	6	7½	9	10½	12	13½	15	16½	18	19	20	21	22	23	24	25	26
54	3	4½	6	7½	9	10½	12	13½	15	16½	18	19½	20½	21½	22½	23½	24½	25½	26½
55	3	4½	6	7½	9	10½	12	13½	15	16½	18	19½	21	22	23	24	25	26	27
56	3	4½	6	7½	9	10½	12	13½	15	16½	18	19½	21	22½	23½	24½	25½	26½	27½
57	3	4½	6	7½	9	10½	12	13½	15	16½	18	19½	21	22½	24	25	26	27	28
58	3	4½	6	7½	9	10½	12	13½	15	16½	18	19½	21	22½	24	25½	26½	27½	28½
59	3	4½	6	7½	9	10½	12	13½	15	16½	18	19½	21	22½	24	25½	27	28	29
60	3	4½	6	7½	9	10½	12	13½	15	16½	18	19½	21	22½	24	25½	27	28½	29½
61+	3	4½	6	7½	9	10½	12	13½	15	16½	18	19½	21	22½	24	25½	27	28½	30

Table 14: Statutory Notice Periods

Period of continuous employment (years)	Minimum period of notice (weeks)
Less than 2 years (but more than 1 month)	1
At least 2 but less than 3	2
At least 3 but less than 4	3
At least 4 but less than 5	4
At least 5 but less than 6	5
At least 6 but less than 7	6
At least 7 but less than 8	7
At least 8 but less than 9	8
At least 9 but less than 10	9
At least 10 but less than 11	10
At least 11 but less than 12	11
12 years or more	12

Statutory Rates

Table 15: National Minimum and Living Wage Rates

Year	Living wage for adults aged 25 and over[1]	National Minimum Wage for workers between the ages of 21 and 24[2]	Development Rate (for 18 to 20 year olds)	16-17 year olds rate	Apprentice rate[3]
01/10/2016 to 31/03/2017[4]	£7.20	£6.95	£5.55	£4.00	£3.40
01/04/2017 to 31/03/2018	£7.50	£7.05	£5.60	£4.05	£3.50
01/04/2018 to 31/03/2019	£7.83	£7.38	£5.90	£4.20	£3.70
01/04/2019 to 31/03/2020	£8.21	£7.70	£6.15	£4.35	£3.90
01/04/2020 to 31/03/2021	£8.72	£8.20	£6.45	£4.55	£4.15
01/04/2021 to 31/03/2022	£8.91	£8.36	£6.56	£4.62	£4.30

[1] The living wage applies to anyone **aged 23 and over** from 1 April 2021.

[2] From 1 April 2021, this rate applies to anyone **aged 21 to 22** inclusive.

[3] This rate is for apprentices under 19 or those in their first year. For anyone over the age of 19, and past their first year, the rate is applicable to the age.

[4] The National Minimum Wage is now reviewed every April to align it with the National Living Wage calendar.

Table 16: Statutory maternity, paternity, adoption, shared parental, parental bereavement and sick pay rates

Date	Statutory Maternity Pay (SMP) (payable for up to 39 weeks)	Ordinary Statutory Paternity Pay (OSPP) (payable for up to 2 weeks)	Statutory Adoption Pay (SAP) (payable for up to 39 weeks)	Statutory Shared Parental Pay (ShPP) (for parents of children due or adopted on or after 5 April 2015) (remaining weeks up to 39)	Statutory Parental Bereavement Pay (for employed parents who lose a child on or after 6 April 2020) (payable for up to 2 weeks)	Statutory Sick Pay (SSP)
06/04/2019 to 05/04/2020	90% of average weekly gross pay for first 6 weeks; and then £148.68 or 90% of average gross weekly earnings (whichever is lower) for the next 33 weeks	£148.68 or 90% of average gross weekly earnings (whichever is lower)	90% of average weekly gross pay for first 6 weeks; and then £148.68 or 90% of average gross weekly earnings (whichever is lower) for the next 33 weeks	£148.68 or 90% of average gross weekly earnings (whichever is lower)	N/A	£94.25 per week
06/04/2020 to 05/04/2021	90% of average weekly gross pay for first 6 weeks; and then £151.20 or 90% of average gross weekly earnings (whichever is lower) for the next 33 weeks	£151.20 or 90% of average gross weekly earnings (whichever is lower)	90% of average weekly gross pay for first 6 weeks; and then £151.20 or 90% of average gross weekly earnings (whichever is lower) for the next 33 weeks	£151.20 or 90% of average gross weekly earnings (whichever is lower)	£151.20 or 90% of average gross weekly earnings (whichever is lower)	£95.85 per week
06/04/2021 to 05/04/2022	90% of average weekly gross pay for first 6 weeks; and then £151.97 or 90% of average gross weekly earnings (whichever is lower) for the next 33 weeks	£151.97 or 90% of average gross weekly earnings (whichever is lower)	90% of average weekly gross pay for first 6 weeks; and then £151.97 or 90% of average gross weekly earnings (whichever is lower) for the next 33 weeks	£151.97 or 90% of average gross weekly earnings (whichever is lower)	£151.97 or 90% of average gross weekly earnings (whichever is lower)	£96.35 per week

Legislation

Table 17: List of abbreviated statutes and statutory instruments	
AWR 2010	Agency Workers Regulations 2010
CA 2020	Coronavirus Act 2020
CAR 2004	Civil Aviation (Working Time) Regulations 2004
CCBR 2007	Companies (Cross-Border Mergers) Regulations 2007
CEC 1975	Colleges of Education (Compensation) Regulations 1975
COMAH 1999	Control of Major Accident Hazards Regulations 1999
CRA(TU)PE 2014	Collective Redundancies and Transfer of Undertakings (Protection of Employment) (Amendment) Regulations 2014
EA 2002	Employment Act 2002
EA 2010	Equality Act 2010
EA 2016	Enterprise Act 2016
EAA 1973	Employment Agencies Act 1973
ECSR 2006	European Cooperative Society (Involvement of Employees) Regulations 2006
EE(RB)R 2003	Employment Equality (Religion or Belief) Regulations 2003
EE(SO)R 2003	Employment Equality (Sexual Orientation) Regulations 2003
EJOs 1994	Employment Tribunals Extension of Jurisdiction (England and Wales) Order 1994(13); and Employment Tribunals Extension of Jurisdiction (Scotland) Order 1994
EOR 2009	Ecclesiastical Offices (Terms of Service) Regulations 2009
ELLR 2009	European Public Limited-Liability Company (Employee Involvement) (Great Britain) Regulations 2009
EPA 1970	Equal Pay Act 1970
EP(RJAIS) Regs 1996	Employment Protection (Recoupment of Jobseeker's Allowance and Income Support) Regulations 1996
ERA 1996	Employment Rights Act 1996
ERelA 1999	Employment Relations Act 1999
ERR 2013	Enterprise and Regulatory Reform Act 2013
EST (PR) Regs 2010	Employee Study and Training (Procedural Requirements) Regulations 2010
EST (ECR) Regulations 2010	Employee Study and Training (Eligibility, Complaints and Remedies) Regulations 2010
ETA 1996	Employment Tribunals Act 1996
ET(I) Order 2013	Employment Tribunals (Interest) Order (Amendment) Order 2013
ET(IADC) Regs 2013	Employment Tribunals (Interest on Awards in Discrimination Cases)(Amendment) Regulations 2013
ETZH C (R) Regs 2015	Exclusivity Terms in Zero Hours Contracts (Redress) Regulations 2015
FA 2017	Finance Act 2017
FTE(PLFT) Regs 2002	Fixed Term Employees (Prevention of less favourable treatment) Regulations 2002
FVR 2004	Fishing Vessels (Working Time: Sea-fishermen) Regulations 2004
FW(PR) Regs 2002	Flexible Working (Procedural Requirements) Regulations 2002
FW(ECR) Regs 2002	Flexible Working (Eligibility, Complaints and Remedies) Regulations 2002
HSCE 1996	Health and Safety (Consultation with Employees) Regulations 1996
HSWA 1974	Health and Safety at Work etc Act 1974
ICE Regs 2004	Information and Consultation of Employees Regulations 2004
ICR 2004	Information and Consultation of Employees Regulations 2004
ITA 1982	Industrial Training Act 1982
IT(IADC) Regs 1996	Industrial Tribunals (Interest on Awards in Discrimination Cases) Regulations 1996
MSR 2003	Merchant Shipping (Working Time: Inland Waterways) Regulations 2003
NMWA 1998	National Minimum Wage Act 1998
OPPS Regs 2006	The Occupational and Personal Pension Schemes (Consultation by Employers and Miscellaneous Amendment) Regulations 2006
OPS(CO)R 1996	Occupational Pension Schemes (Contracting-Out) Regulations 1996

Legislation

Table 17: List of abbreviated statutes and statutory instruments

OPS(DI)R 1996	Occupational Pensions Schemes (Disclosure of Information) Regulations 1996
PSA 1993	Pension Schemes Act 1993
PTW(PLFT) Regs 2000	Part Time Workers (Prevention of less favourable treatment) Regulations 2000
PWER Regs 2016	The Posted Workers (Enforcement of Employment Rights) Regulations 2016
REACHER 2008	REACH Enforcement Regulations 2008
RTR 2005	Road Transport (Working Time) Regulations 2005
SBEE 2015	Small Business, Enterprise and Employment Act 2015
TICE 1999	Transnational Information and Consultation of Employees Regulations 1999
TULR(C)A 1992	Trade Union and Labour Relations (Consolidation) Act 1992
TUPE Regs 2006	The Transfer of Undertakings (Protection of Employment) Regulations 2006
WTR 1998	Working Time Regulations 1998

Table 18: Limitation periods and requisite minimum qualifying periods for claims

Claim	Limitation period (maximum length of time that can elapse for claim to be brought to ET)	Length of service required before a claim can be brought to ET
Discrimination (ss13, 15, 16, 18, 19, 21, 26, 27 EA 2010)	3 months (or 6 months if relating to armed forces service) (s123 EA 2010)	None
Right of union member not to be unjustifiably disciplined (s64 TULR(C)A)	3 months (s66 TULR(C)A)	None
Right of union member to compensation if declared to be unjustifiably disciplined (s67 TULR(C)A)	6 months, but not before 4 weeks (s67(3) TULR(C)A)	None
Right of union member not to suffer deduction of unauthorised or excessive subscriptions (s68 TULR(C)A)	3 months (s68A(1) TULR(C)A)	None
Right of union member not to suffer deduction of contributions to a political fund (s86 TULR(C)A)	3 months (s87(2) TULR(C)A)	None
Right of union member if employer has failed to comply with their right not to suffer deduction of contributions to a political fund (s87(5) TULR(C)A)	6 months but not before 4 weeks (s87(6) TULR(C)A)	None
Refusal of employment on grounds related to trade union membership (s137 TULR(C)A)	3 months (s139(1) TULR(C)A)	None
Right not to be offered inducements relating to union membership or activities (s145A TULR(C)A)	3 months (s145C TULR(C)A)	None
Right not to be offered inducements relating to collective bargaining (s145B TULR(C)A)	3 months (s145C TULR(C)A)	None
Protection from detriment (not dismissal) relating to union membership or activities (s146 TULR(C)A)	3 months (s147(1) TULR(C)A)	None
Time off for union duties (s168 TULR(C)A)	3 months (s171 TULR(C)A)	None
Time off for union learning representatives (s168A TULR(C)A)	3 months (s171 TULR(C)A)	None
Payment for time off for union duties and union learning reps (s169 TULR(C)A)	3 months (s171 TULR(C)A)	None
Time off for union activities (s170 TULR(C)A)	3 months (s171 TULR(C)A)	None
Right not to be excluded or expelled from union (s174 TULR(C)A)	6 months (s175 TULR(C)A)	None

Table 18: Limitation periods and requisite minimum qualifying periods for claims

Claim	Limitation period (maximum length of time that can elapse for claim to be brought to ET)	Length of service required before a claim can be brought to ET
Right to compensation if excluded or expelled from union (s176(2) TULR(C)A)	6 months (but not before 4 weeks) (s176(3) TULR(C)A)	None
Redundancy - right to be consulted (s188 TULR(C)A)	3 months (s189(5) TULR(C)A)	None
Redundancy - right to election of employee reps (s188A TULR(C)A)	3 months (s189(5) TULR(C)A)	None
Redundancy - right to be paid during protected period (s190 TULR(C)A)	3 months (s192(3) TULR(C)A)	None
Right to written statement of particulars (s1(1) ERA), or change in particulars (s4(1) ERA), or itemised pay statement (s8(1) ERA)	During employment or within 3 months of termination (s11(4) ERA)	1 month (s198 ERA) (none in the case of itemised statement)
Right not to suffer unauthorised deductions (normal) (s13(1) ERA), (retail) (s18(1)), not to make payments to employer (normal) (s15(1)), (retail) (s21(1))	3 months (s23 ERA)	None
Right to guarantee payments (s28(1) ERA)	3 months (s34(2) ERA)	1 month (s29 ERA)
Right not to suffer detriment (ss43M, 44, 45, 45A, 46, 47, 47A, 47B, 47C, 47D, 47E, 47F ERA; Reg 4 Exclusivity Terms in Zero Hours Contracts (Redress) Regulations 2015)	3 months (s48(3) ERA; Reg 3 Exclusivity Terms in Zero Hours Contracts (Redress) Regulations 2015 The time limit may be extended under the Exclusivity Terms Act in certain circumstances	None, except: 26 weeks in the case of Ordinary Adoption Leave (pre-5 April 2015 only), Additional Adoption Leave (pre-5 April 2015 only), Ordinary Paternity Leave (birth), Additional Paternity Leave (birth) (pre-5 April 2015 only), Paternity Leave (adoption), Shared Parental Leave; 1 year in the case of Parental Leave (reg 13 Maternity and Parental Leave etc Regs 1999)
Time off for public duties (s50(1) ERA)	3 months (s51(2) ERA)	None
Time off on redundancy to look for work or arrange training (s52(1) ERA) and payment for time off on redundancy to look for work or arrange training (ss53(1) and 53(4) ERA)	3 months (s54(2) ERA)	2 years (s52(2) ERA)
Time off for ante-natal care (s55(1) ERA) and payment for this time off (s56(1) ERA)	3 months (s57(2) ERA)	None
Time off for dependants (s57A ERA)	3 months (s57B(2) ERA)	None
Time off for pension scheme trustees (s58(1) ERA) and payment for this time off (s59(1) ERA)	3 months (s60(2) ERA)	None
Time off for employee representatives (s61(1) ERA) and payment for this time off (s62(1) ERA)	3 months (s63(2) ERA)	None
Time off for young person for study or training (s63A ERA) and payment for this time off (s63B ERA)	3 months (s63C(2) ERA)	None
Time off for study or training (s63D ERA)	3 months (s63I(5) ERA)	26 weeks (s63D(a) ERA)
Payment for suspension on medical grounds (s64(1) ERA) or maternity grounds (s68 ERA)	3 months (s70(2) ERA)	1 month (s65(1) ERA)
Offer of alternative work when suspended on maternity grounds (s67 ERA)	3 months (s70(5) ERA)	None
Right to request flexible working (s80F ERA)	3 months (s80H(5) ERA)	26 weeks (reg 13 Flexible Working (Eligibility etc) Regs 2002
Right of employee to minimum notice period (s86 ERA)	6 years under contract	1 month (s86 ERA 1996)

Table 18: Limitation periods and requisite minimum qualifying periods for claims

Claim	Limitation period (maximum length of time that can elapse for claim to be brought to ET)	Length of service required before a claim can be brought to ET
Right to written reasons for dismissal (s92(1) ERA)	3 months (s93(3) ERA)	1 year (s92(3) ERA)
Unfair dismissal (s94(1) ERA)	3 months (s111(2) ERA) The time limit may be extended in certain circumstances for claims under Reg 2 Exclusivity Terms in Zero Hours Contracts (Redress) Regulations 2015	1 year where period of continuous service started prior to 6 April 2012; 2 years where period of continuous service started on or after 6 April 2012. There is no qualifying period if the principal reasons for dismissal relates to: ERA ss98B; 99; 100 (1); 101; 101A(1); 102; 103; 103A; 104; s104A; 104B; 104C; 104E; 104F; 105; TULR(C)A Sch A1 para 161; ss238A; 152-153; ICE Reg 30 TICE Reg 28; OPPS 2006; Reg 7 PRW Regs; Reg 6 FTE Regs; s12 ERelA 1999; Sch 6 para 13(5) Exclusivity Terms in Zero Hours Contracts (Redress) Regulations 2015 Reg 2
Right to redundancy payment (s135(1) ERA)	6 months (s164 ERA)	2 years (s155 ERA)
Insolvency claim to Secretary of State (s182 ERA)	3 months (s188(2) ERA)	None
Time off for health and safety reps 1996 and payment for time off (Reg 7 HSC Regs)	3 months (Sch 2 HSC Regs 1996)	None
Claims under the Working Time Regulations (Regs 10, 11, 12, 13, 14, 16, 24, 24A, 25, 27, 27A WTR)	3 months (Reg 30(2) WTR)	None
Right to National Minimum Wage (s1(1) NMWA 1998)	3 months (s23(2) ERA) or 6 years under contract	None
Right to access to records in relation to (s10 NMWA)	3 months (s11 NMWA)	None
Right not to suffer detriment for asserting rights in connection with (s23 NMWA)	3 months (s24(2) NMWA)	None
Right to be accompanied at a grievance or disciplinary meeting (s10 ERelA 1999) and right not to suffer detriment in connection with this right (s12 ERelA)	3 months (s11(2) and s12(2) ERelA)	None
Time off for works body member and right to payment during this time off (Regs 25 and 26 TICE 1999)	3 months (Reg 27(2) TICE)	None
Part-time worker discrimination (Regs 5 and 7(2) PTW Regs 2000)	3 months (Reg 8(2) PTW Regs)	None
Fixed term worker discrimination (Regs 3 and 6(2) FTE Regs 2002)	3 months (Reg 7(2) FTE)	None

Table 18: Limitation periods and requisite minimum qualifying periods for claims

Claim	Limitation period (maximum length of time that can elapse for claim to be brought to ET)	Length of service required before a claim can be brought to ET
Right to be accompanied at, or postponement of, flexible working meeting (Reg 14(2) and 14(4) FW(PR) Regs 2002)	3 months (Reg 15(2) FW(PR) Regs)	None
Time off for employee reps (reg 27 ICE Regs 2004) and payment for time off (Reg 28 ICE)	3 months (Reg 29(2) ICE)	None
Right to be informed and /or consulted over TUPE (Reg 13 TUPE 2006) and right to election of employee reps (Reg 14 TUPE)	3 months (Reg 15(12) TUPE)	None
Time off for employee reps (Sch paragraph 2 OPPS Regs 2006) and payment for time off (Sch paragraph 3 OPPS)	3 months (Schedule paragraph 4(2) OPPS)	None
Right not to suffer detriment in connection with employee reps (Schedule paragraph 7 OPPS)	3 months (Schedule paragraph 8(2) OPPS)	None
Breach of Sex Equality Clause (s66 EA 2010) or Maternity Equality Clause (s73 EA 2010)	6 months (or 9 months if relating to armed forces service) (s129 EA 2010)	None
Right to be accompanied to a meeting concerning study and training (Reg 16 EST (PR) Regs 2010)	3 months (Reg 17(2) EST (PR) Regs)	None

Table 19: Matters to which the prescribed element is attributable

See Schedule to Employment Protection (Recoupment of Jobseeker's Allowance and Income Support) Regulations 1996.

Payment	Proceedings	Matter to which prescribed element is attributable
Guarantee payments under section 28.	Complaint under section 34.	Any amount found to be due to the employee and ordered to be paid under section 34(3) for a period before the conclusion of the tribunal proceedings.
Payments under any collective agreement having regard to which the appropriate Minister has made an exemption order under section 35.	Complaint under section 35(4).	Any amount found to be due to the employee and ordered to be paid under section 34(3), as applied by section 35(4), for a period before the conclusion of the tribunal proceedings.
Payments of remuneration in respect of a period of suspension on medical grounds under section 64 and section 108(2).	Complaint under section 70.	Any amount found to be due to the employee and ordered to be paid under section 70(3) for a period before the conclusion of the tribunal proceedings.
Payments of remuneration in respect of a period of suspension on maternity grounds under section 68.	Complaint under section 70.	Any amount found to be due to the employee and ordered to be paid under section 70(3) for a period before the conclusion of the tribunal proceedings.
Payments under an order for reinstatement under section 114(1).	Complaint of unfair dismissal under section 111(1).	Any amount ordered to be paid under section 114(2)(a) in respect of arrears of pay for a period before the conclusion of the tribunal proceedings.
Payments under an order for re-engagement under section 117(8).	Complaint of unfair dismissal under section 111(1).	Any amount ordered to be paid under section 115(2)(d) in respect of arrears of pay for a period before the conclusion of the tribunal proceedings.
Payments under an award of compensation for unfair dismissal in cases falling under section 112(4) (cases where no order for reinstatement or re-engagement has been made).	Complaint of unfair dismissal under section 111(1).	Any amount ordered to be paid and calculated under section 123 in respect of compensation for loss of wages for a period before the conclusion of the tribunal proceedings.
Payments under an award of compensation for unfair dismissal under section 117(3) where reinstatement order not complied with.	Proceedings in respect of non-compliance with order.	Any amount ordered to be paid and calculated under section 123 in respect of compensation for loss of wages for a period before the conclusion of the tribunal proceedings.

Table 19: Matters to which the prescribed element is attributable

See Schedule to Employment Protection (Recoupment of Jobseeker's Allowance and Income Support) Regulations 1996.

Payment	Proceedings	Matter to which prescribed element is attributable
Payments under an award of compensation for unfair dismissal under section 117(3) where re-engagement order not complied with.	Proceedings in respect of non-compliance with order.	Any amount ordered to be paid and calculated under section 123 in respect of compensation for loss of wages for a period before the conclusion of the tribunal proceedings.
Payments under an interim order for reinstatement under section 163(4) of the 1992 Act.	Proceedings on an application for an order for interim relief under section 161(1) of the 1992 Act.	Any amount found to be due to the complainant and ordered to be paid in respect of arrears of pay for the period between the date of termination of employment and the conclusion of the tribunal proceedings.
Payments under an interim order for re-engagement under section 163(5)(a) of the 1992 Act.	Proceedings on an application for an order for interim relief under section 161(1) of the 1992 Act.	Any amount found to be due to the complainant and ordered to be paid in respect of arrears of pay for the period between the date of termination of employment and the conclusion of the tribunal proceedings.
Payments under an order for the continuation of a contract of employment under section 163(5)(b) of the 1992 Act where employee reasonably refuses re-engagement.	Proceedings on an application for an order for interim relief under section 161(1) of the 1992 Act.	Any amount found to be due to the complainant and ordered to be paid in respect of arrears of pay for the period between the date of termination of employment and the conclusion of the tribunal proceedings.
Payments under an order for the continuation of a contract of employment under section 163(6) of the 1992 Act where employer fails to attend or is unwilling to reinstate or re-engage.	Proceedings on an application for an order for interim relief under section 161(1) of the 1992 Act.	Any amount found to be due to the complainant and ordered to be paid in respect of arrears of pay for the period between the date of termination of employment and the conclusion of the tribunal proceedings.
Payments under an order for the continuation of a contract of employment under sections 166(1) and (2) of the 1992 Act where reinstatement or re-engagement order not complied with.	Proceedings in respect of non-compliance with order.	Any amount ordered to be paid to the employee by way of compensation under section 166(1)(b) of the 1992 Act for loss of wages for the period between the date of termination of employment and the conclusion of the tribunal proceedings.
Payments under an order for compensation under sections 166(3)–(5) of the 1992 Act where order for the continuation of contract of employment not complied with.	Proceedings in respect of non-compliance with order.	Any amount ordered to be paid to the employee by way of compensation under section 166(3)–(4) of the 1992 Act for loss of wages for the period between the date of termination of employment and the conclusion of the tribunal proceedings.
Payments under an order under section 192(3) of the 1992 Act on employer's default in respect of remuneration due to employee under protective award.	Complaint under section 192(1) of the 1992 Act.	Any amount ordered to be paid to the employee in respect of so much of the relevant protected period as falls before the date of the conclusion of the tribunal proceedings.

Pensions

Table 20: State pension age for women born on or before 5 December 1953

For women born	Date State Pension age reached
On or before 5 April 1950	Age 60
6 April 1950 to 5 May 1950	6 May 2010
6 May 1950 to 5 June 1950	6 July 2010
6 June 1950 to 5 July 1950	6 September 2010
6 July 1950 to 5 August 1950	6 November 2010

Pensions

Table 20: State pension age for women born on or before 5 December 1953	
For women born	Date State Pension age reached
6 August 1950 to 5 September 1950	6 January 2011
6 September 1950 to 5 October 1950	6 March 2011
6 October 1950 to 5 November 1950	6 May 2011
6 November 1950 to 5 December 1950	6 July 2011
6 December 1950 to 5 January 1951	6 September 2011
6 January 1951 to 5 February 1951	6 November 2011
6 February 1951 to 5 March 1951	6 January 2012
6 March 1951 to 5 April 1951	6 March 2012
6 April 1951 to 5 May 1951	6 May 2012
6 May 1951 to 5 June 1951	6 July 2012
6 June 1951 to 5 July 1951	6 September 2012
6 July 1951 to 5 August 1951	6 November 2012
6 August 1951 to 5 September 1951	6 January 2013
6 September 1951 to 5 October 1951	6 March 2013
6 October 1951 to 5 November 1951	6 May 2013
6 November 1951 to 5 December 1951	6 July 2013
6 December 1951 to 5 January 1952	6 September 2013
6 January 1952 to 5 February 1952	6 November 2013
6 February 1952 to 5 March 1952	6 January 2014
6 March 1952 to 5 April 1952	6 March 2014
6 April 1952 to 5 May 1952	6 May 2014
6 May 1952 to 5 June 1952	6 July 2014
6 June 1952 to 5 July 1952	6 September 2014
6 July 1952 to 5 August 1952	6 November 2014
6 August 1952 to 5 September 1952	6 January 2015
6 September 1952 to 5 October 1952	6 March 2015
6 October 1952 to 5 November 1952	6 May 2015
6 November 1952 to 5 December 1952	6 July 2015
6 December 1952 to 5 January 1953	6 September 2015
6 January 1953 to 5 February 1953	6 November 2015
6 February 1953 to 5 March 1953	6 January 2016
6 March 1953 to 5 April 1953	6 March 2016
6 April 1953 to 5 May 1953	6 July 2016
6 May 1953 to 5 June 1953	6 November 2016
6 June 1953 to 5 July 1953	6 March 2017
6 July 1953 to 5 August 1953	6 July 2017
6 August 1953 to 5 September 1953	6 November 2017
6 September 1953 to 5 October 1953	6 March 2018
6 October 1953 to 5 November 1953	6 July 2018
6 November 1953 to 5 December 1953	6 November 2018

Table 21: State pension age for men and women born after 5 December 1953

For men and women born	Date State Pension age reached
6 December 1953 to 5 January 1954	6 March 2019
6 January 1954 to 5 February 1954	6 May 2019
6 February 1954 to 5 March 1954	6 July 2019
6 March 1954 to 5 April 1954	6 September 2019
6 April 1954 to 5 May 1954	6 November 2019
6 May 1954 to 5 June 1954	6 January 2020
6 June 1954 to 5 July 1954	6 March 2020
6 July 1954 to 5 August 1954	6 May 2020
6 August 1954 to 5 September 1954	6 July 2020
6 September 1954 to 5 October 1954	6 September 2020
6 October 1954 to 5 April 1960	66th birthday
6 April 1960 to 5 May 1960	Age 66 and 1 month
6 May 1960 to 5 June 1960	Age 66 and 2 months
6 June 1960 to 5 July 1960	Age 66 and 3 months
6 July 1960 to 5 August 1960	Age 66 and 4 months
6 August 1960 to 5 September 1960	Age 66 and 5 months
6 September 1960 to 5 October 1960	Age 66 and 6 months
6 October to 5 November 1960	Age 66 and 7 months
6 November 1960 to 5 December 1960	Age 66 and 8 months
6 December 1960 to 5 January 1961	Age 66 and 9 months
6 January 1961 to 5 February 1961	Age 66 and 10 months
6 February 1961 to 5 March 1961	Age 66 and 11 months
6 March 1961 to 5 April 1977	67th birthday
6 April 1977 and 5 May 1977	6 May 2044
6 May 1977 and 5 June 1977	6 July 2044
6 June 1977 and 5 July 1977	6 September 2044
6 July 1977 and 5 August 1977	6 November 2044
6 August 1977 and 5 September 1977	6 January 2045
6 September 1977 and 5 October 1977	6 March 2045
6 October 1977 and 5 November 1977	6 May 2045
6 November 1977 and 5 December 1977	6 July 2045
6 December 1977 and 5 January 1978	6 September 2045
6 January 1978 and 5 February 1978	6 November 2045
6 February 1978 and 5 March 1978	6 January 2046
6 March 1978 and 5 April 1978	6 March 2046
On or after 6 April 1978	68th birthday

Table 22: State pension

	Weekly pension		Number of qualifying years	
	2020/21	2021/22	For full pension	For some pension
Women born before 6 April 1950	£134.25	£137.60	39	10
Women born after 5 April 1950 and before 6 April 1953	£134.25	£137.60	30	1
Women born after 5 April 1953	£175.20	£179.60	35	10
Men born before 6 April 1945	£134.25	£137.60	44	11
Men born after 5 April 1945 and before 6 April 1951	£134.25	£137.60	30	1
Men born after 5 April 1951	£175.20	£179.60	35	10

Table 23: Auto-enrolment rates

Date	Employer minimum contribution	Employee minimum contribution	Total minimum contribution
Before 5 April 2018	1%	1%	2%
6 April 2018 – 5 April 2019	2%	3%	5%
6 April 2019 onwards	3%	5%	8%

Table 24: Auto-enrolment earnings thresholds

Annual earnings	6 April 2019 - 5 April 2020	6 April 2020 - 5 April 2021	6 April 2021 - 5 April 2022
Lower level of qualifying earnings	£6,136	£6,240	£6,240
Earnings trigger for automatic enrolment	£10,000	£10,000	£10,000
Upper level of qualifying earnings	£50,000	£50,000	£50,270

Ogden Tables: 8th edition

The 8th edition of the Ogden Tables was published in July 2020 and are primarily used to assess lump sum damages for personal injury awards but they can also be used to calculate pension loss in certain cases for defined benefit pension schemes. (See Principles For Compensating Pension Loss which was revised in March 2021). All of the Ogden Tables have been summarised to provide only the relevant discount rates, and some (Ogden Tables 3 to 34 which are Tables 26 to 37 below) have been interpolated to provide multipliers in between the ages of 50 and 55 etc.

Ogden Tables 1 and 2
These tables contain the multipliers for men and women, for different discount rates, which are used to calculate life long loss. Table 25 below lists the multipliers for a discount rate of 0% which tells you a person's life expectancy. For example, a woman age 35 would be expected to live a further 54.61 years. This table should be used when the multiplier must be apportioned for variable periods of pension loss (see the example of Rosa in the Principles For Compensating Pension Loss).

Ogden Tables 3 to 18
These tables contain the multipliers for men and women for loss of **earnings** to pension age (or earlier death), for different discount rates. Tables 34 to 37 list the multipliers for discount rates of -0.25% (England & Wales) and -0.75% (Scotland). There is NO 2 year adjustment for loss of earnings.

Ogden Tables 19 to 34
These tables contain the multipliers for men and women for loss of **pension** to death (based on life expectancy projections). Tables 26 to 33 list the multipliers for discount rates of -0.25% (England & Wales) and -0.75% (Scotland), with and without the 2 year adjustment.

Ogden Table 35
This table contains discounting factors for term certain (i.e. factors to discount a sum which has been received early). A positive discount rate assumes that any capital sum paid will be decreased in anticipation of the sum earning interest. A negative discount rate on the other hand assumes that money invested will shrink compared to price inflation, not grow, and so its application will increase the overall sum. Table 38 has reproduced Ogden Table 35 with discount rates of -0.25% (England & Wales) and -0.75% (Scotland).

Ogden Table 36
In cases where pecuniary loss is to be valued for a fixed period, the multipliers in Ogden Table 36 may be used. These make no allowance for mortality or any other contingency but assume that regular frequent payments (e.g. weekly or monthly) will continue throughout the period. For example, if the monthly loss is to continue for 5 years at a discount rate of -0.25%, the correct multiplier will be 5.03. Table 39 has reproduced Ogden Table 36 with discount rates of -0.25% (England & Wales) and -0.75% (Scotland).

Table 25: 8th edition Ogden multipliers for pecuniary loss

This table is a combination of Ogden Tables 1 and 2 with a discount rate of 0%. It shows the life expectancy of men and women which is required when the multiplier must be apportioned for variable periods of pension loss.

Age at date of claim	Multiplier for pecuniary loss for life		Age at date of claim	Multiplier for pecuniary loss for life	
	Men	Women		Men	Women
16	70.76	73.53	59	25.70	28.11
17	69.66	72.44	60	24.76	27.14
18	68.56	71.35	61	23.84	26.18
19	67.46	70.26	62	22.93	25.22
20	66.36	69.17	63	22.02	24.27
21	65.27	68.09	64	21.13	23.34
22	64.17	67.00	65	20.25	22.41
23	63.08	65.91	66	19.39	21.49
24	61.99	64.83	67	18.54	20.58
25	60.90	63.74	68	17.70	19.68
26	59.81	62.65	69	16.88	18.80
27	58.72	61.57	70	16.07	17.92
28	57.63	60.48	71	15.27	17.06
29	56.55	59.40	72	14.49	16.21
30	55.46	58.32	73	13.73	15.38
31	54.38	57.24	74	12.98	14.57
32	53.31	56.16	75	12.25	13.77
33	52.23	55.09	76	11.54	13.00
34	51.16	54.01	77	10.85	12.24
35	50.09	52.94	78	10.19	11.50
36	49.02	51.87	79	9.54	10.79
37	47.96	50.80	80	8.92	10.10
38	46.90	49.73	81	8.33	9.43
39	45.85	48.67	82	7.76	8.79
40	44.80	47.61	83	7.22	8.17
41	43.75	46.55	84	6.70	7.58
42	42.71	45.49	85	6.21	7.01
43	41.68	44.44	86	5.75	6.48
44	40.65	43.39	87	5.32	5.97
45	39.62	42.34	88	4.91	5.49
46	38.59	41.29	89	4.53	5.05
47	37.57	40.25	90	4.18	4.64
48	36.55	39.21	91	3.85	4.26
49	35.54	38.17	92	3.55	3.92
50	34.53	37.14	93	3.27	3.61
51	33.52	36.12	94	3.01	3.32
52	32.52	35.09	95	2.78	3.06
53	31.52	34.08	96	2.57	2.82
54	30.53	33.07	97	2.37	2.60
55	29.55	32.06	98	2.19	2.39
56	28.57	31.06	99	2.03	2.20
57	27.60	30.07	100	1.88	2.03
58	26.64	29.08			

Table 26: 8th edition Ogden multipliers, loss of PENSION, MEN, discount rate: −0.25%, 2 YEAR ADJUSTMENT

Age	Loss of pension from age																									
	52	53	54	55	56	57	58	59	60	61	62	63	64	65	66	67	68	69	70	71	72	73	74	75	76	77
18	42.52	41.47	40.42	39.36	38.29	37.22	36.18	35.12	34.06	33.00	31.92	30.88	29.84	28.79	27.73	26.67	25.65	24.62	23.55	22.55	21.50	20.52	19.53	18.53	17.52	16.50
19	42.29	41.25	40.19	39.14	38.08	37.00	35.96	34.91	33.86	32.79	31.72	30.69	29.64	28.60	27.55	26.48	25.47	24.45	23.38	22.38	21.33	20.36	19.37	18.37	17.37	16.36
20	42.06	41.02	39.97	38.92	37.85	36.79	35.75	34.70	33.65	32.59	31.52	30.49	29.45	28.41	27.35	26.30	25.29	24.27	23.21	22.21	21.17	20.19	19.21	18.22	17.22	16.21
21	41.83	40.80	39.75	38.70	37.64	36.57	35.54	34.50	33.45	32.38	31.32	30.30	29.26	28.22	27.17	26.11	25.11	24.10	23.03	22.04	21.00	20.04	19.06	18.07	17.07	16.06
22	41.60	40.57	39.53	38.49	37.42	36.36	35.33	34.29	33.24	32.19	31.12	30.10	29.07	28.04	26.98	25.93	24.93	23.92	22.86	21.88	20.84	19.87	18.90	17.92	16.92	15.92
23	41.38	40.35	39.31	38.27	37.22	36.15	35.12	34.09	33.04	31.99	30.93	29.91	28.88	27.85	26.81	25.75	24.75	23.75	22.69	21.72	20.68	19.72	18.75	17.77	16.79	15.78
24	41.17	40.13	39.09	38.06	37.00	35.95	34.92	33.88	32.84	31.79	30.74	29.72	28.69	27.67	26.62	25.58	24.58	23.58	22.53	21.55	20.53	19.56	18.60	17.62	16.63	15.65
25	40.94	39.92	38.88	37.84	36.80	35.74	34.72	33.68	32.65	31.60	30.54	29.54	28.51	27.48	26.45	25.40	24.41	23.41	22.36	21.39	20.36	19.42	18.44	17.47	16.50	15.50
26	40.73	39.70	38.68	37.63	36.58	35.54	34.51	33.49	32.45	31.41	30.36	29.34	28.33	27.30	26.26	25.23	24.24	23.24	22.20	21.23	20.21	19.25	18.30	17.33	16.35	15.37
27	40.51	39.49	38.46	37.43	36.38	35.33	34.32	33.29	32.26	31.21	30.17	29.16	28.14	27.13	26.09	25.05	24.07	23.08	22.03	21.06	20.05	19.10	18.14	17.19	16.21	15.23
28	40.30	39.28	38.25	37.22	36.19	35.13	34.11	33.10	32.06	31.03	29.98	28.98	27.96	26.95	25.92	24.88	23.90	22.91	21.87	20.91	19.89	18.95	18.00	17.04	16.07	15.09
29	40.09	39.07	38.04	37.02	35.98	34.94	33.92	32.89	31.87	30.84	29.80	28.79	27.78	26.77	25.75	24.72	23.73	22.74	21.71	20.75	19.74	18.80	17.85	16.89	15.93	14.96
30	39.88	38.87	37.84	36.81	35.78	34.74	33.73	32.71	31.68	30.65	29.61	28.62	27.60	26.59	25.57	24.55	23.57	22.58	21.55	20.59	19.59	18.65	17.70	16.75	15.79	14.82
31	39.66	38.66	37.64	36.61	35.57	34.54	33.54	32.52	31.49	30.46	29.43	28.43	27.43	26.42	25.39	24.37	23.41	22.43	21.39	20.43	19.43	18.56	17.56	16.61	15.65	14.68
32	39.46	38.45	37.44	36.42	35.38	34.34	33.34	32.33	31.32	30.28	29.24	28.26	27.25	26.25	25.23	24.20	23.23	22.27	21.23	20.28	19.28	18.35	17.42	16.48	15.51	14.55
33	39.26	38.25	37.23	36.22	35.19	34.15	33.15	32.14	31.13	30.11	29.07	28.07	27.08	26.08	25.06	24.04	23.07	22.10	21.08	20.14	19.13	18.21	17.27	16.34	15.39	14.42
34	39.06	38.06	37.04	36.02	35.00	33.97	32.96	31.96	30.94	29.92	28.90	27.91	26.91	25.91	24.90	23.88	22.92	21.94	20.93	19.98	18.99	18.06	17.14	16.20	15.25	14.30
35	38.87	37.86	36.86	35.84	34.80	33.78	32.79	31.78	30.76	29.74	28.72	27.74	26.74	25.74	24.73	23.72	22.76	21.79	20.78	19.83	18.84	17.93	17.00	16.06	15.12	14.17
36	38.67	37.68	36.66	35.65	34.63	33.59	32.60	31.60	30.59	29.57	28.54	27.57	26.58	25.58	24.58	23.56	22.60	21.64	20.62	19.69	18.69	17.78	16.86	15.93	14.99	14.04
37	38.48	37.48	36.48	35.47	34.45	33.42	32.42	31.42	30.42	29.41	28.38	27.39	26.41	25.42	24.41	23.41	22.45	21.49	20.48	19.54	18.56	17.64	16.72	15.80	14.87	13.92
38	38.30	37.30	36.30	35.29	34.27	33.25	32.25	31.25	30.25	29.23	28.22	27.24	26.25	25.26	24.26	23.25	22.30	21.34	20.33	19.39	18.42	17.51	16.59	15.67	14.73	13.80
39	38.11	37.12	36.12	35.11	34.09	33.07	32.09	31.08	30.08	29.07	28.05	27.08	26.09	25.10	24.10	23.10	22.15	21.20	20.18	19.26	18.27	17.38	16.46	15.53	14.61	13.67
40	37.94	36.94	35.95	34.94	33.93	32.90	31.92	30.93	29.92	28.91	27.89	26.92	25.94	24.95	23.96	22.95	22.01	21.05	20.05	19.12	18.14	17.24	16.33	15.42	14.48	13.55
41	37.76	36.78	35.78	34.77	33.76	32.74	31.75	30.76	29.76	28.75	27.74	26.76	25.79	24.81	23.80	22.81	21.86	20.91	19.91	18.99	18.01	17.11	16.20	15.29	14.37	13.43
42	37.60	36.61	35.62	34.61	33.60	32.58	31.60	30.60	29.61	28.60	27.58	26.62	25.64	24.66	23.67	22.66	21.73	20.77	19.77	18.85	17.88	16.98	16.08	15.17	14.24	13.32
43	37.44	36.45	35.45	34.45	33.45	32.42	31.44	30.45	29.46	28.45	27.44	26.47	25.50	24.51	23.53	22.53	21.58	20.64	19.64	18.72	17.75	16.86	15.96	15.04	14.13	13.20
44	37.28	36.30	35.30	34.30	33.29	32.28	31.29	30.30	29.31	28.31	27.30	26.33	25.35	24.37	23.39	22.40	21.45	20.50	19.52	18.60	17.63	16.73	15.84	14.93	14.01	13.10
45	37.13	36.14	35.15	34.15	33.14	32.13	31.15	30.16	29.17	28.16	27.16	26.19	25.22	24.24	23.25	22.26	21.33	20.38	19.39	18.47	17.51	16.62	15.71	14.81	13.91	12.98
46	36.98	36.00	35.01	34.01	33.00	31.99	31.01	30.02	29.02	28.03	27.02	26.06	25.09	24.10	23.12	22.13	21.19	20.26	19.26	18.35	17.39	16.50	15.61	14.70	13.79	12.88
47	36.85	35.86	34.87	33.87	32.86	31.85	30.87	29.89	28.90	27.89	26.89	25.92	24.96	23.98	22.99	22.01	21.07	20.13	19.14	18.23	17.27	16.39	15.49	14.59	13.68	12.77
48	36.71	35.73	34.73	33.73	32.74	31.72	30.74	29.76	28.76	27.77	26.76	25.80	24.83	23.85	22.88	21.88	20.95	20.01	19.02	18.12	17.15	16.27	15.38	14.48	13.58	12.66

Table 26: 8th edition Ogden multipliers, loss of PENSION, MEN, discount rate: –0.25%, 2 YEAR ADJUSTMENT

Loss of pension from age

Age	52	53	54	55	56	57	58	59	60	61	62	63	64	65	66	67	68	69	70	71	72	73	74	75	76	77
49	36.59	35.60	34.61	33.61	32.60	31.60	30.61	29.63	28.64	27.64	26.64	25.67	24.71	23.73	22.75	21.77	20.83	19.90	18.92	18.00	17.05	16.16	15.27	14.38	13.47	12.57
50	36.46	35.48	34.49	33.49	32.48	31.47	30.50	29.51	28.52	27.53	26.52	25.56	24.59	23.61	22.64	21.65	20.72	19.78	18.80	17.89	16.93	16.06	15.17	14.28	13.37	12.46
51	36.35	35.36	34.37	33.37	32.37	31.36	30.38	29.40	28.40	27.41	26.41	25.44	24.48	23.50	22.52	21.54	20.61	19.68	18.69	17.79	16.83	15.95	15.07	14.17	13.28	12.37
52	36.24	35.26	34.26	33.27	32.26	31.25	30.27	29.28	28.30	27.30	26.30	25.34	24.37	23.40	22.42	21.43	20.50	19.57	18.59	17.68	16.73	15.85	14.96	14.08	13.18	12.28
53		35.16	34.17	33.16	32.16	31.15	30.17	29.19	28.19	27.20	26.19	25.24	24.27	23.29	22.32	21.33	20.40	19.47	18.49	17.59	16.63	15.75	14.87	13.98	13.09	12.19
54			34.07	33.07	32.06	31.05	30.08	29.09	28.10	27.09	26.10	25.13	24.17	23.20	22.22	21.24	20.31	19.37	18.39	17.48	16.54	15.66	14.78	13.89	12.99	12.10
55				32.99	31.98	30.96	29.99	29.01	28.01	27.02	26.00	25.05	24.08	23.11	22.13	21.14	20.22	19.28	18.30	17.40	16.44	15.57	14.69	13.80	12.91	12.01
56					31.90	30.89	29.91	28.92	27.93	26.93	25.93	24.96	24.00	23.02	22.04	21.06	20.13	19.20	18.22	17.31	16.36	15.48	14.61	13.73	12.83	11.93
57						30.82	29.85	28.86	27.86	26.86	25.85	24.90	23.92	22.95	21.97	20.98	20.06	19.12	18.13	17.23	16.28	15.41	14.52	13.64	12.76	11.85
58							29.79	28.81	27.80	26.79	25.79	24.83	23.87	22.88	21.90	20.91	19.98	19.05	18.07	17.16	16.21	15.34	14.46	13.57	12.68	11.79
59								28.76	27.76	26.75	25.73	24.78	23.81	22.83	21.84	20.85	19.92	18.99	17.99	17.09	16.14	15.27	14.39	13.50	12.61	11.71
60									27.74	26.72	25.70	24.73	23.77	22.79	21.80	20.80	19.87	18.94	17.94	17.04	16.08	15.21	14.33	13.45	12.55	11.65
61										26.71	25.68	24.71	23.74	22.76	21.77	20.77	19.83	18.90	17.90	17.00	16.04	15.16	14.28	13.40	12.50	11.60
62											25.68	24.71	23.73	22.74	21.75	20.75	19.81	18.86	17.87	16.97	16.00	15.12	14.24	13.35	12.46	11.56
63												24.72	23.73	22.74	21.75	20.74	19.80	18.85	17.85	16.95	15.98	15.09	14.20	13.31	12.42	11.52
64													23.76	22.76	21.76	20.75	19.80	18.85	17.85	16.93	15.97	15.08	14.18	13.29	12.39	11.49
65														22.80	21.78	20.77	19.82	18.86	17.86	16.93	15.96	15.08	14.18	13.27	12.37	11.47
66															21.84	20.81	19.86	18.90	17.88	16.95	15.97	15.08	14.18	13.27	12.36	11.45
67																20.88	19.92	18.95	17.92	16.99	16.00	15.10	14.19	13.29	12.37	11.45
68																	20.00	19.02	17.99	17.05	16.05	15.14	14.23	13.31	12.39	11.47
69																		19.12	18.08	17.12	16.12	15.20	14.28	13.35	12.42	11.50
70																			18.19	17.23	16.21	15.28	14.35	13.41	12.48	11.54
71																				17.36	16.34	15.38	14.44	13.49	12.55	11.61
72																					16.48	15.53	14.55	13.60	12.64	11.69
73																						15.68	14.71	13.73	12.76	11.79
74																							14.89	13.90	12.90	11.92
75																								14.09	13.08	12.07
76																									13.30	12.27
77																										12.50

Table 27: 8th edition Ogden multipliers, loss of PENSION, WOMEN, discount rate: −0.25%, 2 YEAR ADJUSTMENT

Loss of pension from age

Age	52	53	54	55	56	57	58	59	60	61	62	63	64	65	66	67	68	69	70	71	72	73	74	75	76	77
18	45.64	44.59	43.52	42.45	41.37	40.27	39.22	38.14	37.06	35.98	34.88	33.82	32.76	31.68	30.60	29.50	28.45	27.39	26.29	25.24	24.16	23.13	22.09	21.04	19.99	18.91
19	45.43	44.36	43.30	42.23	41.15	40.07	39.00	37.94	36.86	35.78	34.70	33.63	32.57	31.49	30.41	29.33	28.27	27.22	26.12	25.08	24.00	22.97	21.94	20.88	19.83	18.78
20	45.20	44.15	43.08	42.02	40.94	39.86	38.80	37.73	36.67	35.58	34.50	33.45	32.37	31.31	30.23	29.14	28.10	27.04	25.95	24.91	23.84	22.81	21.78	20.74	19.68	18.63
21	44.98	43.93	42.87	41.80	40.73	39.65	38.60	37.54	36.46	35.39	34.30	33.25	32.20	31.12	30.06	28.97	27.92	26.88	25.78	24.75	23.67	22.66	21.63	20.58	19.55	18.48
22	44.76	43.71	42.65	41.60	40.52	39.45	38.39	37.33	36.27	35.19	34.12	33.06	32.01	30.95	29.86	28.80	27.75	26.70	25.62	24.58	23.52	22.49	21.47	20.44	19.39	18.35
23	44.54	43.49	42.44	41.38	40.32	39.24	38.19	37.13	36.07	35.01	33.92	32.88	31.82	30.76	29.70	28.61	27.58	26.53	25.45	24.43	23.35	22.34	21.31	20.29	19.26	18.20
24	44.33	43.28	42.22	41.17	40.10	39.04	37.99	36.93	35.87	34.80	33.74	32.69	31.64	30.57	29.52	28.45	27.40	26.37	25.29	24.26	23.20	22.18	21.17	20.14	19.10	18.07
25	44.11	43.07	42.02	40.96	39.90	38.83	37.79	36.74	35.68	34.61	33.54	32.51	31.45	30.40	29.33	28.27	27.24	26.19	25.12	24.10	23.04	22.03	20.99	19.99	18.96	17.92
26	43.89	42.85	41.81	40.75	39.69	38.63	37.59	36.54	35.48	34.42	33.35	32.31	31.28	30.22	29.16	28.09	27.07	26.04	24.96	23.94	22.88	21.88	20.87	19.85	18.82	17.78
27	43.67	42.64	41.60	40.55	39.49	38.42	37.39	36.34	35.29	34.23	33.16	32.13	31.09	30.04	28.98	27.92	26.89	25.87	24.79	23.78	22.72	21.72	20.72	19.70	18.68	17.64
28	43.46	42.42	41.39	40.34	39.29	38.23	37.18	36.15	35.10	34.04	32.98	31.94	30.91	29.86	28.81	27.75	26.73	25.70	24.63	23.63	22.57	21.57	20.57	19.56	18.54	17.51
29	43.25	42.22	41.17	40.13	39.09	38.03	37.00	35.95	34.91	33.85	32.79	31.76	30.72	29.68	28.64	27.58	26.56	25.53	24.47	23.47	22.42	21.42	20.42	19.41	18.40	17.37
30	43.04	42.01	40.97	39.93	38.88	37.83	36.80	35.76	34.71	33.67	32.61	31.58	30.55	29.51	28.46	27.41	26.40	25.37	24.31	23.31	22.27	21.28	20.27	19.26	18.26	17.24
31	42.83	41.80	40.77	39.73	38.68	37.63	36.61	35.57	34.53	33.48	32.43	31.40	30.37	29.33	28.29	27.24	26.23	25.21	24.15	23.14	22.11	21.13	20.13	19.13	18.11	17.10
32	42.62	41.60	40.57	39.53	38.48	37.43	36.41	35.38	34.35	33.29	32.24	31.23	30.20	29.16	28.12	27.07	26.06	25.05	23.99	22.99	21.95	20.98	19.99	18.99	17.98	16.96
33	42.41	41.39	40.37	39.33	38.29	37.24	36.22	35.19	34.16	33.12	32.06	31.04	30.03	28.99	27.95	26.90	25.90	24.89	23.83	22.84	21.80	20.82	19.84	18.84	17.84	16.83
34	42.21	41.19	40.17	39.14	38.10	37.05	36.03	35.00	33.98	32.93	31.89	30.87	29.85	28.82	27.79	26.74	25.74	24.73	23.68	22.69	21.66	20.68	19.69	18.71	17.70	16.70
35	42.01	40.99	39.97	38.94	37.91	36.86	35.84	34.82	33.79	32.76	31.71	30.70	29.68	28.65	27.62	26.58	25.58	24.57	23.52	22.54	21.51	20.54	19.55	18.57	17.57	16.56
36	41.82	40.80	39.78	38.75	37.72	36.68	35.66	34.64	33.62	32.57	31.54	30.53	29.51	28.48	27.46	26.42	25.42	24.42	23.37	22.39	21.36	20.39	19.42	18.43	17.44	16.44
37	41.62	40.61	39.59	38.56	37.53	36.49	35.48	34.46	33.43	32.41	31.36	30.36	29.34	28.32	27.29	26.26	25.27	24.26	23.22	22.24	21.22	20.25	19.28	18.29	17.30	16.31
38	41.43	40.42	39.40	38.38	37.35	36.31	35.30	34.28	33.26	32.23	31.20	30.18	29.18	28.16	27.13	26.10	25.11	24.11	23.07	22.09	21.08	20.11	19.14	18.16	17.17	16.18
39	41.23	40.23	39.21	38.20	37.17	36.13	35.12	34.11	33.09	32.06	31.02	30.03	29.01	27.99	26.97	25.94	24.96	23.96	22.92	21.95	20.93	19.98	19.00	18.02	17.05	16.05
40	41.05	40.04	39.03	38.01	36.99	35.96	34.95	33.93	32.91	31.89	30.86	29.85	28.86	27.83	26.81	25.79	24.80	23.81	22.78	21.80	20.79	19.83	18.87	17.90	16.91	15.93
41	40.86	39.86	38.85	37.84	36.80	35.78	34.78	33.77	32.75	31.72	30.69	29.70	28.69	27.68	26.66	25.63	24.66	23.66	22.63	21.66	20.65	19.70	18.73	17.77	16.79	15.80
42	40.68	39.68	38.67	37.65	36.64	35.60	34.61	33.60	32.58	31.56	30.53	29.53	28.54	27.52	26.51	25.48	24.50	23.52	22.49	21.52	20.51	19.56	18.60	17.64	16.66	15.68
43	40.50	39.50	38.50	37.49	36.46	35.44	34.43	33.43	32.43	31.40	30.37	29.38	28.38	27.37	26.36	25.34	24.36	23.37	22.35	21.38	20.38	19.43	18.47	17.51	16.54	15.56
44	40.33	39.33	38.32	37.31	36.30	35.27	34.28	33.26	32.26	31.25	30.22	29.22	28.23	27.22	26.21	25.19	24.22	23.23	22.21	21.25	20.24	19.30	18.34	17.39	16.41	15.44
45	40.16	39.16	38.16	37.15	36.13	35.11	34.11	33.12	32.10	31.08	30.07	29.08	28.08	27.07	26.07	25.05	24.07	23.10	22.08	21.11	20.12	19.17	18.22	17.26	16.30	15.32
46	39.99	39.00	38.00	36.99	35.97	34.95	33.96	32.95	31.95	30.93	29.91	28.93	27.93	26.93	25.92	24.91	23.94	22.96	21.94	20.98	19.98	19.05	18.09	17.14	16.17	15.21
47	39.83	38.83	37.84	36.83	35.82	34.79	33.80	32.81	31.80	30.79	29.76	28.78	27.79	26.79	25.79	24.77	23.80	22.83	21.81	20.85	19.86	18.91	17.98	17.02	16.06	15.09
48	39.67	38.68	37.68	36.68	35.67	34.65	33.65	32.65	31.65	30.64	29.63	28.63	27.65	26.66	25.64	24.64	23.67	22.69	21.68	20.73	19.73	18.80	17.85	16.90	15.94	14.98

Table 27: 8th edition Ogden multipliers, loss of PENSION, WOMEN, discount rate: –0.25%, 2 YEAR ADJUSTMENT

Loss of pension from age

Age	52	53	54	55	56	57	58	59	60	61	62	63	64	65	66	67	68	69	70	71	72	73	74	75	76	77
49	39.52	38.53	37.53	36.52	35.52	34.50	33.51	32.51	31.51	30.50	29.48	28.51	27.51	26.51	25.52	24.50	23.54	22.57	21.55	20.60	19.61	18.67	17.74	16.78	15.83	14.87
50	39.37	38.38	37.39	36.39	35.37	34.36	33.37	32.37	31.37	30.36	29.35	28.36	27.38	26.38	25.38	24.38	23.41	22.44	21.43	20.48	19.49	18.56	17.62	16.67	15.72	14.76
51	39.22	38.24	37.25	36.24	35.24	34.21	33.23	32.24	31.24	30.23	29.21	28.24	27.25	26.26	25.26	24.25	23.29	22.32	21.30	20.36	19.37	18.44	17.51	16.56	15.61	14.65
52	39.09	38.10	37.11	36.11	35.10	34.09	33.09	32.11	31.11	30.10	29.09	28.11	27.13	26.13	25.13	24.13	23.17	22.20	21.19	20.25	19.26	18.33	17.39	16.45	15.51	14.55
53		37.98	36.98	35.98	34.98	33.96	32.98	31.98	30.98	29.98	28.96	27.99	27.00	26.01	25.02	24.01	23.05	22.09	21.08	20.13	19.15	18.22	17.29	16.35	15.40	14.45
54			36.87	35.86	34.85	33.84	32.86	31.87	30.86	29.86	28.85	27.87	26.89	25.90	24.90	23.90	22.94	21.98	20.97	20.02	19.04	18.12	17.19	16.24	15.30	14.35
55				35.75	34.74	33.72	32.75	31.76	30.76	29.75	28.73	27.77	26.78	25.80	24.79	23.79	22.84	21.87	20.86	19.92	18.93	18.02	17.09	16.15	15.20	14.25
56					34.64	33.62	32.64	31.66	30.65	29.65	28.63	27.65	26.68	25.68	24.70	23.69	22.73	21.77	20.76	19.83	18.84	17.91	16.99	16.05	15.12	14.16
57						33.53	32.55	31.55	30.56	29.55	28.54	27.56	26.58	25.60	24.59	23.60	22.64	21.67	20.67	19.73	18.75	17.83	16.89	15.97	15.02	14.08
58							32.46	31.47	30.47	29.47	28.45	27.48	26.49	25.50	24.51	23.50	22.56	21.59	20.58	19.64	18.66	17.74	16.82	15.88	14.94	13.99
59								31.40	30.40	29.38	28.38	27.40	26.42	25.43	24.43	23.43	22.47	21.51	20.51	19.56	18.58	17.66	16.73	15.80	14.86	13.92
60									30.33	29.32	28.30	27.34	26.35	25.35	24.36	23.35	22.40	21.43	20.43	19.49	18.50	17.58	16.66	15.73	14.79	13.84
61										29.27	28.25	27.27	26.30	25.29	24.29	23.29	22.33	21.37	20.37	19.42	18.44	17.51	16.59	15.65	14.72	13.78
62											28.20	27.23	26.24	25.25	24.24	23.23	22.28	21.31	20.30	19.36	18.38	17.46	16.52	15.59	14.65	13.71
63												27.19	26.21	25.21	24.21	23.19	22.23	21.27	20.26	19.32	18.33	17.40	16.48	15.54	14.60	13.65
64													26.18	25.18	24.18	23.17	22.20	21.23	20.22	19.28	18.29	17.36	16.43	15.49	14.55	13.60
65														25.17	24.16	23.15	22.18	21.20	20.19	19.24	18.26	17.33	16.39	15.45	14.51	13.56
66															24.16	23.14	22.17	21.20	20.18	19.22	18.23	17.30	16.37	15.42	14.48	13.53
67																23.15	22.18	21.20	20.17	19.21	18.22	17.29	16.35	15.40	14.45	13.50
68																	22.20	21.22	20.18	19.23	18.22	17.29	16.34	15.39	14.44	13.48
69																		21.25	20.21	19.25	18.24	17.29	16.35	15.40	14.44	13.48
70																			20.26	19.29	18.27	17.33	16.37	15.42	14.45	13.48
71																				19.36	18.33	17.37	16.42	15.44	14.48	13.51
72																					18.41	17.45	16.47	15.50	14.52	13.55
73																						17.54	16.56	15.58	14.59	13.59
74																							16.67	15.68	14.68	13.68
75																								15.81	14.79	13.78
76																									14.94	13.91
77																										14.07

Table 28: 8th edition Ogden multipliers, loss of PENSION, MEN, discount rate: −0.25%, NO 2 YEAR ADJUSTMENT

Age	Loss of pension from age																									
	50	51	52	53	54	55	56	57	58	59	60	61	62	63	64	65	66	67	68	69	70	71	72	73	74	75
16	42.52	41.47	40.42	39.36	38.29	37.22	36.18	35.12	34.06	33.00	31.92	30.88	29.84	28.79	27.73	26.67	25.65	24.62	23.55	22.55	21.50	20.52	19.53	18.53	17.52	16.50
17	42.29	41.25	40.19	39.14	38.08	37.00	35.96	34.91	33.86	32.79	31.72	30.69	29.64	28.60	27.55	26.48	25.47	24.45	23.38	22.38	21.33	20.36	19.37	18.37	17.37	16.36
18	42.06	41.02	39.97	38.92	37.85	36.79	35.75	34.70	33.65	32.59	31.52	30.49	29.45	28.41	27.35	26.30	25.29	24.27	23.21	22.21	21.17	20.19	19.21	18.22	17.22	16.21
19	41.83	40.80	39.75	38.70	37.64	36.57	35.54	34.50	33.45	32.38	31.32	30.30	29.26	28.22	27.17	26.11	25.11	24.10	23.03	22.04	21.00	20.04	19.06	18.07	17.07	16.06
20	41.60	40.57	39.53	38.49	37.42	36.36	35.33	34.29	33.24	32.19	31.12	30.10	29.07	28.04	26.98	25.93	24.93	23.92	22.86	21.88	20.84	19.87	18.90	17.92	16.92	15.92
21	41.38	40.35	39.31	38.27	37.22	36.15	35.12	34.09	33.04	31.99	30.93	29.91	28.88	27.85	26.81	25.75	24.75	23.75	22.69	21.72	20.68	19.72	18.75	17.77	16.79	15.78
22	41.17	40.13	39.09	38.06	37.00	35.95	34.92	33.88	32.84	31.79	30.74	29.72	28.69	27.67	26.62	25.58	24.58	23.58	22.53	21.55	20.53	19.56	18.60	17.62	16.63	15.65
23	40.94	39.92	38.88	37.84	36.80	35.74	34.72	33.68	32.65	31.60	30.54	29.54	28.51	27.48	26.45	25.40	24.41	23.41	22.36	21.39	20.36	19.42	18.44	17.47	16.50	15.50
24	40.73	39.70	38.68	37.63	36.58	35.54	34.51	33.49	32.45	31.41	30.36	29.34	28.33	27.30	26.26	25.23	24.24	23.24	22.20	21.23	20.21	19.25	18.30	17.33	16.35	15.37
25	40.51	39.49	38.46	37.43	36.38	35.33	34.32	33.29	32.26	31.21	30.17	29.16	28.14	27.13	26.09	25.05	24.07	23.08	22.03	21.06	20.05	19.10	18.14	17.19	16.21	15.23
26	40.30	39.28	38.25	37.22	36.19	35.13	34.11	33.10	32.06	31.03	29.98	28.98	27.96	26.95	25.92	24.88	23.90	22.91	21.87	20.91	19.89	18.95	18.00	17.04	16.07	15.09
27	40.09	39.07	38.04	37.02	35.98	34.94	33.92	32.89	31.87	30.84	29.80	28.79	27.78	26.77	25.75	24.72	23.73	22.74	21.71	20.75	19.74	18.80	17.85	16.89	15.93	14.96
28	39.88	38.87	37.84	36.81	35.78	34.74	33.73	32.71	31.68	30.65	29.61	28.62	27.60	26.59	25.57	24.55	23.57	22.58	21.55	20.59	19.59	18.65	17.70	16.75	15.79	14.82
29	39.66	38.66	37.64	36.61	35.57	34.54	33.54	32.52	31.49	30.46	29.43	28.43	27.43	26.42	25.39	24.37	23.41	22.43	21.39	20.43	19.43	18.51	17.56	16.61	15.65	14.68
30	39.46	38.45	37.44	36.42	35.38	34.34	33.34	32.33	31.32	30.28	29.24	28.26	27.25	26.25	25.23	24.20	23.23	22.27	21.23	20.28	19.28	18.35	17.42	16.48	15.51	14.55
31	39.26	38.25	37.23	36.22	35.19	34.15	33.15	32.14	31.13	30.11	29.07	28.07	27.08	26.08	25.06	24.04	23.07	22.10	21.08	20.14	19.13	18.21	17.27	16.34	15.39	14.42
32	39.06	38.06	37.04	36.02	35.00	33.97	32.96	31.96	30.94	29.92	28.90	27.91	26.91	25.91	24.90	23.88	22.92	21.94	20.93	19.98	18.99	18.06	17.14	16.20	15.25	14.30
33	38.87	37.86	36.86	35.84	34.80	33.78	32.79	31.78	30.76	29.74	28.72	27.74	26.74	25.74	24.73	23.72	22.76	21.79	20.78	19.83	18.84	17.93	17.00	16.06	15.12	14.17
34	38.67	37.68	36.66	35.65	34.63	33.59	32.60	31.60	30.59	29.57	28.54	27.57	26.58	25.58	24.58	23.56	22.60	21.64	20.62	19.69	18.69	17.78	16.86	15.93	14.99	14.04
35	38.48	37.48	36.48	35.47	34.45	33.42	32.42	31.42	30.42	29.41	28.38	27.39	26.41	25.42	24.41	23.41	22.45	21.49	20.48	19.54	18.56	17.64	16.72	15.80	14.87	13.92
36	38.30	37.30	36.30	35.29	34.27	33.25	32.25	31.25	30.25	29.23	28.22	27.25	26.25	25.26	24.26	23.25	22.30	21.34	20.33	19.39	18.42	17.51	16.59	15.67	14.73	13.80
37	38.11	37.12	36.12	35.11	34.09	33.07	32.09	31.08	30.08	29.07	28.05	27.08	26.09	25.10	24.10	23.10	22.15	21.20	20.18	19.26	18.27	17.38	16.46	15.53	14.61	13.67
38	37.94	36.94	35.95	34.94	33.93	32.90	31.92	30.93	29.92	28.91	27.89	26.92	25.94	24.95	23.96	22.95	22.01	21.05	20.05	19.12	18.14	17.24	16.33	15.42	14.48	13.55
39	37.76	36.78	35.78	34.77	33.76	32.74	31.75	30.76	29.76	28.75	27.74	26.76	25.79	24.81	23.80	22.81	21.86	20.91	20.01	18.99	18.01	17.11	16.20	15.29	14.37	13.43
40	37.60	36.61	35.62	34.61	33.60	32.58	31.60	30.60	29.61	28.60	27.58	26.62	25.64	24.66	23.67	22.66	21.73	20.77	19.77	18.85	17.88	16.98	16.08	15.17	14.24	13.32
41	37.44	36.45	35.45	34.45	33.45	32.42	31.44	30.45	29.46	28.45	27.44	26.47	25.50	24.51	23.53	22.53	21.58	20.64	19.64	18.72	17.75	16.86	15.96	15.04	14.13	13.20
42	37.28	36.30	35.30	34.30	33.29	32.28	31.29	30.30	29.31	28.31	27.30	26.33	25.35	24.37	23.39	22.40	21.45	20.50	19.52	18.60	17.63	16.72	15.84	14.93	14.01	13.10
43	37.13	36.14	35.15	34.15	33.14	32.13	31.15	30.16	29.17	28.16	27.16	26.19	25.22	24.24	23.25	22.26	21.33	20.38	19.39	18.47	17.51	16.62	15.71	14.81	13.91	12.98
44	36.98	36.00	35.01	34.01	33.00	31.99	31.01	30.02	29.02	28.03	27.02	26.06	25.09	24.10	23.12	22.13	21.19	20.26	19.26	18.35	17.39	16.50	15.61	14.70	13.79	12.88
45	36.85	35.86	34.87	33.87	32.86	31.85	30.87	29.89	28.90	27.89	26.89	25.92	24.96	23.98	22.99	22.01	21.07	20.13	19.14	18.23	17.27	16.39	15.49	14.59	13.68	12.77
46	36.71	35.73	34.73	33.73	32.74	31.72	30.74	29.76	28.76	27.77	26.76	25.80	24.83	23.85	22.88	21.88	20.95	20.01	19.02	18.12	17.15	16.27	15.38	14.48	13.58	12.66

Table 28: 8th edition Ogden multipliers, loss of PENSION, MEN, discount rate: −0.25%, NO 2 YEAR ADJUSTMENT

Loss of pension from age

Age	50	51	52	53	54	55	56	57	58	59	60	61	62	63	64	65	66	67	68	69	70	71	72	73	74	75
47	36.59	35.60	34.61	33.61	32.60	31.60	30.61	29.63	28.64	27.64	26.64	25.67	24.71	23.73	22.75	21.77	20.83	19.90	18.92	18.00	17.05	16.16	15.27	14.38	13.47	12.57
48	36.46	35.48	34.49	33.49	32.48	31.47	30.50	29.51	28.52	27.53	26.52	25.56	24.59	23.61	22.64	21.65	20.72	19.78	18.80	17.89	16.93	16.06	15.17	14.28	13.37	12.46
49	36.35	35.36	34.37	33.37	32.37	31.36	30.38	29.40	28.40	27.41	26.41	25.44	24.48	23.50	22.52	21.54	20.61	19.68	18.69	17.79	16.83	15.95	15.07	14.17	13.28	12.37
50	36.24	35.26	34.26	33.27	32.26	31.25	30.27	29.28	28.30	27.30	26.30	25.34	24.37	23.40	22.42	21.43	20.50	19.57	18.59	17.68	16.73	15.85	14.96	14.08	13.18	12.28
51		35.16	34.17	33.16	32.16	31.15	30.17	29.19	28.19	27.20	26.19	25.24	24.27	23.29	22.32	21.33	20.40	19.47	18.49	17.59	16.63	15.75	14.87	13.98	13.09	12.19
52			34.07	33.07	32.06	31.05	30.08	29.09	28.10	27.09	26.10	25.13	24.17	23.20	22.22	21.24	20.31	19.37	18.39	17.48	16.54	15.66	14.78	13.89	12.99	12.10
53				32.99	31.98	30.96	29.99	29.01	28.01	27.02	26.00	25.05	24.08	23.11	22.13	21.14	20.22	19.28	18.30	17.40	16.44	15.57	14.69	13.80	12.91	12.01
54					31.90	30.89	29.91	28.92	27.93	26.93	25.93	24.96	24.00	23.02	22.04	21.06	20.13	19.20	18.22	17.31	16.36	15.48	14.61	13.73	12.83	11.93
55						30.82	29.85	28.86	27.86	26.86	25.85	24.90	23.92	22.95	21.97	20.98	20.06	19.12	18.13	17.23	16.28	15.41	14.52	13.64	12.76	11.85
56							29.79	28.81	27.80	26.79	25.79	24.83	23.87	22.88	21.90	20.91	19.98	19.05	18.07	17.16	16.21	15.34	14.46	13.57	12.68	11.79
57								28.76	27.76	26.75	25.73	24.78	23.81	22.83	21.84	20.85	19.92	18.99	17.99	17.09	16.14	15.27	14.39	13.50	12.61	11.71
58									27.74	26.72	25.70	24.73	23.77	22.79	21.80	20.80	19.87	18.94	17.94	17.04	16.08	15.21	14.33	13.45	12.55	11.65
59										26.71	25.68	24.71	23.74	22.76	21.77	20.77	19.83	18.90	17.90	17.00	16.04	15.16	14.28	13.40	12.50	11.60
60											25.68	24.71	23.73	22.74	21.75	20.75	19.81	18.86	17.87	16.97	16.00	15.12	14.24	13.35	12.46	11.56
61												24.72	23.73	22.74	21.75	20.74	19.80	18.85	17.85	16.95	15.98	15.09	14.20	13.31	12.42	11.52
62													23.76	22.76	21.76	20.75	19.80	18.85	17.85	16.93	15.97	15.08	14.18	13.29	12.39	11.49
63														22.80	21.78	20.77	19.82	18.86	17.86	16.93	15.96	15.08	14.18	13.27	12.37	11.47
64															21.84	20.81	19.86	18.90	17.88	16.95	15.97	15.08	14.18	13.27	12.36	11.45
65																20.88	19.92	18.95	17.92	16.99	16.00	15.10	14.19	13.29	12.37	11.45
66																	20.00	19.02	17.99	17.05	16.05	15.14	14.23	13.31	12.39	11.47
67																		19.12	18.08	17.12	16.12	15.20	14.28	13.35	12.42	11.50
68																			18.19	17.23	16.21	15.28	14.35	13.41	12.48	11.54
69																				17.36	16.34	15.38	14.44	13.49	12.55	11.61
70																					16.48	15.53	14.55	13.60	12.64	11.69
71																						15.68	14.71	13.73	12.76	11.79
72																							14.89	13.90	12.90	11.92
73																								14.09	13.08	12.07
74																									13.30	12.27
75																										12.50

Table 29: 8th edition Ogden multipliers, loss of PENSION, WOMEN, discount rate: −0.25%, NO 2 YEAR ADJUSTMENT

Loss of pension from age

Age	50	51	52	53	54	55	56	57	58	59	60	61	62	63	64	65	66	67	68	69	70	71	72	73	74	75
16	45.64	44.59	43.52	42.45	41.37	40.27	39.22	38.14	37.06	35.98	34.88	33.82	32.76	31.68	30.60	29.50	28.45	27.39	26.29	25.24	24.16	23.13	22.09	21.04	19.99	18.91
17	45.43	44.36	43.30	42.23	41.15	40.07	39.00	37.94	36.86	35.78	34.70	33.63	32.57	31.49	30.41	29.33	28.27	27.22	26.12	25.08	24.00	22.97	21.94	20.88	19.83	18.78
18	45.20	44.15	43.08	42.02	40.94	39.86	38.80	37.73	36.67	35.58	34.50	33.45	32.37	31.31	30.23	29.14	28.10	27.04	25.95	24.91	23.84	22.81	21.78	20.74	19.68	18.63
19	44.98	43.93	42.87	41.80	40.73	39.65	38.60	37.54	36.46	35.39	34.30	33.25	32.20	31.12	30.06	28.97	27.92	26.88	25.78	24.75	23.67	22.66	21.63	20.58	19.55	18.48
20	44.76	43.71	42.65	41.60	40.52	39.45	38.39	37.33	36.27	35.19	34.12	33.06	32.01	30.95	29.86	28.80	27.75	26.70	25.62	24.58	23.52	22.49	21.47	20.44	19.39	18.35
21	44.54	43.49	42.44	41.38	40.32	39.24	38.19	37.13	36.07	35.01	33.92	32.88	31.82	30.76	29.70	28.61	27.58	26.53	25.45	24.43	23.35	22.34	21.31	20.29	19.26	18.20
22	44.33	43.28	42.22	41.17	40.10	39.04	37.99	36.93	35.87	34.80	33.74	32.69	31.64	30.57	29.52	28.45	27.40	26.37	25.29	24.26	23.20	22.18	21.17	20.14	19.10	18.07
23	44.11	43.07	42.02	40.96	39.90	38.83	37.79	36.74	35.68	34.61	33.54	32.51	31.45	30.40	29.33	28.27	27.24	26.19	25.12	24.10	23.04	22.03	21.01	19.99	18.96	17.92
24	43.89	42.85	41.81	40.75	39.69	38.63	37.59	36.54	35.48	34.42	33.35	32.31	31.28	30.22	29.16	28.09	27.07	26.04	24.96	23.94	22.88	21.88	20.87	19.85	18.82	17.78
25	43.67	42.64	41.60	40.55	39.49	38.42	37.39	36.34	35.29	34.23	33.16	32.13	31.09	30.04	28.98	27.92	26.89	25.87	24.79	23.78	22.72	21.72	20.72	19.70	18.68	17.64
26	43.46	42.42	41.39	40.34	39.29	38.23	37.18	36.15	35.10	34.04	32.98	31.94	30.91	29.86	28.81	27.75	26.73	25.70	24.63	23.63	22.57	21.57	20.57	19.56	18.54	17.51
27	43.25	42.22	41.17	40.13	39.09	38.03	37.00	35.95	34.91	33.85	32.79	31.76	30.72	29.68	28.64	27.58	26.56	25.53	24.47	23.47	22.42	21.42	20.42	19.41	18.40	17.37
28	43.04	42.01	40.97	39.93	38.88	37.83	36.80	35.76	34.71	33.67	32.61	31.58	30.55	29.51	28.46	27.41	26.40	25.37	24.31	23.31	22.27	21.28	20.27	19.26	18.26	17.24
29	42.83	41.80	40.77	39.73	38.68	37.63	36.61	35.57	34.53	33.48	32.43	31.40	30.37	29.33	28.29	27.24	26.23	25.21	24.15	23.14	22.11	21.13	20.13	19.13	18.11	17.10
30	42.62	41.60	40.57	39.53	38.48	37.43	36.41	35.38	34.35	33.29	32.24	31.23	30.20	29.16	28.12	27.07	26.06	25.05	23.99	22.99	21.95	20.98	19.99	18.99	17.98	16.96
31	42.41	41.39	40.37	39.33	38.29	37.24	36.22	35.19	34.16	33.12	32.06	31.04	30.03	28.99	27.95	26.90	25.90	24.89	23.83	22.84	21.80	20.82	19.84	18.84	17.84	16.83
32	42.21	41.19	40.17	39.14	38.10	37.05	36.03	35.00	33.98	32.93	31.89	30.87	29.85	28.82	27.79	26.74	25.74	24.73	23.68	22.69	21.66	20.68	19.69	18.71	17.70	16.70
33	42.01	40.99	39.97	38.94	37.91	36.86	35.84	34.82	33.79	32.76	31.71	30.70	29.68	28.65	27.62	26.58	25.58	24.57	23.52	22.54	21.51	20.54	19.55	18.57	17.57	16.56
34	41.82	40.80	39.78	38.75	37.72	36.68	35.66	34.64	33.62	32.57	31.54	30.53	29.51	28.48	27.46	26.42	25.42	24.42	23.37	22.39	21.36	20.39	19.42	18.43	17.44	16.44
35	41.62	40.61	39.59	38.56	37.53	36.49	35.48	34.46	33.43	32.41	31.36	30.36	29.34	28.32	27.29	26.26	25.27	24.26	23.22	22.24	21.22	20.25	19.28	18.29	17.30	16.31
36	41.43	40.42	39.40	38.38	37.35	36.30	35.30	34.28	33.26	32.23	31.20	30.18	29.18	28.16	27.13	26.10	25.11	24.11	23.07	22.09	21.08	20.11	19.14	18.16	17.17	16.18
37	41.23	40.23	39.21	38.20	37.17	36.13	35.12	34.11	33.09	32.06	31.02	30.03	29.01	27.99	26.97	25.94	24.96	23.96	22.92	21.95	20.93	19.98	19.00	18.02	17.05	16.05
38	41.05	40.04	39.03	38.01	36.99	35.96	34.95	33.93	32.91	31.89	30.86	29.85	28.86	27.83	26.81	25.79	24.80	23.81	22.78	21.80	20.79	19.83	18.87	17.90	16.91	15.93
39	40.86	39.86	38.85	37.84	36.80	35.78	34.78	33.77	32.75	31.72	30.69	29.70	28.69	27.68	26.66	25.63	24.66	23.66	22.63	21.66	20.65	19.70	18.73	17.77	16.79	15.80
40	40.68	39.68	38.67	37.65	36.64	35.60	34.61	33.60	32.58	31.56	30.53	29.53	28.54	27.52	26.51	25.48	24.50	23.52	22.49	21.52	20.51	19.56	18.60	17.64	16.66	15.68
41	40.50	39.50	38.50	37.49	36.46	35.44	34.43	33.43	32.43	31.40	30.37	29.38	28.38	27.37	26.36	25.34	24.36	23.37	22.35	21.38	20.38	19.43	18.47	17.51	16.54	15.56
42	40.33	39.33	38.32	37.31	36.30	35.27	34.28	33.26	32.26	31.25	30.22	29.22	28.23	27.22	26.21	25.19	24.22	23.23	22.21	21.25	20.24	19.30	18.34	17.39	16.41	15.44
43	40.16	39.16	38.16	37.15	36.13	35.11	34.11	33.12	32.10	31.08	30.07	29.08	28.08	27.07	26.07	25.05	24.07	23.10	22.08	21.11	20.12	19.17	18.22	17.26	16.30	15.32
44	39.99	39.00	38.00	36.99	35.97	34.95	33.96	32.95	31.95	30.93	29.91	28.93	27.93	26.93	25.92	24.91	23.94	22.96	21.94	20.98	19.98	19.05	18.09	17.14	16.17	15.21
45	39.83	38.83	37.84	36.83	35.82	34.79	33.80	32.81	31.80	30.79	29.76	28.78	27.79	26.79	25.79	24.77	23.80	22.83	21.81	20.85	19.86	18.91	17.98	17.02	16.06	15.09
46	39.67	38.68	37.68	36.68	35.67	34.65	33.65	32.65	31.65	30.64	29.63	28.63	27.65	26.66	25.64	24.64	23.67	22.69	21.68	20.73	19.73	18.80	17.85	16.90	15.94	14.98

Table 29: 8th edition Ogden multipliers, loss of PENSION, WOMEN, discount rate: −0.25%, NO 2 YEAR ADJUSTMENT

Loss of pension from age

Age	50	51	52	53	54	55	56	57	58	59	60	61	62	63	64	65	66	67	68	69	70	71	72	73	74	75
47	39.52	38.53	37.53	36.52	35.52	34.50	33.51	32.51	31.51	30.50	29.48	28.51	27.51	26.51	25.52	24.50	23.54	22.57	21.55	20.60	19.61	18.67	17.74	16.78	15.83	14.87
48	39.37	38.38	37.39	36.39	35.37	34.36	33.37	32.37	31.37	30.36	29.35	28.36	27.38	26.38	25.38	24.38	23.41	22.44	21.43	20.48	19.49	18.56	17.62	16.67	15.72	14.76
49	39.22	38.24	37.25	36.24	35.24	34.21	33.23	32.24	31.24	30.23	29.21	28.24	27.25	26.26	25.26	24.25	23.29	22.32	21.30	20.36	19.37	18.44	17.51	16.56	15.61	14.65
50	39.09	38.10	37.11	36.11	35.10	34.09	33.09	32.11	31.11	30.10	29.09	28.11	27.13	26.13	25.13	24.13	23.17	22.20	21.19	20.25	19.26	18.33	17.39	16.45	15.51	14.55
51		37.98	36.98	35.98	34.98	33.96	32.98	31.98	30.98	29.98	28.96	27.99	27.00	26.01	25.02	24.01	23.05	22.09	21.08	20.13	19.15	18.22	17.29	16.35	15.40	14.45
52			36.87	35.86	34.85	33.84	32.86	31.87	30.86	29.86	28.85	27.87	26.89	25.90	24.90	23.90	22.94	21.98	20.97	20.02	19.04	18.12	17.19	16.24	15.30	14.35
53				35.75	34.74	33.72	32.75	31.76	30.76	29.75	28.73	27.77	26.78	25.80	24.79	23.79	22.84	21.87	20.86	19.92	18.93	18.02	17.09	16.15	15.20	14.25
54					34.64	33.62	32.64	31.66	30.65	29.65	28.63	27.65	26.68	25.68	24.70	23.69	22.73	21.77	20.76	19.83	18.84	17.91	16.99	16.05	15.12	14.16
55						33.53	32.55	31.55	30.56	29.55	28.54	27.56	26.58	25.60	24.59	23.60	22.64	21.67	20.67	19.73	18.75	17.83	16.89	15.97	15.02	14.08
56							32.46	31.47	30.47	29.47	28.45	27.48	26.49	25.50	24.51	23.50	22.56	21.59	20.58	19.64	18.66	17.74	16.82	15.88	14.94	13.99
57								31.40	30.40	29.38	28.38	27.40	26.42	25.43	24.43	23.43	22.47	21.51	20.51	19.56	18.58	17.66	16.73	15.80	14.86	13.92
58									30.33	29.32	28.30	27.34	26.35	25.35	24.36	23.35	22.40	21.43	20.43	19.49	18.50	17.58	16.66	15.73	14.79	13.84
59										29.27	28.25	27.27	26.30	25.29	24.29	23.29	22.33	21.37	20.37	19.42	18.44	17.51	16.59	15.65	14.72	13.78
60											28.20	27.23	26.24	25.25	24.24	23.23	22.28	21.31	20.30	19.36	18.38	17.46	16.52	15.59	14.65	13.71
61												27.19	26.21	25.21	24.21	23.19	22.23	21.27	20.26	19.32	18.33	17.40	16.48	15.54	14.60	13.65
62													26.18	25.18	24.18	23.17	22.20	21.23	20.22	19.28	18.29	17.36	16.43	15.49	14.55	13.60
63														25.17	24.16	23.15	22.18	21.20	20.19	19.24	18.26	17.33	16.39	15.45	14.51	13.56
64															24.16	23.14	22.17	21.20	20.18	19.22	18.23	17.30	16.37	15.42	14.48	13.53
65																23.15	22.18	21.20	20.17	19.21	18.22	17.29	16.35	15.40	14.45	13.50
66																	22.20	21.22	20.18	19.23	18.22	17.29	16.34	15.39	14.44	13.48
67																		21.25	20.21	19.25	18.24	17.29	16.35	15.40	14.44	13.48
68																			20.26	19.29	18.27	17.33	16.37	15.42	14.45	13.48
69																				19.36	18.33	17.37	16.42	15.44	14.48	13.51
70																					18.41	17.45	16.47	15.50	14.52	13.55
71																						17.54	16.56	15.58	14.59	13.59
72																							16.67	15.68	14.68	13.68
73																								15.81	14.79	13.78
74																									14.94	13.91
75																										14.07

Table 30: 8th edition Ogden multipliers, loss of PENSION, MEN, discount rate: –0.75%, 2 YEAR ADJUSTMENT

Loss of pension from age

Age	52	53	54	55	56	57	58	59	60	61	62	63	64	65	66	67	68	69	70	71	72	73	74	75	76	77
18	56.21	55.00	53.75	52.48	51.18	49.85	48.60	47.33	46.02	44.69	43.32	42.05	40.75	39.43	38.07	36.68	35.41	34.09	32.67	31.39	29.99	28.73	27.43	26.10	24.74	23.35
19	55.62	54.40	53.17	51.91	50.62	49.30	48.06	46.79	45.50	44.18	42.83	41.56	40.27	38.96	37.62	36.24	34.97	33.67	32.26	30.99	29.61	28.35	27.06	25.75	24.40	23.03
20	55.03	53.83	52.59	51.35	50.06	48.76	47.53	46.27	44.99	43.68	42.34	41.09	39.80	38.50	37.16	35.81	34.54	33.26	31.86	30.60	29.23	27.98	26.70	25.40	24.07	22.71
21	54.44	53.25	52.04	50.79	49.52	48.22	47.00	45.76	44.48	43.18	41.85	40.61	39.34	38.05	36.72	35.37	34.13	32.85	31.46	30.20	28.85	27.62	26.35	25.06	23.73	22.39
22	53.86	52.68	51.48	50.24	48.98	47.69	46.48	45.24	43.98	42.69	41.37	40.14	38.88	37.60	36.29	34.94	33.70	32.44	31.06	29.83	28.47	27.25	26.00	24.73	23.41	22.07
23	53.30	52.12	50.92	49.70	48.45	47.17	45.96	44.74	43.49	42.21	40.90	39.67	38.43	37.16	35.85	34.53	33.29	32.04	30.68	29.46	28.12	26.89	25.66	24.39	23.10	21.77
24	52.74	51.57	50.37	49.16	47.93	46.66	45.46	44.24	43.00	41.73	40.44	39.22	37.98	36.71	35.43	34.11	32.89	31.64	30.30	29.07	27.76	26.55	25.31	24.06	22.77	21.47
25	52.18	51.03	49.84	48.63	47.40	46.15	44.96	43.75	42.51	41.26	39.97	38.77	37.54	36.28	35.00	33.70	32.49	31.25	29.91	28.71	27.39	26.21	24.98	23.73	22.47	21.16
26	51.63	50.48	49.31	48.11	46.88	45.64	44.47	43.27	42.03	40.79	39.52	38.32	37.10	35.85	34.59	33.29	32.09	30.87	29.54	28.34	27.04	25.85	24.66	23.42	22.15	20.87
27	51.09	49.95	48.78	47.60	46.38	45.14	43.97	42.79	41.57	40.32	39.06	37.88	36.67	35.44	34.17	32.89	31.70	30.49	29.16	27.98	26.69	25.52	24.32	23.10	21.85	20.57
28	50.55	49.42	48.26	47.08	45.88	44.65	43.49	42.31	41.10	39.88	38.61	37.44	36.24	35.01	33.77	32.49	31.31	30.11	28.80	27.63	26.34	25.18	24.00	22.78	21.55	20.28
29	50.02	48.90	47.75	46.58	45.38	44.17	43.02	41.84	40.64	39.42	38.18	37.01	35.82	34.61	33.36	32.10	30.93	29.74	28.44	27.28	26.01	24.85	23.67	22.47	21.25	20.00
30	49.50	48.38	47.25	46.08	44.89	43.68	42.55	41.38	40.19	38.98	37.74	36.59	35.40	34.19	32.97	31.71	30.55	29.37	28.08	26.93	25.67	24.53	23.36	22.17	20.95	19.71
31	48.98	47.88	46.74	45.59	44.41	43.21	42.08	40.93	39.75	38.54	37.31	36.16	34.99	33.80	32.57	31.33	30.18	29.01	27.73	26.59	25.34	24.21	23.05	21.87	20.66	19.43
32	48.47	47.37	46.25	45.10	43.94	42.74	41.62	40.47	39.30	38.11	36.89	35.75	34.59	33.40	32.19	30.95	29.81	28.65	27.38	26.25	25.01	23.89	22.75	21.58	20.38	19.15
33	47.97	46.88	45.76	44.63	43.46	42.29	41.17	40.03	38.87	37.68	36.48	35.34	34.19	33.01	31.80	30.59	29.45	28.30	27.05	25.92	24.69	23.58	22.44	21.28	20.10	18.89
34	47.47	46.39	45.29	44.16	43.00	41.82	40.73	39.59	38.44	37.26	36.06	34.95	33.80	32.62	31.44	30.21	29.10	27.95	26.70	25.59	24.37	23.27	22.15	21.00	19.82	18.62
35	46.99	45.91	44.82	43.69	42.55	41.38	40.28	39.17	38.02	36.85	35.66	34.54	33.42	32.25	31.06	29.86	28.74	27.61	26.37	25.27	24.06	22.97	21.85	20.71	19.55	18.36
36	46.51	45.44	44.35	43.24	42.10	40.94	39.85	38.74	37.61	36.44	35.26	34.16	33.03	31.88	30.71	29.50	28.40	27.27	26.04	24.95	23.75	22.67	21.56	20.44	19.28	18.10
37	46.04	44.98	43.90	42.79	41.67	40.51	39.43	38.32	37.19	36.05	34.87	33.77	32.66	31.51	30.35	29.16	28.06	26.94	25.72	24.64	23.45	22.38	21.28	20.16	19.02	17.85
38	45.58	44.52	43.45	42.35	41.23	40.09	39.01	37.91	36.80	35.65	34.49	33.40	32.29	31.15	30.00	28.82	27.73	26.62	25.41	24.33	23.15	22.09	21.00	19.89	18.75	17.60
39	45.12	44.08	43.01	41.92	40.81	39.67	38.61	37.51	36.40	35.27	34.11	33.03	31.92	30.80	29.65	28.48	27.41	26.30	25.10	24.03	22.86	21.80	20.73	19.63	18.50	17.35
40	44.68	43.64	42.58	41.49	40.39	39.26	38.20	37.12	36.01	34.88	33.74	32.67	31.57	30.45	29.32	28.15	27.08	25.99	24.79	23.73	22.57	21.53	20.46	19.36	18.25	17.11
41	44.24	43.21	42.16	41.09	39.98	38.86	37.81	36.73	35.64	34.51	33.37	32.31	31.23	30.12	28.97	27.83	26.76	25.68	24.50	23.44	22.29	21.25	20.19	19.11	18.00	16.88
42	43.81	42.79	41.74	40.67	39.59	38.46	37.42	36.35	35.27	34.15	33.01	31.96	30.88	29.78	28.66	27.50	26.46	25.37	24.20	23.16	22.01	20.98	19.93	18.86	17.77	16.64
43	43.40	42.38	41.34	40.28	39.19	38.09	37.04	35.98	34.90	33.80	32.67	31.61	30.55	29.45	28.34	27.20	26.14	25.09	23.92	22.88	21.75	20.72	19.68	18.61	17.52	16.42
44	42.99	41.98	40.94	39.89	38.81	37.71	36.68	35.62	34.55	33.44	32.33	31.28	30.21	29.13	28.02	26.90	25.85	24.79	23.64	22.60	21.48	20.47	19.43	18.37	17.29	16.19
45	42.59	41.58	40.56	39.51	38.44	37.34	36.31	35.27	34.19	33.11	31.99	30.96	29.90	28.82	27.72	26.59	25.57	24.51	23.36	22.34	21.21	20.21	19.19	18.13	17.07	15.97
46	42.20	41.20	40.18	39.13	38.07	36.99	35.96	34.92	33.86	32.77	31.67	30.63	29.59	28.51	27.42	26.31	25.27	24.23	23.09	22.08	20.97	19.96	18.94	17.90	16.84	15.76
47	41.82	40.82	39.81	38.77	37.71	36.64	35.62	34.58	33.52	32.45	31.35	30.32	29.27	28.21	27.13	26.02	25.00	23.95	22.83	21.82	20.72	19.73	18.71	17.68	16.62	15.55
48	41.45	40.46	39.45	38.42	37.37	36.29	35.28	34.25	33.20	32.13	31.04	30.02	28.98	27.92	26.84	25.74	24.73	23.69	22.57	21.56	20.47	19.49	18.49	17.45	16.41	15.34

Table 30: 8th edition Ogden multipliers, loss of PENSION, MEN, discount rate: −0.75%, 2 YEAR ADJUSTMENT

Loss of pension from age

Age	52	53	54	55	56	57	58	59	60	61	62	63	64	65	66	67	68	69	70	71	72	73	74	75	76	77
49	41.09	40.10	39.10	38.07	37.03	35.96	34.95	33.93	32.89	31.82	30.73	29.72	28.69	27.63	26.56	25.47	24.46	23.43	22.32	21.32	20.23	19.25	18.26	17.24	16.20	15.14
50	40.74	39.76	38.75	37.73	36.70	35.64	34.63	33.61	32.57	31.52	30.44	29.42	28.40	27.35	26.29	25.20	24.20	23.18	22.07	21.08	20.00	19.02	18.03	17.02	16.00	14.95
51	40.40	39.42	38.42	37.41	36.37	35.32	34.33	33.31	32.27	31.22	30.15	29.15	28.12	27.08	26.02	24.94	23.94	22.93	21.83	20.84	19.77	18.81	17.82	16.82	15.79	14.76
52	40.06	39.10	38.10	37.09	36.06	35.01	34.02	33.01	31.98	30.93	29.86	28.87	27.85	26.81	25.76	24.69	23.70	22.69	21.59	20.61	19.55	18.59	17.61	16.61	15.60	14.56
53		38.77	37.79	36.78	35.75	34.71	33.73	32.72	31.70	30.66	29.59	28.60	27.59	26.56	25.51	24.44	23.46	22.45	21.36	20.39	19.33	18.38	17.41	16.42	15.41	14.38
54			37.49	36.49	35.46	34.42	33.44	32.45	31.43	30.38	29.33	28.34	27.33	26.31	25.26	24.20	23.22	22.23	21.14	20.18	19.12	18.17	17.21	16.22	15.22	14.20
55				36.20	35.18	34.14	33.17	32.18	31.16	30.13	29.07	28.09	27.09	26.07	25.03	23.97	23.00	22.01	20.93	19.96	18.92	17.98	17.02	16.04	15.04	14.03
56					34.92	33.88	32.91	31.92	30.91	29.88	28.83	27.85	26.86	25.84	24.80	23.75	22.78	21.79	20.72	19.77	18.72	17.79	16.83	15.86	14.87	13.86
57						33.63	32.67	31.68	30.67	29.65	28.60	27.63	26.63	25.62	24.59	23.54	22.58	21.59	20.52	19.58	18.54	17.60	16.66	15.69	14.71	13.70
58							32.44	31.46	30.45	29.42	28.38	27.42	26.43	25.42	24.39	23.34	22.38	21.40	20.34	19.38	18.36	17.44	16.49	15.52	14.54	13.55
59								31.25	30.24	29.22	28.17	27.21	26.23	25.22	24.20	23.15	22.20	21.22	20.16	19.22	18.18	17.27	16.33	15.37	14.39	13.40
60									30.05	29.03	27.99	27.02	26.05	25.05	24.02	22.98	22.02	21.06	19.99	19.05	18.03	17.10	16.18	15.23	14.26	13.26
61										28.86	27.82	26.86	25.88	24.88	23.86	22.82	21.87	20.90	19.84	18.91	17.88	16.97	16.03	15.08	14.12	13.14
62											27.67	26.71	25.73	24.73	23.72	22.68	21.73	20.76	19.71	18.77	17.75	16.83	15.90	14.95	13.99	13.02
63												26.58	25.60	24.60	23.59	22.55	21.60	20.63	19.58	18.65	17.63	16.71	15.78	14.84	13.88	12.90
64													25.49	24.50	23.47	22.44	21.49	20.52	19.47	18.53	17.52	16.61	15.68	14.74	13.77	12.80
65														24.41	23.39	22.34	21.40	20.43	19.38	18.44	17.42	16.51	15.59	14.64	13.69	12.71
66															23.32	22.28	21.32	20.36	19.31	18.37	17.35	16.43	15.51	14.56	13.61	12.64
67																22.23	21.28	20.30	19.25	18.32	17.29	16.37	15.44	14.50	13.54	12.57
68																	21.25	20.28	19.22	18.28	17.26	16.33	15.40	14.45	13.50	12.52
69																		20.27	19.21	18.26	17.24	16.32	15.37	14.42	13.46	12.49
70																			19.23	18.28	17.24	16.31	15.37	14.41	13.45	12.47
71																				18.32	17.28	16.33	15.39	14.43	13.45	12.47
72																					17.34	16.39	15.43	14.46	13.48	12.49
73																						16.48	15.51	14.52	13.54	12.54
74																							15.61	14.62	13.62	12.61
75																								14.75	13.74	12.71
76																									13.88	12.85
77																										13.02

Table 31: 8th edition Ogden multipliers, loss of PENSION, WOMEN, discount rate: −0.75%, 2 YEAR ADJUSTMENT

Loss of pension from age

Age	52	53	54	55	56	57	58	59	60	61	62	63	64	65	66	67	68	69	70	71	72	73	74	75	76	77
18	60.62	59.38	58.12	56.83	55.51	54.17	52.90	51.59	50.26	48.91	47.53	46.23	44.88	43.53	42.14	40.73	39.41	38.04	36.58	35.25	33.81	32.48	31.10	29.71	28.29	26.84
19	60.01	58.78	57.52	56.24	54.94	53.61	52.34	51.05	49.73	48.39	47.02	45.72	44.40	43.05	41.68	40.27	38.95	37.61	36.17	34.83	33.41	32.08	30.73	29.35	27.94	26.50
20	59.41	58.19	56.94	55.67	54.37	53.05	51.80	50.51	49.21	47.87	46.51	45.23	43.91	42.58	41.21	39.82	38.51	37.18	35.74	34.43	33.01	31.70	30.35	28.99	27.59	26.16
21	58.81	57.60	56.36	55.09	53.81	52.50	51.25	49.99	48.69	47.36	46.01	44.73	43.44	42.11	40.75	39.37	38.07	36.75	35.33	34.02	32.62	31.31	29.99	28.63	27.24	25.83
22	58.21	57.01	55.79	54.54	53.25	51.95	50.72	49.45	48.17	46.86	45.52	44.25	42.95	41.64	40.30	38.93	37.64	36.33	34.92	33.63	32.23	30.94	29.61	28.27	26.90	25.50
23	57.63	56.43	55.22	53.97	52.71	51.41	50.18	48.94	47.66	46.36	45.03	43.77	42.49	41.18	39.85	38.49	37.21	35.91	34.51	33.23	31.85	30.56	29.26	27.92	26.56	25.17
24	57.05	55.86	54.65	53.42	52.16	50.89	49.66	48.42	47.15	45.86	44.55	43.30	42.02	40.72	39.40	38.06	36.79	35.50	34.12	32.84	31.47	30.20	28.90	27.57	26.22	24.85
25	56.47	55.30	54.09	52.87	51.63	50.35	49.15	47.91	46.65	45.37	44.06	42.83	41.56	40.28	38.96	37.62	36.37	35.09	33.71	32.45	31.09	29.83	28.55	27.23	25.89	24.52
26	55.90	54.73	53.55	52.33	51.09	49.83	48.63	47.41	46.15	44.89	43.59	42.36	41.11	39.83	38.53	37.20	35.95	34.69	33.32	32.07	30.72	29.47	28.19	26.89	25.57	24.21
27	55.34	54.18	52.99	51.79	50.56	49.31	48.12	46.90	45.67	44.40	43.12	41.90	40.65	39.39	38.09	36.78	35.54	34.28	32.93	31.69	30.35	29.11	27.85	26.56	25.24	23.90
28	54.78	53.63	52.45	51.26	50.04	48.79	47.62	46.41	45.18	43.93	42.65	41.44	40.21	38.95	37.67	36.36	35.14	33.88	32.54	31.32	29.99	28.76	27.50	26.22	24.92	23.59
29	54.22	53.09	51.92	50.73	49.52	48.29	47.11	45.92	44.70	43.45	42.19	40.99	39.77	38.52	37.24	35.95	34.73	33.50	32.16	30.94	29.63	28.41	27.17	25.90	24.60	23.28
30	53.67	52.54	51.39	50.22	49.00	47.78	46.62	45.43	44.23	42.99	41.73	40.54	39.33	38.09	36.83	35.54	34.34	33.10	31.78	30.57	29.27	28.07	26.83	25.57	24.29	22.98
31	53.13	52.01	50.87	49.70	48.51	47.28	46.13	44.96	43.75	42.53	41.28	40.10	38.90	37.67	36.42	35.14	33.94	32.73	31.41	30.21	28.91	27.72	26.50	25.25	23.98	22.68
32	52.60	51.48	50.35	49.19	48.00	46.80	45.65	44.48	43.29	42.07	40.84	39.66	38.47	37.25	36.01	34.74	33.56	32.35	31.05	29.85	28.57	27.38	26.17	24.94	23.67	22.39
33	52.07	50.97	49.84	48.69	47.52	46.31	45.18	44.01	42.84	41.63	40.39	39.24	38.05	36.85	35.61	34.35	33.17	31.97	30.68	29.50	28.22	27.05	25.84	24.63	23.37	22.09
34	51.56	50.45	49.34	48.19	47.03	45.84	44.71	43.56	42.38	41.19	39.96	38.81	37.64	36.43	35.22	33.96	32.80	31.60	30.32	29.16	27.89	26.72	25.53	24.31	23.08	21.81
35	51.05	49.96	48.84	47.70	46.55	45.37	44.25	43.10	41.94	40.74	39.54	38.39	37.22	36.04	34.82	33.59	32.42	31.24	29.98	28.80	27.56	26.40	25.21	24.01	22.77	21.53
36	50.53	49.46	48.35	47.22	46.07	44.90	43.79	42.66	41.50	40.32	39.11	37.98	36.82	35.64	34.44	33.20	32.06	30.88	29.62	28.47	27.22	26.08	24.91	23.71	22.49	21.24
37	50.04	48.96	47.87	46.75	45.61	44.44	43.34	42.22	41.06	39.89	38.70	37.57	36.42	35.24	34.05	32.84	31.69	30.53	29.28	28.13	26.90	25.76	24.60	23.41	22.20	20.97
38	49.55	48.48	47.39	46.29	45.14	43.99	42.89	41.78	40.64	39.47	38.29	37.17	36.02	34.87	33.67	32.47	31.34	30.18	28.94	27.80	26.58	25.45	24.29	23.13	21.92	20.70
39	49.05	48.00	46.92	45.81	44.70	43.54	42.46	41.34	40.21	39.07	37.88	36.77	35.64	34.48	33.31	32.10	30.98	29.84	28.60	27.48	26.26	25.14	24.00	22.83	21.65	20.43
40	48.58	47.52	46.46	45.36	44.24	43.11	42.02	40.92	39.80	38.65	37.49	36.38	35.26	34.11	32.93	31.75	30.63	29.50	28.28	27.15	25.95	24.84	23.71	22.55	21.36	20.17
41	48.11	47.06	45.99	44.91	43.80	42.67	41.60	40.50	39.39	38.25	37.09	36.00	34.88	33.74	32.58	31.39	30.29	29.16	27.95	26.84	25.64	24.54	23.42	22.27	21.10	19.90
42	47.64	46.61	45.55	44.46	43.37	42.24	41.18	40.09	38.98	37.85	36.70	35.61	34.51	33.37	32.23	31.05	29.95	28.83	27.62	26.53	25.34	24.24	23.13	21.99	20.84	19.65
43	47.19	46.15	45.11	44.03	42.93	41.82	40.76	39.69	38.59	37.46	36.32	35.24	34.14	33.02	31.87	30.71	29.62	28.50	27.31	26.22	25.04	23.96	22.85	21.72	20.57	19.40
44	46.73	45.72	44.67	43.60	42.52	41.40	40.36	39.28	38.19	37.08	35.94	34.87	33.78	32.66	31.53	30.37	29.29	28.19	27.00	25.92	24.75	23.67	22.58	21.45	20.31	19.15
45	46.29	45.27	44.25	43.18	42.10	41.00	39.95	38.90	37.81	36.70	35.57	34.51	33.43	32.32	31.19	30.04	28.97	27.88	26.69	25.61	24.46	23.39	22.30	21.19	20.06	18.90
46	45.86	44.85	43.81	42.77	41.70	40.60	39.57	38.50	37.43	36.33	35.21	34.15	33.08	31.98	30.86	29.71	28.65	27.56	26.39	25.33	24.17	23.12	22.03	20.94	19.81	18.66
47	45.43	44.43	43.41	42.36	41.30	40.21	39.18	38.13	37.06	35.97	34.85	33.81	32.73	31.64	30.54	29.40	28.33	27.26	26.10	25.05	23.90	22.84	21.78	20.68	19.57	18.43
48	45.02	44.02	43.00	41.96	40.90	39.83	38.80	37.76	36.70	35.61	34.51	33.46	32.40	31.32	30.21	29.09	28.04	26.96	25.81	24.75	23.63	22.58	21.51	20.43	19.32	18.20

Table 31: 8th edition Ogden multipliers, loss of PENSION, WOMEN, discount rate: −0.75%, 2 YEAR ADJUSTMENT

Loss of pension from age

Age	52	53	54	55	56	57	58	59	60	61	62	63	64	65	66	67	68	69	70	71	72	73	74	75	76	77
49	44.60	43.62	42.60	41.58	40.52	39.44	38.44	37.39	36.34	35.26	34.16	33.13	32.07	31.00	29.90	28.78	27.74	26.67	25.52	24.48	23.35	22.32	21.26	20.19	19.09	17.96
50	44.21	43.22	42.22	41.19	40.15	39.08	38.07	37.05	35.99	34.92	33.83	32.80	31.75	30.67	29.59	28.48	27.44	26.39	25.25	24.21	23.09	22.06	21.02	19.95	18.86	17.75
51	43.82	42.84	41.84	40.83	39.77	38.72	37.72	36.69	35.65	34.58	33.50	32.48	31.44	30.38	29.28	28.19	27.16	26.11	24.98	23.94	22.83	21.81	20.77	19.71	18.63	17.53
52	43.43	42.47	41.47	40.46	39.43	38.36	37.37	36.36	35.32	34.26	33.17	32.16	31.13	30.07	29.00	27.89	26.88	25.83	24.70	23.69	22.58	21.56	20.53	19.48	18.41	17.31
53		42.10	41.12	40.11	39.08	38.03	37.03	36.02	34.99	33.94	32.87	31.85	30.83	29.78	28.71	27.62	26.59	25.57	24.45	23.44	22.34	21.33	20.30	19.26	18.19	17.10
54			40.76	39.76	38.74	37.70	36.71	35.70	34.68	33.63	32.57	31.56	30.53	29.49	28.43	27.35	26.34	25.30	24.20	23.18	22.10	21.10	20.07	19.03	17.98	16.90
55				39.43	38.41	37.37	36.40	35.40	34.37	33.33	32.27	31.28	30.26	29.21	28.16	27.08	26.08	25.06	23.95	22.94	21.86	20.87	19.86	18.82	17.77	16.70
56					38.09	37.06	36.09	35.10	34.08	33.04	31.98	31.00	29.99	28.95	27.89	26.82	25.83	24.81	23.71	22.71	21.63	20.65	19.65	18.62	17.56	16.50
57						36.76	35.80	34.81	33.80	32.77	31.71	30.72	29.72	28.70	27.65	26.57	25.58	24.57	23.48	22.49	21.41	20.43	19.44	18.42	17.38	16.31
58							35.51	34.53	33.52	32.50	31.45	30.47	29.46	28.45	27.41	26.34	25.35	24.34	23.26	22.28	21.21	20.22	19.23	18.22	17.20	16.14
59								34.27	33.27	32.24	31.20	30.22	29.23	28.21	27.17	26.12	25.13	24.13	23.05	22.06	21.01	20.04	19.04	18.04	17.01	15.97
60									33.02	32.00	30.96	29.99	29.00	27.98	26.95	25.90	24.92	23.92	22.85	21.87	20.81	19.85	18.86	17.85	16.84	15.80
61										31.78	30.74	29.77	28.78	27.77	26.74	25.69	24.72	23.73	22.65	21.68	20.63	19.66	18.69	17.69	16.67	15.64
62											30.53	29.57	28.58	27.57	26.55	25.50	24.53	23.54	22.47	21.51	20.46	19.50	18.52	17.52	16.51	15.48
63												29.37	28.39	27.39	26.36	25.32	24.35	23.36	22.30	21.34	20.30	19.34	18.36	17.37	16.36	15.34
64													28.22	27.22	26.20	25.15	24.19	23.20	22.14	21.18	20.14	19.19	18.22	17.23	16.23	15.20
65														27.06	26.04	25.01	24.04	23.06	22.00	21.03	20.00	19.05	18.08	17.10	16.09	15.08
66															25.91	24.87	23.91	22.92	21.87	20.91	19.87	18.92	17.96	16.98	15.98	14.96
67																24.75	23.79	22.81	21.75	20.79	19.76	18.81	17.84	16.86	15.87	14.86
68																	23.69	22.71	21.65	20.69	19.66	18.71	17.75	16.77	15.77	14.76
69																		22.63	21.57	20.62	19.58	18.63	17.66	16.68	15.69	14.68
70																			21.51	20.55	19.52	18.57	17.60	16.62	15.62	14.61
71																				20.51	19.47	18.53	17.56	16.57	15.57	14.56
72																					19.45	18.50	17.53	16.54	15.54	14.52
73																						18.50	17.53	16.54	15.53	14.51
74																							17.55	16.55	15.54	14.52
75																								16.60	15.58	14.55
76																									15.65	14.61
77																										14.70

Tables

Table 32: 8th edition Ogden multipliers, loss of PENSION, MEN, discount rate: −0.75%, NO 2 YEAR ADJUSTMENT

Age	Loss of pension from age																									
---	50	51	52	53	54	55	56	57	58	59	60	61	62	63	64	65	66	67	68	69	70	71	72	73	74	75
16	56.21	55.00	53.75	52.48	51.18	49.85	48.60	47.33	46.02	44.69	43.32	42.05	40.75	39.43	38.07	36.68	35.41	34.09	32.67	31.39	29.99	28.73	27.43	26.10	24.74	23.35
17	55.62	54.40	53.17	51.91	50.62	49.30	48.06	46.79	45.50	44.18	42.83	41.56	40.27	38.96	37.62	36.24	34.97	33.67	32.26	30.99	29.61	28.35	27.06	25.75	24.40	23.03
18	55.03	53.83	52.59	51.35	50.06	48.76	47.53	46.27	44.99	43.68	42.34	41.09	39.80	38.50	37.16	35.81	34.54	33.26	31.86	30.60	29.23	27.98	26.70	25.40	24.07	22.71
19	54.44	53.25	52.04	50.79	49.52	48.22	47.00	45.76	44.48	43.18	41.85	40.61	39.34	38.05	36.72	35.37	34.13	32.85	31.46	30.20	28.85	27.62	26.35	25.06	23.73	22.39
20	53.86	52.68	51.48	50.24	48.98	47.69	46.48	45.24	43.98	42.69	41.37	40.14	38.88	37.60	36.29	34.94	33.70	32.44	31.06	29.83	28.47	27.25	26.00	24.73	23.41	22.07
21	53.30	52.12	50.92	49.70	48.45	47.17	45.96	44.74	43.49	42.21	40.90	39.67	38.43	37.16	35.85	34.53	33.29	32.04	30.68	29.46	28.12	26.89	25.66	24.39	23.10	21.77
22	52.74	51.57	50.37	49.16	47.93	46.66	45.46	44.24	43.00	41.73	40.44	39.22	37.98	36.71	35.43	34.11	32.89	31.64	30.30	29.07	27.76	26.55	25.31	24.06	22.77	21.47
23	52.18	51.03	49.84	48.63	47.40	46.15	44.96	43.75	42.51	41.26	39.97	38.77	37.54	36.28	35.00	33.70	32.49	31.25	29.91	28.71	27.39	26.21	24.98	23.73	22.47	21.16
24	51.63	50.48	49.31	48.11	46.88	45.64	44.47	43.27	42.03	40.79	39.52	38.32	37.10	35.85	34.59	33.29	32.09	30.87	29.54	28.34	27.04	25.85	24.66	23.42	22.15	20.87
25	51.09	49.95	48.78	47.60	46.38	45.14	43.97	42.79	41.57	40.32	39.06	37.88	36.67	35.44	34.17	32.89	31.70	30.49	29.16	27.98	26.69	25.52	24.32	23.10	21.85	20.57
26	50.55	49.42	48.26	47.08	45.88	44.65	43.49	42.31	41.10	39.88	38.61	37.44	36.24	35.01	33.77	32.49	31.31	30.11	28.80	27.63	26.34	25.18	24.00	22.78	21.55	20.28
27	50.02	48.90	47.75	46.58	45.38	44.17	43.02	41.84	40.64	39.42	38.18	37.01	35.82	34.61	33.36	32.10	30.93	29.74	28.44	27.28	26.01	24.85	23.67	22.47	21.25	20.00
28	49.50	48.38	47.25	46.08	44.89	43.68	42.55	41.38	40.19	38.98	37.74	36.59	35.40	34.19	32.97	31.71	30.55	29.37	28.08	26.93	25.67	24.53	23.36	22.17	20.95	19.71
29	48.98	47.88	46.74	45.59	44.41	43.21	42.08	40.93	39.75	38.54	37.31	36.16	34.99	33.80	32.57	31.33	30.18	29.01	27.73	26.59	25.34	24.21	23.05	21.87	20.66	19.43
30	48.47	47.37	46.25	45.10	43.94	42.74	41.62	40.47	39.30	38.11	36.89	35.75	34.59	33.40	32.19	30.95	29.81	28.65	27.38	26.25	25.01	23.89	22.75	21.58	20.38	19.15
31	47.97	46.88	45.76	44.63	43.46	42.29	41.17	40.03	38.87	37.68	36.48	35.34	34.19	33.01	31.80	30.59	29.45	28.30	27.05	25.92	24.69	23.58	22.44	21.28	20.10	18.89
32	47.47	46.39	45.29	44.16	43.00	41.82	40.73	39.59	38.44	37.26	36.06	34.95	33.80	32.62	31.44	30.21	29.10	27.95	26.70	25.59	24.37	23.27	22.15	21.00	19.82	18.62
33	46.99	45.91	44.82	43.69	42.55	41.38	40.28	39.17	38.02	36.85	35.66	34.54	33.42	32.25	31.06	29.86	28.74	27.61	26.37	25.27	24.06	22.97	21.85	20.71	19.55	18.36
34	46.51	45.44	44.35	43.24	42.10	40.94	39.85	38.74	37.61	36.44	35.26	34.16	33.03	31.88	30.71	29.50	28.40	27.27	26.04	24.95	23.75	22.67	21.56	20.44	19.28	18.10
35	46.04	44.98	43.90	42.79	41.67	40.51	39.43	38.32	37.19	36.05	34.87	33.77	32.66	31.51	30.35	29.16	28.06	26.94	25.72	24.64	23.45	22.38	21.28	20.16	19.02	17.85
36	45.58	44.52	43.45	42.35	41.23	40.09	39.01	37.91	36.80	35.65	34.49	33.40	32.29	31.15	30.00	28.82	27.73	26.62	25.41	24.33	23.15	22.09	21.00	19.89	18.75	17.60
37	45.12	44.08	43.01	41.92	40.81	39.67	38.61	37.51	36.40	35.27	34.11	33.03	31.92	30.80	29.65	28.48	27.41	26.30	25.10	24.03	22.86	21.80	20.73	19.63	18.50	17.35
38	44.68	43.64	42.58	41.49	40.39	39.26	38.20	37.12	36.01	34.88	33.74	32.67	31.57	30.45	29.32	28.15	27.08	25.99	24.79	23.73	22.57	21.53	20.46	19.36	18.25	17.11
39	44.24	43.21	42.16	41.09	39.98	38.86	37.81	36.73	35.64	34.51	33.37	32.31	31.23	30.12	28.97	27.83	26.76	25.68	24.51	23.44	22.29	21.25	20.19	19.11	18.00	16.88
40	43.81	42.79	41.74	40.67	39.59	38.46	37.42	36.35	35.27	34.15	33.01	31.96	30.88	29.78	28.66	27.50	26.46	25.37	24.20	23.16	22.01	20.98	19.93	18.86	17.77	16.64
41	43.40	42.38	41.34	40.28	39.19	38.09	37.04	35.98	34.90	33.80	32.67	31.61	30.55	29.45	28.34	27.20	26.14	25.09	23.92	22.88	21.75	20.72	19.68	18.61	17.52	16.42
42	42.99	41.98	40.94	39.89	38.81	37.71	36.68	35.62	34.55	33.44	32.33	31.28	30.21	29.13	28.02	26.90	25.85	24.79	23.64	22.60	21.48	20.47	19.43	18.37	17.29	16.19
43	42.59	41.58	40.56	39.51	38.44	37.34	36.31	35.27	34.19	33.11	31.99	30.96	29.90	28.82	27.72	26.59	25.57	24.51	23.36	22.34	21.21	20.21	19.19	18.13	17.07	15.97
44	42.20	41.20	40.18	39.13	38.07	36.99	35.96	34.92	33.86	32.77	31.67	30.63	29.59	28.51	27.42	26.31	25.27	24.23	23.09	22.08	20.97	19.96	18.94	17.90	16.84	15.76
45	41.82	40.82	39.81	38.77	37.71	36.64	35.62	34.58	33.52	32.45	31.35	30.32	29.27	28.21	27.13	26.02	25.00	23.95	22.83	21.82	20.72	19.73	18.71	17.68	16.62	15.55
46	41.45	40.46	39.45	38.42	37.37	36.29	35.28	34.25	33.20	32.13	31.04	30.02	28.98	27.92	26.84	25.74	24.73	23.69	22.57	21.56	20.47	19.49	18.49	17.45	16.41	15.34

Table 32: 8th edition Ogden multipliers, loss of PENSION, MEN, discount rate: −0.75%, NO 2 YEAR ADJUSTMENT

Loss of pension from age

Age	50	51	52	53	54	55	56	57	58	59	60	61	62	63	64	65	66	67	68	69	70	71	72	73	74	75
47	41.09	40.10	39.10	38.07	37.03	35.96	34.95	33.93	32.89	31.82	30.73	29.72	28.69	27.63	26.56	25.47	24.46	23.43	22.32	21.32	20.23	19.25	18.26	17.24	16.20	15.14
48	40.74	39.76	38.75	37.73	36.70	35.64	34.63	33.61	32.57	31.52	30.44	29.42	28.40	27.35	26.29	25.20	24.20	23.18	22.07	21.08	20.00	19.02	18.03	17.02	16.00	14.95
49	40.40	39.42	38.42	37.41	36.37	35.32	34.33	33.31	32.27	31.22	30.15	29.15	28.12	27.08	26.02	24.94	23.94	22.93	21.83	20.84	19.77	18.81	17.82	16.82	15.79	14.76
50	40.06	39.10	38.10	37.09	36.06	35.01	34.02	33.01	31.98	30.93	29.86	28.87	27.85	26.81	25.76	24.69	23.70	22.69	21.59	20.61	19.55	18.59	17.61	16.61	15.60	14.56
51		38.77	37.79	36.78	35.75	34.71	33.73	32.72	31.70	30.66	29.59	28.60	27.59	26.56	25.51	24.44	23.46	22.45	21.36	20.39	19.33	18.38	17.41	16.42	15.41	14.38
52			37.49	36.49	35.46	34.42	33.44	32.45	31.43	30.38	29.33	28.34	27.33	26.31	25.26	24.20	23.22	22.23	21.14	20.18	19.12	18.17	17.21	16.22	15.22	14.20
53				36.20	35.18	34.14	33.17	32.18	31.16	30.13	29.07	28.09	27.09	26.07	25.03	23.97	23.00	22.01	20.93	19.96	18.92	17.98	17.02	16.04	15.04	14.03
54					34.92	33.88	32.91	31.92	30.91	29.88	28.83	27.85	26.86	25.84	24.80	23.75	22.78	21.79	20.72	19.77	18.72	17.79	16.83	15.86	14.87	13.86
55						33.63	32.67	31.68	30.67	29.65	28.60	27.63	26.63	25.62	24.59	23.54	22.58	21.59	20.52	19.58	18.54	17.60	16.66	15.69	14.71	13.70
56							32.44	31.46	30.45	29.42	28.38	27.42	26.43	25.42	24.39	23.34	22.38	21.40	20.34	19.38	18.36	17.44	16.49	15.52	14.54	13.55
57								31.25	30.24	29.22	28.17	27.21	26.23	25.22	24.20	23.15	22.20	21.22	20.16	19.22	18.18	17.27	16.33	15.37	14.39	13.40
58									30.05	29.03	27.99	27.02	26.05	25.05	24.02	22.98	22.02	21.06	19.99	19.05	18.03	17.10	16.18	15.23	14.26	13.26
59										28.86	27.82	26.86	25.88	24.88	23.86	22.82	21.87	20.90	19.84	18.91	17.88	16.97	16.03	15.08	14.12	13.14
60											27.67	26.71	25.73	24.73	23.72	22.68	21.73	20.76	19.71	18.77	17.75	16.83	15.90	14.95	13.99	13.02
61												26.58	25.60	24.60	23.59	22.55	21.60	20.63	19.58	18.65	17.63	16.71	15.78	14.84	13.88	12.90
62													25.49	24.50	23.47	22.44	21.49	20.52	19.47	18.53	17.52	16.61	15.68	14.74	13.77	12.80
63														24.41	23.39	22.34	21.40	20.43	19.38	18.44	17.42	16.51	15.59	14.64	13.69	12.71
64															23.32	22.28	21.32	20.36	19.31	18.37	17.35	16.43	15.51	14.56	13.61	12.64
65																22.23	21.28	20.30	19.25	18.32	17.29	16.37	15.44	14.50	13.54	12.57
66																	21.25	20.28	19.22	18.28	17.26	16.33	15.40	14.45	13.50	12.52
67																		20.27	19.21	18.26	17.24	16.32	15.37	14.42	13.46	12.49
68																			19.23	18.28	17.24	16.31	15.37	14.41	13.45	12.47
69																				18.32	17.28	16.33	15.39	14.43	13.45	12.47
70																					17.34	16.39	15.43	14.46	13.48	12.49
71																						16.48	15.51	14.52	13.54	12.54
72																							15.61	14.62	13.62	12.61
73																								14.75	13.74	12.71
74																									13.88	12.85
75																										13.02

Table 33: 8th edition Ogden multipliers, loss of PENSION, WOMEN, discount rate: −0.75%, NO 2 YEAR ADJUSTMENT

Age	Loss of pension from age																									
	50	51	52	53	54	55	56	57	58	59	60	61	62	63	64	65	66	67	68	69	70	71	72	73	74	75
16	60.62	59.38	58.12	56.83	55.51	54.17	52.90	51.59	50.26	48.91	47.53	46.23	44.88	43.53	42.14	40.73	39.41	38.04	36.58	35.25	33.81	32.48	31.10	29.71	28.29	26.84
17	60.01	58.78	57.52	56.24	54.94	53.61	52.34	51.05	49.73	48.39	47.02	45.72	44.40	43.05	41.68	40.27	38.95	37.61	36.17	34.83	33.41	32.08	30.73	29.35	27.94	26.50
18	59.41	58.19	56.94	55.67	54.37	53.05	51.80	50.51	49.21	47.87	46.51	45.23	43.91	42.58	41.21	39.82	38.51	37.18	35.74	34.43	33.01	31.70	30.35	28.99	27.59	26.16
19	58.81	57.60	56.36	55.09	53.81	52.50	51.25	49.99	48.69	47.36	46.01	44.73	43.44	42.11	40.75	39.37	38.07	36.75	35.33	34.02	32.62	31.31	29.99	28.63	27.24	25.83
20	58.21	57.01	55.79	54.54	53.25	51.95	50.72	49.45	48.17	46.86	45.52	44.25	42.95	41.64	40.30	38.93	37.64	36.33	34.92	33.63	32.23	30.94	29.61	28.27	26.90	25.50
21	57.63	56.43	55.22	53.97	52.71	51.41	50.18	48.94	47.66	46.36	45.03	43.77	42.49	41.18	39.85	38.49	37.21	35.91	34.51	33.23	31.85	30.56	29.26	27.92	26.56	25.17
22	57.05	55.86	54.65	53.42	52.16	50.89	49.66	48.42	47.15	45.86	44.55	43.30	42.02	40.72	39.40	38.06	36.79	35.50	34.12	32.84	31.47	30.20	28.90	27.57	26.22	24.85
23	56.47	55.30	54.09	52.87	51.63	50.35	49.15	47.91	46.65	45.37	44.06	42.83	41.56	40.28	38.96	37.62	36.37	35.09	33.71	32.45	31.09	29.83	28.55	27.23	25.89	24.52
24	55.90	54.73	53.55	52.33	51.09	49.83	48.63	47.41	46.15	44.89	43.59	42.36	41.11	39.83	38.53	37.20	35.95	34.69	33.32	32.07	30.72	29.47	28.19	26.89	25.57	24.21
25	55.34	54.18	52.99	51.79	50.56	49.31	48.12	46.90	45.67	44.40	43.12	41.90	40.65	39.39	38.09	36.78	35.54	34.28	32.93	31.69	30.35	29.11	27.85	26.56	25.25	23.90
26	54.78	53.63	52.45	51.26	50.04	48.79	47.62	46.41	45.18	43.93	42.65	41.44	40.21	38.95	37.67	36.36	35.14	33.88	32.54	31.32	29.99	28.76	27.50	26.22	24.92	23.59
27	54.22	53.09	51.92	50.73	49.52	48.29	47.11	45.92	44.70	43.45	42.19	40.99	39.77	38.52	37.24	35.95	34.73	33.50	32.16	30.94	29.63	28.41	27.17	25.90	24.60	23.28
28	53.67	52.54	51.39	50.22	49.00	47.78	46.62	45.43	44.23	42.99	41.73	40.54	39.33	38.09	36.83	35.54	34.34	33.10	31.78	30.57	29.27	28.07	26.83	25.57	24.29	22.98
29	53.13	52.01	50.87	49.70	48.51	47.28	46.13	44.96	43.75	42.53	41.28	40.10	38.90	37.67	36.42	35.14	33.94	32.73	31.41	30.21	28.91	27.72	26.50	25.25	23.98	22.68
30	52.60	51.48	50.35	49.19	48.00	46.80	45.65	44.48	43.29	42.07	40.84	39.66	38.47	37.25	36.01	34.74	33.56	32.35	31.05	29.85	28.57	27.38	26.17	24.94	23.67	22.39
31	52.07	50.97	49.84	48.69	47.52	46.31	45.18	44.01	42.84	41.63	40.39	39.24	38.05	36.85	35.61	34.35	33.17	31.97	30.68	29.50	28.22	27.05	25.84	24.63	23.37	22.09
32	51.56	50.45	49.34	48.19	47.03	45.84	44.71	43.56	42.38	41.19	39.96	38.81	37.64	36.43	35.22	33.96	32.80	31.60	30.32	29.16	27.89	26.72	25.53	24.31	23.08	21.81
33	51.05	49.96	48.84	47.70	46.55	45.37	44.25	43.10	41.94	40.74	39.54	38.39	37.22	36.04	34.82	33.59	32.42	31.24	29.98	28.80	27.56	26.40	25.21	24.01	22.77	21.53
34	50.53	49.46	48.35	47.22	46.07	44.90	43.79	42.66	41.50	40.32	39.11	37.98	36.82	35.64	34.44	33.20	32.06	30.88	29.62	28.47	27.22	26.08	24.91	23.71	22.49	21.24
35	50.04	48.96	47.87	46.75	45.61	44.44	43.34	42.22	41.06	39.89	38.70	37.57	36.42	35.24	34.05	32.84	31.69	30.53	29.28	28.13	26.90	25.76	24.60	23.41	22.20	20.97
36	49.55	48.48	47.39	46.29	45.14	43.99	42.89	41.78	40.64	39.47	38.29	37.17	36.02	34.87	33.67	32.47	31.34	30.18	28.94	27.80	26.58	25.45	24.29	23.13	21.92	20.70
37	49.05	48.00	46.92	45.81	44.70	43.54	42.46	41.34	40.21	39.07	37.88	36.77	35.64	34.48	33.31	32.10	30.98	29.84	28.60	27.48	26.26	25.14	24.00	22.83	21.65	20.43
38	48.58	47.52	46.46	45.36	44.24	43.11	42.02	40.92	39.80	38.65	37.49	36.38	35.26	34.11	32.93	31.75	30.63	29.50	28.28	27.15	25.95	24.84	23.71	22.55	21.36	20.17
39	48.11	47.06	45.99	44.91	43.80	42.67	41.60	40.50	39.39	38.25	37.09	36.00	34.88	33.74	32.58	31.39	30.29	29.16	27.95	26.84	25.64	24.54	23.42	22.27	21.10	19.90
40	47.64	46.61	45.55	44.46	43.37	42.24	41.18	40.09	38.98	37.85	36.70	35.61	34.51	33.37	32.23	31.05	29.95	28.83	27.62	26.53	25.34	24.24	23.13	21.99	20.84	19.65
41	47.19	46.15	45.11	44.03	42.93	41.82	40.76	39.69	38.59	37.46	36.32	35.24	34.14	33.02	31.87	30.71	29.62	28.50	27.31	26.22	25.04	23.96	22.85	21.72	20.57	19.40
42	46.73	45.72	44.67	43.60	42.52	41.40	40.36	39.28	38.19	37.08	35.94	34.87	33.78	32.66	31.53	30.37	29.29	28.19	27.00	25.92	24.75	23.67	22.58	21.45	20.31	19.15
43	46.29	45.27	44.25	43.18	42.10	41.00	39.95	38.90	37.81	36.70	35.57	34.51	33.43	32.32	31.19	30.04	28.97	27.88	26.69	25.61	24.46	23.39	22.30	21.19	20.06	18.90
44	45.86	44.85	43.81	42.77	41.70	40.60	39.57	38.50	37.43	36.33	35.21	34.15	33.08	31.98	30.86	29.71	28.65	27.56	26.39	25.33	24.17	23.12	22.03	20.94	19.81	18.66
45	45.43	44.43	43.41	42.36	41.30	40.21	39.18	38.13	37.06	35.97	34.85	33.81	32.73	31.64	30.54	29.40	28.33	27.26	26.10	25.05	23.90	22.84	21.78	20.68	19.57	18.43
46	45.02	44.02	43.00	41.96	40.90	39.83	38.80	37.76	36.70	35.61	34.51	33.46	32.40	31.32	30.21	29.09	28.04	26.96	25.81	24.75	23.63	22.58	21.51	20.43	19.32	18.20

Table 33: 8th edition Ogden multipliers, loss of PENSION, WOMEN, discount rate: −0.75%, NO 2 YEAR ADJUSTMENT

Loss of pension from age

Age	50	51	52	53	54	55	56	57	58	59	60	61	62	63	64	65	66	67	68	69	70	71	72	73	74	75
47	44.60	43.62	42.60	41.58	40.52	39.44	38.44	37.39	36.34	35.26	34.16	33.13	32.07	31.00	29.90	28.78	27.74	26.67	25.52	24.48	23.35	22.32	21.26	20.19	19.09	17.96
48	44.21	43.22	42.22	41.19	40.15	39.08	38.07	37.05	35.99	34.92	33.83	32.80	31.75	30.67	29.59	28.48	27.44	26.39	25.25	24.21	23.09	22.06	21.02	19.95	18.86	17.75
49	43.82	42.84	41.84	40.83	39.77	38.72	37.72	36.69	35.65	34.58	33.50	32.48	31.44	30.38	29.28	28.19	27.16	26.11	24.98	23.94	22.83	21.81	20.77	19.71	18.63	17.53
50	43.43	42.47	41.47	40.46	39.43	38.36	37.37	36.36	35.32	34.26	33.17	32.16	31.13	30.07	29.00	27.89	26.88	25.83	24.70	23.69	22.58	21.56	20.53	19.48	18.41	17.31
51		42.10	41.12	40.11	39.08	38.03	37.03	36.02	34.99	33.94	32.87	31.85	30.83	29.78	28.71	27.62	26.59	25.57	24.45	23.44	22.34	21.33	20.30	19.26	18.19	17.10
52			40.76	39.76	38.74	37.70	36.71	35.70	34.68	33.63	32.57	31.56	30.53	29.49	28.43	27.35	26.34	25.30	24.20	23.18	22.10	21.10	20.07	19.03	17.98	16.90
53				39.43	38.41	37.37	36.40	35.40	34.37	33.33	32.27	31.28	30.26	29.21	28.16	27.08	26.08	25.06	23.95	22.94	21.86	20.87	19.86	18.82	17.77	16.70
54					38.09	37.06	36.09	35.10	34.08	33.04	31.98	31.00	29.99	28.95	27.89	26.82	25.83	24.81	23.71	22.71	21.63	20.65	19.65	18.62	17.56	16.50
55						36.76	35.80	34.81	33.80	32.77	31.71	30.72	29.72	28.70	27.65	26.57	25.58	24.57	23.48	22.49	21.41	20.43	19.44	18.42	17.38	16.31
56							35.51	34.53	33.52	32.50	31.45	30.47	29.46	28.45	27.41	26.34	25.35	24.34	23.26	22.28	21.21	20.22	19.23	18.22	17.20	16.14
57								34.27	33.27	32.24	31.20	30.22	29.23	28.21	27.17	26.12	25.13	24.13	23.05	22.06	21.01	20.04	19.04	18.04	17.01	15.97
58									33.02	32.00	30.96	29.99	29.00	27.98	26.95	25.90	24.92	23.92	22.85	21.87	20.81	19.85	18.86	17.85	16.84	15.80
59										31.78	30.74	29.77	28.78	27.77	26.74	25.69	24.72	23.73	22.65	21.68	20.63	19.66	18.69	17.69	16.67	15.64
60											30.53	29.57	28.58	27.57	26.55	25.50	24.53	23.54	22.47	21.51	20.46	19.50	18.52	17.52	16.51	15.48
61												29.37	28.39	27.39	26.36	25.32	24.35	23.36	22.30	21.34	20.30	19.34	18.36	17.37	16.36	15.34
62													28.22	27.22	26.20	25.15	24.19	23.20	22.14	21.18	20.14	19.19	18.22	17.23	16.23	15.20
63														27.06	26.04	25.01	24.04	23.06	22.00	21.03	20.00	19.05	18.08	17.10	16.09	15.08
64															25.91	24.87	23.91	22.92	21.87	20.91	19.87	18.92	17.96	16.98	15.98	14.96
65																24.75	23.79	22.81	21.75	20.79	19.76	18.81	17.84	16.86	15.87	14.86
66																	23.69	22.71	21.65	20.69	19.66	18.71	17.75	16.77	15.77	14.76
67																		22.63	21.57	20.62	19.58	18.63	17.66	16.68	15.69	14.68
68																			21.51	20.55	19.52	18.57	17.60	16.62	15.62	14.61
69																				20.51	19.47	18.53	17.56	16.57	15.57	14.56
70																					19.45	18.50	17.53	16.54	15.54	14.52
71																						18.50	17.53	16.54	15.53	14.51
72																							17.55	16.55	15.54	14.52
73																								16.60	15.58	14.55
74																									15.65	14.61
75																										14.70

Table 34: 8th edition Ogden multipliers, loss of EARNINGS, MEN, discount rate: −0.25%, NO 2 YEAR ADJUSTMENT

Loss of earnings to pension age

Age	50	51	52	53	54	55	56	57	58	59	60	61	62	63	64	65	66	67	68	69	70	71	72	73	74	75
16	35.18	36.24	37.30	38.36	39.42	40.48	41.54	42.60	43.66	44.72	45.78	46.83	47.89	48.94	49.99	51.03	52.08	53.11	54.15	55.17	56.20	57.21	58.22	59.22	60.21	61.20
17	34.09	35.15	36.21	37.26	38.32	39.38	40.44	41.49	42.55	43.61	44.66	45.71	46.76	47.81	48.86	49.90	50.94	51.97	53.00	54.03	55.05	56.06	57.06	58.06	59.05	60.02
18	33.01	34.06	35.12	36.17	37.23	38.28	39.34	40.39	41.44	42.50	43.55	44.60	45.65	46.69	47.73	48.77	49.81	50.84	51.86	52.88	53.90	54.91	55.91	56.90	57.88	58.86
19	31.93	32.98	34.04	35.09	36.14	37.19	38.24	39.29	40.34	41.39	42.44	43.49	44.53	45.57	46.61	47.65	48.68	49.71	50.73	51.75	52.76	53.76	54.76	55.75	56.73	57.70
20	30.86	31.91	32.96	34.01	35.05	36.10	37.15	38.20	39.25	40.29	41.34	42.38	43.42	44.46	45.50	46.53	47.56	48.58	49.60	50.61	51.62	52.62	53.62	54.60	55.58	56.54
21	29.79	30.83	31.88	32.93	33.97	35.02	36.07	37.11	38.16	39.20	40.24	41.28	42.32	43.36	44.39	45.42	46.44	47.46	48.48	49.49	50.49	51.49	52.48	53.46	54.43	55.39
22	28.72	29.77	30.81	31.85	32.90	33.94	34.98	36.03	37.07	38.11	39.15	40.18	41.22	42.25	43.28	44.31	45.33	46.35	47.36	48.36	49.36	50.36	51.34	52.32	53.29	54.24
23	27.66	28.70	29.74	30.78	31.82	32.86	33.90	34.94	35.98	37.02	38.06	39.09	40.12	41.15	42.18	43.20	44.22	45.23	46.24	47.24	48.24	49.23	50.21	51.18	52.15	53.10
24	26.60	27.64	28.67	29.71	30.75	31.79	32.83	33.86	34.90	35.93	36.97	38.00	39.03	40.05	41.08	42.10	43.11	44.12	45.13	46.13	47.12	48.11	49.08	50.05	51.01	51.96
25	25.54	26.58	27.61	28.65	29.68	30.72	31.75	32.79	33.82	34.85	35.88	36.91	37.94	38.96	39.98	41.00	42.01	43.02	44.02	45.01	46.00	46.99	47.96	48.92	49.88	50.82
26	24.48	25.52	26.55	27.58	28.62	29.65	30.68	31.71	32.74	33.77	34.80	35.83	36.85	37.87	38.89	39.90	40.91	41.91	42.91	43.90	44.89	45.87	46.84	47.80	48.75	49.69
27	23.43	24.46	25.49	26.52	27.55	28.58	29.61	30.64	31.67	32.70	33.72	34.74	35.76	36.78	37.80	38.80	39.81	40.81	41.81	42.80	43.78	44.75	45.72	46.68	47.63	48.56
28	22.38	23.41	24.44	25.47	26.49	27.52	28.55	29.58	30.60	31.62	32.65	33.67	34.68	35.70	36.71	37.71	38.72	39.71	40.71	41.69	42.67	43.64	44.61	45.56	46.50	47.44
29	21.34	22.36	23.39	24.41	25.44	26.46	27.49	28.51	29.53	30.56	31.57	32.59	33.61	34.62	35.63	36.63	37.63	38.62	39.61	40.59	41.57	42.54	43.50	44.45	45.39	46.32
30	20.29	21.32	22.34	23.36	24.39	25.41	26.43	27.45	28.47	29.49	30.51	31.52	32.53	33.54	34.55	35.55	36.54	37.53	38.52	39.50	40.47	41.44	42.39	43.34	44.27	45.20
31	19.25	20.28	21.30	22.32	23.34	24.36	25.38	26.40	27.41	28.43	29.44	30.46	31.46	32.47	33.47	34.47	35.46	36.45	37.43	38.41	39.38	40.34	41.29	42.24	43.17	44.09
32	18.22	19.24	20.26	21.27	22.29	23.31	24.33	25.34	26.36	27.37	28.38	29.39	30.40	31.40	32.40	33.40	34.39	35.37	36.35	37.32	38.29	39.25	40.20	41.14	42.06	42.98
33	17.18	18.20	19.22	20.23	21.25	22.27	23.28	24.29	25.31	26.32	27.33	28.33	29.34	30.34	31.33	32.33	33.31	34.30	35.27	36.24	37.21	38.16	39.11	40.04	40.97	41.88
34	16.15	17.17	18.18	19.20	20.21	21.23	22.24	23.25	24.26	25.27	26.28	27.28	28.28	29.28	30.27	31.26	32.25	33.23	34.20	35.17	36.13	37.08	38.02	38.95	39.87	40.78
35	15.13	16.14	17.15	18.16	19.18	20.19	21.20	22.21	23.22	24.22	25.23	26.23	27.23	28.22	29.21	30.20	31.18	32.16	33.13	34.10	35.05	36.00	36.94	37.87	38.79	39.69
36	14.10	15.11	16.12	17.13	18.14	19.15	20.16	21.17	22.18	23.18	24.18	25.18	26.18	27.17	28.16	29.15	30.12	31.10	32.07	33.03	33.98	34.93	35.86	36.79	37.70	38.60
37	13.08	14.09	15.10	16.11	17.12	18.12	19.13	20.14	21.14	22.14	23.14	24.14	25.13	26.12	27.11	28.09	29.07	30.04	31.01	31.97	32.92	33.86	34.79	35.71	36.62	37.52
38	12.06	13.07	14.08	15.08	16.09	17.10	18.10	19.11	20.11	21.11	22.11	23.10	24.09	25.08	26.07	27.05	28.02	28.99	29.95	30.91	31.86	32.80	33.73	34.64	35.55	36.45
39	11.05	12.05	13.06	14.06	15.07	16.07	17.08	18.08	19.08	20.08	21.07	22.07	23.06	24.04	25.03	26.00	26.98	27.94	28.90	29.86	30.80	31.74	32.67	33.58	34.49	35.38
40	10.03	11.04	12.04	13.05	14.05	15.05	16.06	17.06	18.05	19.05	20.05	21.04	22.03	23.01	23.99	24.97	25.94	26.90	27.86	28.81	29.75	30.69	31.61	32.52	33.43	34.31
41	9.02	10.03	11.03	12.03	13.04	14.04	15.04	16.04	17.03	18.03	19.02	20.01	21.00	21.98	22.96	23.93	24.90	25.86	26.82	27.77	28.71	29.64	30.56	31.47	32.37	33.26
42	8.02	9.02	10.02	11.02	12.02	13.02	14.02	15.02	16.02	17.01	18.00	18.99	19.97	20.96	21.93	22.90	23.87	24.83	25.78	26.73	27.67	28.60	29.52	30.42	31.32	32.20
43	7.01	8.01	9.01	10.01	11.01	12.01	13.01	14.01	15.00	15.99	16.98	17.97	18.95	19.93	20.91	21.88	22.84	23.80	24.75	25.70	26.63	27.56	28.48	29.38	30.28	31.16
44	6.01	7.01	8.01	9.01	10.01	11.00	12.00	13.00	13.99	14.98	15.97	16.96	17.94	18.92	19.89	20.86	21.82	22.78	23.73	24.67	25.60	26.53	27.44	28.35	29.24	30.11
45	5.00	6.00	7.00	8.00	9.00	10.00	10.99	11.99	12.98	13.97	14.96	15.94	16.93	17.90	18.87	19.84	20.80	21.76	22.71	23.65	24.58	25.50	26.41	27.31	28.20	29.08
46	4.00	5.00	6.00	7.00	8.00	8.99	9.99	10.98	11.97	12.96	13.95	14.94	15.92	16.89	17.86	18.83	19.79	20.74	21.69	22.63	23.56	24.48	25.39	26.29	27.17	28.05

Table 34: 8th edition Ogden multipliers, loss of EARNINGS, MEN, discount rate: −0.25%, NO 2 YEAR ADJUSTMENT

Loss of earnings to pension age

Age	50	51	52	53	54	55	56	57	58	59	60	61	62	63	64	65	66	67	68	69	70	71	72	73	74	75
47	3.00	4.00	5.00	6.00	6.99	7.99	8.99	9.98	10.97	11.96	12.95	13.93	14.91	15.88	16.85	17.82	18.78	19.73	20.67	21.61	22.54	23.46	24.37	25.26	26.15	27.02
48	2.00	3.00	4.00	5.00	5.99	6.99	7.98	8.98	9.97	10.96	11.94	12.93	13.90	14.88	15.85	16.81	17.77	18.72	19.66	20.60	21.53	22.44	23.35	24.25	25.13	26.00
49	1.00	2.00	3.00	4.00	4.99	5.99	6.98	7.98	8.97	9.96	10.94	11.92	12.90	13.88	14.84	15.81	16.76	17.71	18.66	19.59	20.52	21.43	22.34	23.23	24.11	24.98
50		1.00	2.00	3.00	3.99	4.99	5.99	6.98	7.97	8.96	9.94	10.92	11.90	12.88	13.84	14.81	15.76	16.71	17.65	18.59	19.51	20.43	21.33	22.22	23.10	23.96
51			1.00	2.00	3.00	3.99	4.99	5.98	6.97	7.96	8.95	9.93	10.91	11.88	12.85	13.81	14.76	15.71	16.65	17.59	18.51	19.42	20.33	21.22	22.09	22.95
52				1.00	2.00	3.00	3.99	4.98	5.98	6.96	7.95	8.93	9.91	10.88	11.85	12.81	13.77	14.72	15.66	16.59	17.51	18.42	19.33	20.21	21.09	21.95
53					1.00	2.00	2.99	3.99	4.98	5.97	6.96	7.94	8.92	9.89	10.86	11.82	12.77	13.72	14.66	15.60	16.52	17.43	18.33	19.22	20.09	20.95
54						1.00	2.00	2.99	3.99	4.98	5.96	6.95	7.92	8.90	9.87	10.83	11.78	12.73	13.67	14.60	15.53	16.44	17.34	18.22	19.10	19.96
55							1.00	2.00	2.99	3.98	4.97	5.95	6.93	7.91	8.88	9.84	10.80	11.75	12.69	13.62	14.54	15.45	16.35	17.24	18.11	18.97
56								1.00	2.00	2.99	3.98	4.96	5.95	6.92	7.89	8.86	9.81	10.76	11.70	12.64	13.56	14.47	15.37	16.26	17.13	17.98
57									1.00	1.99	2.99	3.97	4.96	5.93	6.91	7.87	8.83	9.78	10.73	11.66	12.58	13.49	14.39	15.28	16.15	17.01
58										1.00	1.99	2.98	3.97	4.95	5.92	6.89	7.85	8.81	9.75	10.68	11.61	12.52	13.42	14.31	15.18	16.04
59											1.00	1.99	2.98	3.96	4.94	5.91	6.88	7.83	8.78	9.71	10.64	11.56	12.46	13.35	14.22	15.08
60												1.00	1.99	2.98	3.96	4.93	5.90	6.86	7.81	8.75	9.68	10.59	11.50	12.39	13.26	14.12
61													1.00	1.99	2.97	3.95	4.92	5.89	6.84	7.78	8.71	9.63	10.54	11.44	12.31	13.17
62														1.00	1.99	2.97	3.95	4.91	5.87	6.82	7.75	8.68	9.59	10.49	11.37	12.23
63															1.00	1.99	2.97	3.94	4.90	5.86	6.80	7.73	8.64	9.54	10.43	11.29
64																1.00	1.98	2.96	3.93	4.89	5.84	6.77	7.69	8.60	9.49	10.36
65																	1.00	1.98	2.96	3.92	4.88	5.82	6.75	7.66	8.55	9.43
66																		1.00	1.98	2.95	3.92	4.86	5.80	6.72	7.62	8.50
67																			0.99	1.98	2.95	3.91	4.85	5.77	6.68	7.57
68																				0.99	1.98	2.94	3.89	4.83	5.75	6.65
69																					0.99	1.97	2.94	3.88	4.81	5.72
70																						0.99	1.97	2.93	3.87	4.79
71																							0.99	1.97	2.92	3.85
72																								0.99	1.96	2.91
73																									0.99	1.96
74																										0.99

Tables

Table 35: 8th edition Ogden multipliers, loss of EARNINGS, WOMEN, discount rate: −0.25%, NO 2 YEAR ADJUSTMENT

Loss of earnings to pension age

Age	50	51	52	53	54	55	56	57	58	59	60	61	62	63	64	65	66	67	68	69	70	71	72	73	74	75
16	35.31	36.38	37.45	38.53	39.60	40.68	41.76	42.83	43.91	44.99	46.07	47.15	48.22	49.30	50.38	51.45	52.52	53.60	54.66	55.73	56.79	57.85	58.91	59.96	61.00	62.04
17	34.22	35.29	36.36	37.43	38.51	39.58	40.65	41.73	42.80	43.88	44.95	46.03	47.10	48.18	49.25	50.32	51.39	52.46	53.53	54.59	55.65	56.70	57.75	58.80	59.84	60.87
18	33.14	34.21	35.27	36.34	37.41	38.48	39.55	40.63	41.70	42.77	43.84	44.92	45.99	47.06	48.13	49.20	50.26	51.33	52.39	53.45	54.50	55.56	56.60	57.65	58.68	59.71
19	32.06	33.12	34.19	35.26	36.32	37.39	38.46	39.53	40.60	41.67	42.74	43.81	44.87	45.94	47.01	48.07	49.14	50.20	51.26	52.31	53.37	54.41	55.46	56.50	57.53	58.56
20	30.99	32.05	33.11	34.17	35.24	36.30	37.37	38.43	39.50	40.57	41.63	42.70	43.76	44.83	45.89	46.95	48.01	49.07	50.13	51.18	52.23	53.27	54.32	55.35	56.38	57.40
21	29.91	30.97	32.03	33.09	34.15	35.21	36.28	37.34	38.40	39.47	40.53	41.59	42.66	43.72	44.78	45.84	46.89	47.95	49.00	50.05	51.10	52.14	53.18	54.21	55.23	56.25
22	28.84	29.90	30.95	32.01	33.07	34.13	35.19	36.25	37.31	38.37	39.43	40.49	41.55	42.61	43.67	44.72	45.78	46.83	47.88	48.92	49.97	51.01	52.04	53.07	54.09	55.10
23	27.77	28.83	29.88	30.94	31.99	33.05	34.11	35.16	36.22	37.28	38.34	39.40	40.45	41.51	42.56	43.61	44.66	45.71	46.76	47.80	48.84	49.88	50.91	51.93	52.95	53.96
24	26.71	27.76	28.81	29.86	30.92	31.97	33.03	34.08	35.14	36.19	37.25	38.30	39.35	40.41	41.46	42.51	43.55	44.60	45.64	46.68	47.72	48.75	49.77	50.80	51.81	52.82
25	25.65	26.70	27.74	28.79	29.84	30.90	31.95	33.00	34.05	35.10	36.16	37.21	38.26	39.31	40.36	41.40	42.45	43.49	44.53	45.56	46.60	47.62	48.65	49.66	50.67	51.68
26	24.59	25.63	26.68	27.73	28.77	29.82	30.87	31.92	32.97	34.02	35.07	36.12	37.17	38.21	39.26	40.30	41.34	42.38	43.42	44.45	45.48	46.50	47.52	48.54	49.54	50.54
27	23.53	24.57	25.62	26.66	27.71	28.75	29.80	30.85	31.89	32.94	33.99	35.03	36.08	37.12	38.16	39.20	40.24	41.28	42.31	43.34	44.36	45.39	46.40	47.41	48.42	49.41
28	22.48	23.52	24.56	25.60	26.64	27.69	28.73	29.78	30.82	31.86	32.91	33.95	34.99	36.03	37.07	38.11	39.14	40.18	41.21	42.23	43.25	44.27	45.29	46.29	47.29	48.28
29	21.43	22.47	23.50	24.54	25.58	26.63	27.67	28.71	29.75	30.79	31.83	32.87	33.91	34.95	35.98	37.02	38.05	39.08	40.11	41.13	42.15	43.16	44.17	45.18	46.17	47.16
30	20.38	21.42	22.45	23.49	24.53	25.57	26.60	27.64	28.68	29.72	30.76	31.80	32.83	33.87	34.90	35.93	36.96	37.99	39.01	40.03	41.05	42.06	43.06	44.06	45.06	46.04
31	19.34	20.37	21.40	22.44	23.47	24.51	25.55	26.58	27.62	28.65	29.69	30.72	31.76	32.79	33.82	34.85	35.87	36.90	37.92	38.94	39.95	40.96	41.96	42.95	43.94	44.92
32	18.30	19.33	20.36	21.39	22.42	23.46	24.49	25.52	26.56	27.59	28.62	29.66	30.69	31.72	32.74	33.77	34.79	35.81	36.83	37.84	38.85	39.86	40.86	41.85	42.84	43.81
33	17.26	18.29	19.32	20.35	21.38	22.41	23.44	24.47	25.50	26.53	27.56	28.59	29.62	30.65	31.67	32.69	33.71	34.73	35.75	36.76	37.76	38.76	39.76	40.75	41.73	42.71
34	16.22	17.25	18.28	19.30	20.33	21.36	22.39	23.42	24.45	25.47	26.50	27.53	28.55	29.58	30.60	31.62	32.64	33.65	34.67	35.67	36.68	37.67	38.67	39.65	40.63	41.60
35	15.19	16.22	17.24	18.26	19.29	20.32	21.34	22.37	23.40	24.42	25.45	26.47	27.49	28.52	29.54	30.55	31.57	32.58	33.59	34.59	35.59	36.59	37.58	38.56	39.54	40.50
36	14.16	15.18	16.21	17.23	18.25	19.28	20.30	21.32	22.35	23.37	24.39	25.42	26.44	27.46	28.47	29.49	30.50	31.51	32.52	33.52	34.51	35.51	36.49	37.47	38.45	39.41
37	13.14	14.15	15.18	16.20	17.22	18.24	19.26	20.28	21.30	22.33	23.35	24.37	25.38	26.40	27.41	28.43	29.44	30.44	31.45	32.44	33.44	34.43	35.41	36.39	37.36	38.32
38	12.11	13.13	14.15	15.17	16.19	17.20	18.22	19.24	20.26	21.28	22.30	23.32	24.33	25.35	26.36	27.37	28.38	29.38	30.38	31.38	32.37	33.35	34.34	35.31	36.27	37.23
39	11.09	12.11	13.13	14.14	15.16	16.17	17.19	18.21	19.23	20.24	21.26	22.27	23.29	24.30	25.31	26.32	27.32	28.32	29.32	30.31	31.30	32.29	33.26	34.23	35.20	36.15
40	10.07	11.09	12.10	13.11	14.13	15.15	16.16	17.18	18.19	19.21	20.22	21.23	22.24	23.25	24.26	25.27	26.27	27.27	28.26	29.25	30.24	31.22	32.19	33.16	34.12	35.07
41	9.06	10.07	11.08	12.09	13.11	14.12	15.13	16.15	17.16	18.17	19.19	20.20	21.20	22.21	23.22	24.22	25.22	26.22	27.21	28.20	29.18	30.16	31.13	32.09	33.05	34.00
42	8.04	9.05	10.06	11.07	12.09	13.10	14.11	15.12	16.13	17.14	18.15	19.16	20.17	21.17	22.18	23.18	24.17	25.17	26.16	27.14	28.13	29.10	30.07	31.03	31.99	32.93
43	7.03	8.04	9.05	10.06	11.07	12.08	13.09	14.10	15.11	16.12	17.12	18.13	19.14	20.14	21.14	22.14	23.13	24.12	25.11	26.10	27.07	28.05	29.01	29.97	30.92	31.87
44	6.02	7.03	8.04	9.04	10.05	11.06	12.07	13.08	14.09	15.09	16.10	17.10	18.11	19.11	20.11	21.10	22.10	23.08	24.07	25.05	26.03	27.00	27.96	28.92	29.87	30.80
45	5.01	6.02	7.03	8.03	9.04	10.05	11.05	12.06	13.07	14.07	15.08	16.08	17.08	18.08	19.08	20.07	21.06	22.05	23.03	24.01	24.98	25.95	26.91	27.87	28.81	29.75
46	4.01	5.01	6.02	7.02	8.03	9.03	10.04	11.04	12.05	13.05	14.05	15.06	16.06	17.05	18.05	19.04	20.03	21.02	22.00	22.97	23.95	24.91	25.87	26.82	27.76	28.70

Table 35: 8th edition Ogden multipliers, loss of EARNINGS, WOMEN, discount rate: –0.25%, NO 2 YEAR ADJUSTMENT

Loss of earnings to pension age

Age	50	51	52	53	54	55	56	57	58	59	60	61	62	63	64	65	66	67	68	69	70	71	72	73	74	75
47	3.00	4.01	5.01	6.01	7.02	8.02	9.03	10.03	11.03	12.04	13.04	14.04	15.04	16.03	17.02	18.02	19.00	19.99	20.97	21.94	22.91	23.87	24.83	25.78	26.72	27.65
48	2.00	3.00	4.01	5.01	6.01	7.01	8.02	9.02	10.02	11.02	12.02	13.02	14.02	15.01	16.00	16.99	17.98	18.96	19.94	20.91	21.88	22.84	23.79	24.74	25.68	26.61
49	1.00	2.00	3.00	4.00	5.01	6.01	7.01	8.01	9.01	10.01	11.01	12.01	13.00	14.00	14.99	15.97	16.96	17.94	18.92	19.89	20.85	21.81	22.76	23.71	24.64	25.57
50		1.00	2.00	3.00	4.00	5.00	6.01	7.01	8.01	9.00	10.00	11.00	11.99	12.98	13.97	14.96	15.94	16.92	17.90	18.87	19.83	20.79	21.74	22.68	23.61	24.54
51			1.00	2.00	3.00	4.00	5.00	6.00	7.00	8.00	9.00	9.99	10.98	11.97	12.96	13.95	14.93	15.91	16.88	17.85	18.81	19.77	20.72	21.66	22.59	23.51
52				1.00	2.00	3.00	4.00	5.00	6.00	7.00	7.99	8.99	9.98	10.97	11.96	12.94	13.92	14.90	15.87	16.84	17.80	18.75	19.70	20.64	21.57	22.49
53					1.00	2.00	3.00	4.00	5.00	5.99	6.99	7.98	8.97	9.96	10.95	11.93	12.91	13.89	14.86	15.83	16.79	17.74	18.69	19.62	20.55	21.47
54						1.00	2.00	3.00	4.00	4.99	5.99	6.98	7.97	8.96	9.95	10.93	11.91	12.89	13.86	14.82	15.78	16.73	17.68	18.61	19.54	20.46
55							1.00	2.00	3.00	3.99	4.99	5.98	6.97	7.96	8.95	9.93	10.91	11.89	12.86	13.82	14.78	15.73	16.67	17.61	18.53	19.45
56								1.00	2.00	3.00	3.99	4.99	5.98	6.97	7.95	8.94	9.91	10.89	11.86	12.82	13.78	14.73	15.67	16.61	17.53	18.45
57									1.00	2.00	2.99	3.99	4.98	5.97	6.96	7.94	8.92	9.89	10.86	11.83	12.79	13.74	14.68	15.61	16.54	17.45
58										1.00	2.00	2.99	3.99	4.98	5.96	6.95	7.93	8.90	9.87	10.84	11.80	12.75	13.69	14.62	15.55	16.46
59											1.00	2.00	2.99	3.98	4.97	5.96	6.94	7.91	8.88	9.85	10.81	11.76	12.70	13.64	14.56	15.47
60												1.00	2.00	2.99	3.98	4.97	5.95	6.93	7.90	8.86	9.82	10.78	11.72	12.66	13.58	14.49
61													1.00	1.99	2.99	3.98	4.96	5.94	6.91	7.88	8.84	9.80	10.74	11.68	12.60	13.52
62														1.00	1.99	2.98	3.97	4.95	5.93	6.90	7.86	8.82	9.77	10.70	11.63	12.55
63															1.00	1.99	2.98	3.97	4.95	5.92	6.88	7.84	8.79	9.73	10.66	11.58
64																1.00	1.99	2.98	3.96	4.94	5.91	6.87	7.82	8.76	9.69	10.61
65																	1.00	1.99	2.98	3.96	4.93	5.89	6.85	7.80	8.73	9.65
66																		1.00	1.99	2.97	3.95	4.92	5.88	6.83	7.77	8.69
67																			1.00	1.99	2.97	3.94	4.91	5.86	6.80	7.73
68																				1.00	1.99	2.97	3.94	4.90	5.84	6.78
69																					1.00	1.98	2.96	3.93	4.88	5.82
70																						1.00	1.98	2.95	3.92	4.86
71																							0.99	1.98	2.95	3.91
72																								0.99	1.97	2.94
73																									0.99	1.97
74																										0.99

Table 36: 8th edition Ogden multipliers, loss of EARNINGS, MEN, discount rate: −0.75%, NO 2 YEAR ADJUSTMENT

Loss of earnings to pension age

Age	50	51	52	53	54	55	56	57	58	59	60	61	62	63	64	65	66	67	68	69	70	71	72	73	74	75
16	38.40	39.66	40.92	42.20	43.48	44.76	46.06	47.36	48.66	49.97	51.29	52.61	53.93	55.26	56.59	57.93	59.27	60.60	61.94	63.28	64.62	65.95	67.29	68.62	69.94	71.26
17	37.11	38.36	39.62	40.88	42.15	43.43	44.71	46.00	47.30	48.60	49.90	51.21	52.53	53.85	55.17	56.49	57.81	59.14	60.47	61.80	63.12	64.45	65.77	67.08	68.40	69.70
18	35.84	37.08	38.33	39.58	40.84	42.11	43.38	44.66	45.95	47.24	48.53	49.83	51.13	52.44	53.75	55.06	56.38	57.69	59.01	60.32	61.64	62.95	64.26	65.57	66.87	68.16
19	34.58	35.81	37.05	38.29	39.54	40.80	42.06	43.33	44.61	45.89	47.17	48.46	49.75	51.05	52.35	53.65	54.95	56.26	57.56	58.87	60.17	61.47	62.77	64.06	65.35	66.63
20	33.33	34.55	35.78	37.01	38.25	39.50	40.76	42.01	43.28	44.55	45.82	47.10	48.39	49.67	50.96	52.25	53.54	54.84	56.13	57.42	58.72	60.01	61.29	62.57	63.85	65.12
21	32.09	33.30	34.52	35.75	36.98	38.22	39.46	40.71	41.96	43.22	44.49	45.76	47.03	48.30	49.58	50.86	52.14	53.43	54.71	55.99	57.27	58.55	59.83	61.10	62.36	63.62
22	30.86	32.06	33.27	34.49	35.71	36.94	38.17	39.41	40.66	41.91	43.16	44.42	45.68	46.95	48.22	49.49	50.76	52.03	53.30	54.57	55.84	57.11	58.38	59.63	60.89	62.13
23	29.64	30.83	32.03	33.24	34.45	35.67	36.90	38.13	39.36	40.60	41.85	43.10	44.35	45.61	46.86	48.12	49.38	50.64	51.91	53.17	54.43	55.68	56.93	58.18	59.42	60.66
24	28.43	29.61	30.80	32.00	33.21	34.42	35.63	36.85	38.08	39.31	40.54	41.78	43.03	44.27	45.52	46.77	48.02	49.27	50.52	51.77	53.02	54.26	55.51	56.74	57.97	59.19
25	27.22	28.40	29.58	30.77	31.97	33.17	34.38	35.59	36.80	38.02	39.25	40.48	41.71	42.95	44.18	45.42	46.66	47.91	49.15	50.39	51.62	52.86	54.09	55.31	56.53	57.74
26	26.03	27.20	28.37	29.55	30.74	31.93	33.13	34.33	35.54	36.75	37.97	39.19	40.41	41.63	42.86	44.09	45.32	46.55	47.78	49.01	50.24	51.46	52.68	53.90	55.10	56.30
27	24.85	26.01	27.17	28.34	29.52	30.70	31.89	33.09	34.28	35.49	36.69	37.90	39.12	40.33	41.55	42.77	43.99	45.21	46.43	47.65	48.86	50.08	51.29	52.49	53.69	54.87
28	23.67	24.82	25.98	27.14	28.31	29.49	30.67	31.85	33.04	34.23	35.43	36.63	37.83	39.04	40.25	41.46	42.67	43.88	45.09	46.30	47.50	48.70	49.90	51.10	52.28	53.46
29	22.51	23.65	24.80	25.95	27.11	28.28	29.45	30.62	31.80	32.99	34.18	35.37	36.56	37.76	38.96	40.16	41.36	42.56	43.76	44.96	46.15	47.34	48.53	49.71	50.89	52.06
30	21.35	22.49	23.63	24.77	25.92	27.08	28.24	29.41	30.58	31.76	32.93	34.12	35.30	36.49	37.68	38.87	40.06	41.25	42.44	43.63	44.81	46.00	47.17	48.35	49.51	50.67
31	20.21	21.33	22.46	23.60	24.74	25.89	27.05	28.20	29.37	30.53	31.70	32.88	34.05	35.23	36.41	37.59	38.77	39.95	41.13	42.31	43.49	44.66	45.83	46.99	48.14	49.29
32	19.07	20.19	21.31	22.44	23.58	24.72	25.86	27.01	28.16	29.32	30.48	31.65	32.81	33.98	35.15	36.33	37.50	38.67	39.84	41.01	42.17	43.34	44.49	45.65	46.79	47.92
33	17.94	19.05	20.17	21.29	22.42	23.55	24.68	25.82	26.97	28.12	29.27	30.43	31.59	32.75	33.91	35.07	36.23	37.40	38.56	39.72	40.87	42.02	43.17	44.31	45.45	46.57
34	16.82	17.93	19.03	20.15	21.26	22.39	23.52	24.65	25.79	26.93	28.07	29.22	30.37	31.52	32.67	33.83	34.98	36.13	37.29	38.44	39.58	40.72	41.86	42.99	44.12	45.23
35	15.71	16.81	17.91	19.01	20.12	21.24	22.36	23.48	24.61	25.75	26.88	28.02	29.16	30.30	31.45	32.59	33.74	34.88	36.03	37.17	38.30	39.44	40.56	41.69	42.80	43.90
36	14.61	15.70	16.79	17.89	18.99	20.10	21.21	22.33	23.45	24.57	25.70	26.83	27.97	29.10	30.24	31.37	32.51	33.64	34.78	35.91	37.04	38.16	39.28	40.39	41.50	42.59
37	13.52	14.60	15.68	16.77	17.87	18.97	20.07	21.18	22.30	23.41	24.53	25.66	26.78	27.91	29.03	30.16	31.29	32.42	33.54	34.66	35.78	36.90	38.01	39.11	40.20	41.29
38	12.43	13.51	14.59	15.67	16.76	17.85	18.95	20.05	21.15	22.26	23.37	24.49	25.61	26.72	27.84	28.96	30.08	31.20	32.32	33.43	34.54	35.65	36.75	37.84	38.92	40.00
39	11.36	12.42	13.50	14.57	15.65	16.74	17.83	18.92	20.02	21.12	22.23	23.33	24.44	25.55	26.66	27.77	28.88	29.99	31.10	32.21	33.31	34.41	35.50	36.58	37.66	38.72
40	10.29	11.35	12.41	13.48	14.56	15.64	16.72	17.81	18.90	19.99	21.09	22.19	23.29	24.39	25.49	26.60	27.70	28.80	29.90	31.00	32.09	33.18	34.26	35.34	36.41	37.46
41	9.23	10.28	11.34	12.40	13.47	14.54	15.62	16.70	17.78	18.87	19.96	21.05	22.14	23.24	24.33	25.43	26.52	27.62	28.71	29.80	30.88	31.96	33.04	34.11	35.16	36.21
42	8.18	9.23	10.28	11.33	12.39	13.46	14.53	15.60	16.68	17.76	18.84	19.92	21.01	22.10	23.19	24.27	25.36	26.45	27.53	28.61	29.69	30.76	31.83	32.89	33.94	34.98
43	7.13	8.17	9.22	10.27	11.32	12.38	13.44	14.51	15.58	16.65	17.73	18.81	19.89	20.97	22.05	23.13	24.21	25.29	26.36	27.44	28.51	29.57	30.63	31.68	32.72	33.75
44	6.10	7.13	8.17	9.22	10.26	11.31	12.37	13.43	14.49	15.56	16.63	17.70	18.77	19.85	20.92	21.99	23.07	24.14	25.21	26.27	27.33	28.39	29.44	30.48	31.52	32.54
45	5.07	6.09	7.13	8.16	9.21	10.25	11.30	12.36	13.41	14.47	15.54	16.60	17.67	18.73	19.80	20.87	21.93	23.00	24.06	25.12	26.17	27.22	28.26	29.30	30.32	31.34
46	4.04	5.06	6.09	7.12	8.16	9.20	10.24	11.29	12.34	13.40	14.45	15.51	16.57	17.63	18.69	19.75	20.81	21.87	22.92	23.97	25.02	26.06	27.10	28.12	29.14	30.15

Table 36: 8th edition Ogden multipliers, loss of EARNINGS, MEN, discount rate: −0.75%, NO 2 YEAR ADJUSTMENT

Loss of earnings to pension age

Age	50	51	52	53	54	55	56	57	58	59	60	61	62	63	64	65	66	67	68	69	70	71	72	73	74	75
47	3.02	4.04	5.06	6.09	7.12	8.15	9.19	10.23	11.28	12.33	13.38	14.43	15.48	16.54	17.59	18.64	19.70	20.75	21.79	22.84	23.88	24.91	25.94	26.96	27.97	28.97
48	2.01	3.02	4.04	5.06	6.08	7.11	8.15	9.18	10.22	11.27	12.31	13.36	14.40	15.45	16.50	17.55	18.59	19.64	20.68	21.71	22.75	23.77	24.79	25.81	26.81	27.80
49	1.00	2.01	3.02	4.04	5.06	6.08	7.11	8.14	9.17	10.21	11.25	12.29	13.33	14.37	15.42	16.46	17.50	18.53	19.57	20.60	21.63	22.65	23.66	24.66	25.66	26.64
50		1.00	2.01	3.02	4.04	5.05	6.08	7.10	8.13	9.16	10.20	11.23	12.27	13.30	14.34	15.37	16.41	17.44	18.47	19.49	20.51	21.53	22.53	23.53	24.52	25.50
51			1.00	2.01	3.02	4.03	5.05	6.07	7.10	8.12	9.15	10.18	11.21	12.24	13.27	14.30	15.33	16.36	17.38	18.40	19.41	20.42	21.42	22.41	23.39	24.36
52				1.00	2.01	3.02	4.03	5.05	6.07	7.09	8.11	9.14	10.16	11.19	12.21	13.24	14.26	15.28	16.30	17.31	18.32	19.32	20.31	21.30	22.27	23.24
53					1.00	2.01	3.02	4.03	5.04	6.06	7.08	8.10	9.12	10.14	11.16	12.18	13.20	14.21	15.22	16.23	17.23	18.23	19.22	20.20	21.16	22.12
54						1.00	2.01	3.01	4.03	5.04	6.05	7.07	8.09	9.10	10.12	11.13	12.14	13.15	14.16	15.16	16.16	17.15	18.13	19.10	20.07	21.02
55							1.00	2.01	3.01	4.02	5.03	6.04	7.06	8.07	9.08	10.09	11.10	12.10	13.11	14.10	15.09	16.08	17.06	18.02	18.98	19.93
56								1.00	2.01	3.01	4.02	5.03	6.04	7.04	8.05	9.06	10.06	11.06	12.06	13.05	14.04	15.02	15.99	16.96	17.91	18.85
57									1.00	2.00	3.01	4.01	5.02	6.02	7.03	8.03	9.03	10.03	11.02	12.01	13.00	13.97	14.94	15.90	16.85	17.78
58										1.00	2.00	3.01	4.01	5.01	6.01	7.01	8.01	9.01	10.00	10.98	11.96	12.93	13.90	14.85	15.80	16.73
59											1.00	2.00	3.00	4.00	5.00	6.00	7.00	7.99	8.98	9.96	10.94	11.91	12.87	13.82	14.76	15.68
60												1.00	2.00	3.00	4.00	4.99	5.99	6.98	7.96	8.95	9.92	10.89	11.85	12.79	13.73	14.65
61													1.00	2.00	3.00	3.99	4.99	5.97	6.96	7.94	8.91	9.88	10.83	11.78	12.72	13.64
62														1.00	2.00	2.99	3.99	4.98	5.96	6.94	7.91	8.88	9.83	10.78	11.71	12.63
63															1.00	2.00	2.99	3.98	4.96	5.94	6.92	7.88	8.84	9.78	10.71	11.63
64																1.00	1.99	2.99	3.97	4.95	5.93	6.89	7.85	8.79	9.72	10.64
65																	1.00	1.99	2.98	3.96	4.94	5.91	6.86	7.81	8.74	9.66
66																		1.00	1.99	2.98	3.95	4.92	5.88	6.83	7.77	8.69
67																			1.00	1.99	2.97	3.94	4.91	5.86	6.80	7.72
68																				1.00	1.99	2.96	3.93	4.89	5.83	6.76
69																					1.00	1.98	2.96	3.92	4.87	5.81
70																						0.99	1.98	2.95	3.91	4.85
71																							0.99	1.98	2.94	3.89
72																								0.99	1.97	2.93
73																									0.99	1.97
74																										0.99

Tables

Table 37: 8th edition Ogden multipliers, loss of EARNINGS, WOMEN, discount rate: −0.75%, NO 2 YEAR ADJUSTMENT

Loss of earnings to pension age

Age	50	51	52	53	54	55	56	57	58	59	60	61	62	63	64	65	66	67	68	69	70	71	72	73	74	75
16	38.54	39.82	41.10	42.39	43.69	44.99	46.31	47.63	48.96	50.29	51.63	52.98	54.34	55.70	57.06	58.43	59.81	61.19	62.58	63.96	65.35	66.75	68.14	69.54	70.93	72.32
17	37.26	38.52	39.80	41.08	42.37	43.66	44.97	46.28	47.59	48.92	50.25	51.59	52.93	54.28	55.64	57.00	58.36	59.73	61.10	62.48	63.86	65.24	66.62	68.01	69.39	70.77
18	35.98	37.24	38.50	39.77	41.05	42.34	43.63	44.93	46.24	47.56	48.88	50.20	51.54	52.88	54.22	55.57	56.92	58.28	59.65	61.01	62.38	63.75	65.12	66.49	67.86	69.23
19	34.72	35.97	37.22	38.48	39.75	41.03	42.31	43.60	44.90	46.20	47.52	48.83	50.16	51.48	52.82	54.16	55.50	56.85	58.20	59.55	60.91	62.27	63.63	64.99	66.34	67.70
20	33.47	34.70	35.95	37.20	38.46	39.73	41.00	42.28	43.57	44.86	46.16	47.47	48.78	50.10	51.42	52.75	54.09	55.42	56.76	58.10	59.45	60.80	62.15	63.49	64.84	66.18
21	32.22	33.45	34.69	35.93	37.18	38.44	39.70	40.97	42.25	43.53	44.82	46.12	47.42	48.73	50.04	51.36	52.68	54.01	55.34	56.67	58.00	59.34	60.68	62.01	63.35	64.68
22	30.99	32.21	33.43	34.67	35.91	37.15	38.41	39.67	40.94	42.21	43.49	44.78	46.07	47.37	48.67	49.98	51.29	52.60	53.92	55.24	56.57	57.89	59.22	60.54	61.87	63.19
23	29.76	30.97	32.19	33.41	34.64	35.88	37.13	38.38	39.64	40.90	42.17	43.45	44.73	46.02	47.31	48.61	49.91	51.21	52.52	53.83	55.14	56.46	57.77	59.08	60.40	61.71
24	28.55	29.75	30.96	32.17	33.39	34.62	35.86	37.10	38.35	39.60	40.86	42.13	43.40	44.68	45.96	47.25	48.54	49.83	51.13	52.43	53.73	55.03	56.34	57.64	58.94	60.24
25	27.34	28.53	29.73	30.94	32.15	33.37	34.59	35.83	37.07	38.31	39.56	40.82	42.08	43.35	44.62	45.90	47.18	48.46	49.75	51.04	52.33	53.62	54.91	56.20	57.49	58.78
26	26.14	27.33	28.52	29.71	30.91	32.13	33.34	34.57	35.79	37.03	38.27	39.52	40.77	42.03	43.29	44.56	45.83	47.10	48.38	49.65	50.93	52.22	53.50	54.78	56.06	57.33
27	24.96	26.13	27.31	28.50	29.69	30.89	32.10	33.31	34.53	35.76	36.99	38.23	39.47	40.72	41.97	43.23	44.49	45.75	47.02	48.28	49.55	50.82	52.09	53.36	54.63	55.90
28	23.78	24.94	26.11	27.29	28.48	29.67	30.87	32.07	33.28	34.50	35.72	36.95	38.18	39.42	40.66	41.91	43.16	44.41	45.67	46.93	48.18	49.44	50.70	51.96	53.22	54.47
29	22.61	23.76	24.93	26.10	27.27	28.46	29.64	30.84	32.04	33.25	34.46	35.68	36.90	38.13	39.37	40.60	41.84	43.08	44.33	45.58	46.83	48.08	49.33	50.57	51.82	53.06
30	21.45	22.59	23.75	24.91	26.08	27.25	28.43	29.62	30.81	32.01	33.21	34.42	35.64	36.86	38.08	39.31	40.54	41.77	43.00	44.24	45.48	46.72	47.96	49.20	50.43	51.66
31	20.30	21.44	22.58	23.73	24.89	26.06	27.23	28.41	29.59	30.78	31.98	33.18	34.38	35.59	36.80	38.02	39.24	40.46	41.69	42.92	44.15	45.38	46.60	47.83	49.06	50.28
32	19.15	20.28	21.42	22.57	23.72	24.87	26.04	27.21	28.38	29.56	30.75	31.94	33.13	34.33	35.54	36.75	37.96	39.17	40.39	41.60	42.82	44.04	45.26	46.48	47.69	48.90
33	18.02	19.14	20.27	21.41	22.55	23.70	24.85	26.01	27.18	28.35	29.53	30.71	31.90	33.09	34.28	35.48	36.68	37.89	39.09	40.30	41.51	42.72	43.93	45.14	46.34	47.54
34	16.90	18.01	19.13	20.26	21.39	22.53	23.68	24.83	25.99	27.15	28.32	29.49	30.67	31.85	33.04	34.23	35.42	36.61	37.81	39.01	40.21	41.41	42.61	43.80	45.00	46.19
35	15.78	16.89	18.00	19.12	20.25	21.38	22.52	23.66	24.81	25.96	27.12	28.29	29.45	30.63	31.80	32.98	34.17	35.35	36.54	37.73	38.92	40.11	41.30	42.48	43.67	44.85
36	14.67	15.77	16.88	17.99	19.11	20.23	21.36	22.50	23.64	24.78	25.93	27.09	28.25	29.41	30.58	31.75	32.93	34.10	35.28	36.46	37.64	38.82	40.00	41.18	42.35	43.52
37	13.58	14.67	15.76	16.87	17.98	19.09	20.21	21.34	22.47	23.61	24.75	25.90	27.05	28.21	29.37	30.53	31.69	32.86	34.03	35.20	36.37	37.54	38.71	39.88	41.04	42.20
38	12.49	13.57	14.66	15.75	16.86	17.96	19.08	20.20	21.32	22.45	23.58	24.72	25.87	27.01	28.16	29.32	30.47	31.63	32.79	33.95	35.12	36.28	37.44	38.59	39.75	40.90
39	11.40	12.48	13.56	14.65	15.74	16.84	17.95	19.06	20.18	21.30	22.42	23.55	24.69	25.83	26.97	28.12	29.26	30.41	31.56	32.72	33.87	35.02	36.17	37.32	38.47	39.61
40	10.33	11.40	12.47	13.56	14.64	15.73	16.83	17.93	19.04	20.16	21.27	22.40	23.52	24.65	25.79	26.92	28.06	29.20	30.35	31.49	32.63	33.78	34.92	36.06	37.19	38.32
41	9.26	10.33	11.39	12.47	13.55	14.63	15.72	16.82	17.92	19.02	20.13	21.25	22.37	23.49	24.61	25.74	26.87	28.01	29.14	30.27	31.41	32.54	33.68	34.81	35.93	37.05
42	8.21	9.26	10.32	11.39	12.46	13.54	14.62	15.71	16.80	17.90	19.00	20.11	21.22	22.33	23.45	24.57	25.69	26.82	27.94	29.07	30.19	31.32	32.44	33.57	34.68	35.79
43	7.16	8.20	9.26	10.32	11.38	12.46	13.53	14.61	15.69	16.78	17.88	18.98	20.08	21.19	22.30	23.41	24.52	25.64	26.76	27.87	28.99	30.11	31.22	32.34	33.44	34.55
44	6.11	7.15	8.20	9.25	10.31	11.37	12.44	13.51	14.59	15.68	16.76	17.86	18.95	20.05	21.15	22.26	23.36	24.47	25.58	26.69	27.80	28.91	30.01	31.12	32.22	33.31
45	5.08	6.11	7.15	8.20	9.25	10.30	11.36	12.43	13.50	14.58	15.66	16.74	17.83	18.92	20.02	21.11	22.21	23.31	24.41	25.51	26.61	27.72	28.81	29.91	31.00	32.08
46	4.05	5.08	6.11	7.15	8.19	9.24	10.30	11.36	12.42	13.49	14.56	15.64	16.72	17.80	18.89	19.98	21.07	22.16	23.26	24.35	25.44	26.53	27.62	28.71	29.79	30.87

Table 37: 8th edition Ogden multipliers, loss of EARNINGS, WOMEN, discount rate: −0.75%, NO 2 YEAR ADJUSTMENT

Loss of earnings to pension age

Age	50	51	52	53	54	55	56	57	58	59	60	61	62	63	64	65	66	67	68	69	70	71	72	73	74	75
47	3.03	4.05	5.07	6.11	7.14	8.19	9.23	10.29	11.35	12.41	13.47	14.54	15.62	16.69	17.77	18.85	19.94	21.02	22.11	23.19	24.28	25.36	26.45	27.52	28.60	29.67
48	2.01	3.03	4.05	5.07	6.10	7.14	8.18	9.23	10.28	11.33	12.39	13.46	14.52	15.59	16.66	17.74	18.82	19.89	20.97	22.05	23.13	24.20	25.28	26.35	27.41	28.47
49	1.00	2.01	3.03	4.05	5.07	6.10	7.14	8.18	9.22	10.27	11.32	12.38	13.44	14.50	15.57	16.63	17.70	18.77	19.84	20.91	21.99	23.05	24.12	25.18	26.24	27.29
50		1.00	2.01	3.02	4.04	5.07	6.10	7.13	8.17	9.21	10.26	11.31	12.36	13.42	14.48	15.54	16.60	17.66	18.73	19.79	20.85	21.92	22.97	24.03	25.08	26.12
51			1.00	2.01	3.02	4.04	5.07	6.09	7.13	8.16	9.20	10.25	11.29	12.34	13.39	14.45	15.50	16.56	17.62	18.68	19.73	20.79	21.84	22.89	23.93	24.97
52				1.00	2.01	3.02	4.04	5.06	6.09	7.12	8.15	9.19	10.23	11.28	12.32	13.37	14.42	15.47	16.52	17.57	18.62	19.67	20.71	21.75	22.79	23.82
53					1.00	2.01	3.02	4.04	5.06	6.08	7.11	8.15	9.18	10.22	11.26	12.30	13.34	14.39	15.43	16.48	17.52	18.56	19.60	20.63	21.66	22.68
54						1.00	2.01	3.02	4.04	5.06	6.08	7.11	8.14	9.17	10.20	11.24	12.28	13.31	14.35	15.39	16.43	17.46	18.49	19.52	20.54	21.56
55							1.00	2.01	3.02	4.03	5.05	6.07	7.10	8.13	9.15	10.19	11.22	12.25	13.28	14.31	15.35	16.37	17.40	18.42	19.44	20.45
56								1.00	2.01	3.02	4.03	5.05	6.07	7.09	8.11	9.14	10.17	11.19	12.22	13.25	14.27	15.30	16.32	17.33	18.34	19.34
57									1.00	2.01	3.02	4.03	5.04	6.06	7.08	8.10	9.12	10.15	11.17	12.19	13.21	14.23	15.24	16.25	17.26	18.25
58										1.00	2.01	3.02	4.03	5.04	6.05	7.07	8.09	9.11	10.12	11.14	12.16	13.17	14.18	15.18	16.18	17.17
59											1.00	2.01	3.01	4.02	5.03	6.05	7.06	8.07	9.09	10.10	11.11	12.12	13.12	14.12	15.12	16.10
60												1.00	2.01	3.01	4.02	5.03	6.04	7.05	8.06	9.07	10.07	11.08	12.08	13.07	14.06	15.05
61													1.00	2.00	3.01	4.02	5.02	6.03	7.04	8.04	9.04	10.04	11.04	12.03	13.02	14.00
62														1.00	2.00	3.01	4.01	5.02	6.02	7.02	8.02	9.02	10.01	11.00	11.98	12.96
63															1.00	2.00	3.00	4.01	5.01	6.01	7.01	8.00	8.99	9.98	10.96	11.93
64																1.00	2.00	3.00	4.00	5.00	6.00	6.99	7.98	8.96	9.94	10.91
65																	1.00	2.00	3.00	4.00	4.99	5.98	6.97	7.95	8.93	9.89
66																		1.00	2.00	3.00	3.99	4.98	5.97	6.95	7.92	8.89
67																			1.00	2.00	2.99	3.98	4.97	5.95	6.92	7.89
68																				1.00	1.99	2.99	3.98	4.96	5.93	6.90
69																					1.00	1.99	2.98	3.97	4.94	5.91
70																						1.00	1.99	2.98	3.96	4.93
71																							1.00	1.99	2.97	3.94
72																								1.00	1.98	2.96
73																									1.00	1.98
74																										0.99

Table 38 (8th edition Ogden Table 35): Discounting factors for term certain

Factor to discount value of multiplier for a period of deferment.

	Discount Rate				Discount Rate	
Term	−0.75%	−0.25%		Term	−0.75%	−0.25%
1	1.0076	1.0025		41	1.3616	1.1081
2	1.0152	1.0050		42	1.3719	1.1109
3	1.0228	1.0075		43	1.3823	1.1136
4	1.0306	1.0101		44	1.3927	1.1164
5	1.0384	1.0126		45	1.4032	1.1192
6	1.0462	1.0151		46	1.4138	1.1220
7	1.0541	1.0177		47	1.4245	1.1248
8	1.0621	1.0202		48	1.4353	1.1277
9	1.0701	1.0228		49	1.4461	1.1305
10	1.0782	1.0253		50	1.4570	1.1333
11	1.0863	1.0279		51	1.4681	1.1362
12	1.0945	1.0305		52	1.4792	1.1390
13	1.1028	1.0331		53	1.4903	1.1419
14	1.1112	1.0357		54	1.5016	1.1447
15	1.1195	1.0383		55	1.5129	1.1476
16	1.1280	1.0409		56	1.5244	1.1505
17	1.1365	1.0435		57	1.5359	1.1534
18	1.1451	1.0461		58	1.5475	1.1562
19	1.1538	1.0487		59	1.5592	1.1591
20	1.1625	1.0513		60	1.5710	1.1621
21	1.1713	1.0540		61	1.5828	1.1650
22	1.1801	1.0566		62	1.5948	1.1679
23	1.1890	1.0593		63	1.6069	1.1708
24	1.1980	1.0619		64	1.6190	1.1737
25	1.2071	1.0646		65	1.6312	1.1767
26	1.2162	1.0672		66	1.6436	1.1796
27	1.2254	1.0699		67	1.6560	1.1826
28	1.2347	1.0726		68	1.6685	1.1856
29	1.2440	1.0753		69	1.6811	1.1885
30	1.2534	1.0780		70	1.6938	1.1915
31	1.2629	1.0807		71	1.7066	1.1945
32	1.2724	1.0834		72	1.7195	1.1975
33	1.2820	1.0861		73	1.7325	1.2005
34	1.2917	1.0888		74	1.7456	1.2035
35	1.3015	1.0916		75	1.7588	1.2065
36	1.3113	1.0943		76	1.7721	1.2095
37	1.3212	1.0970		77	1.7855	1.2126
38	1.3312	1.0998		78	1.7990	1.2156
39	1.3413	1.1025		79	1.8125	1.2187
40	1.3514	1.1053		80	1.8262	1.2217

Table 39 (8ᵗʰ edition Ogden Table 36): Multipliers for pecuniary loss for term certain

Multiplier for regular frequent payments for a term certain.

	Discount Rate				Discount Rate	
Term	**−0.75%**	**−0.25%**		**Term**	**−0.75%**	**−0.25%**
1	1.00	1.00		41	48.03	43.18
2	2.02	2.01		42	49.40	44.29
3	3.03	3.01		43	50.78	45.40
4	4.06	4.02		44	52.16	46.51
5	5.10	5.03		45	53.56	47.63
6	6.14	6.05		46	54.97	48.75
7	7.19	7.06		47	56.39	49.88
8	8.25	8.08		48	57.82	51.00
9	9.31	9.10		49	59.26	52.13
10	10.39	10.13		50	60.71	53.26
11	11.47	11.15		51	62.17	54.40
12	12.56	12.18		52	63.65	55.54
13	13.66	13.21		53	65.13	56.68
14	14.76	14.25		54	66.63	57.82
15	15.88	15.29		55	68.14	58.97
16	17.00	16.32		56	69.65	60.11
17	18.14	17.37		57	71.18	61.27
18	19.28	18.41		58	72.73	62.42
19	20.43	19.46		59	74.28	63.58
20	21.58	20.51		60	75.84	64.74
21	22.75	21.56		61	77.42	65.90
22	23.93	22.62		62	79.01	67.07
23	25.11	23.67		63	80.61	68.24
24	26.30	24.74		64	82.22	69.41
25	27.51	25.80		65	83.85	70.59
26	28.72	26.86		66	85.49	71.76
27	29.94	27.93		67	87.14	72.95
28	31.17	29.00		68	88.80	74.13
29	32.41	30.08		69	90.47	75.32
30	33.66	31.16		70	92.16	76.51
31	34.92	32.23		71	93.86	77.70
32	36.18	33.32		72	95.57	78.90
33	37.46	34.40		73	97.30	80.10
34	38.75	35.49		74	99.04	81.30
35	40.04	36.58		75	100.79	82.50
36	41.35	37.67		76	102.56	83.71
37	42.67	38.77		77	104.33	84.92
38	43.99	39.87		78	106.13	86.14
39	45.33	40.97		79	107.93	87.35
40	46.68	42.07		80	109.75	88.57

APPENDIX 1: Presidential Guidance - General Case Management

This guidance was re-issued on 22 January 2018 and updated on 23 March 2018.

GUIDANCE NOTE 6

REMEDY

What is remedy?

1) After an Employment Tribunal has decided whether the claimant's claim succeeds it will consider how the successful party should be compensated. This part of the judgment is called "Remedy". Sometimes it is done immediately after the merits or liability judgment, but in long or complex cases it may be adjourned to another day.

2) The Tribunal has different powers for each different type of claim. It must calculate loss and order an appropriate remedy for each part of a successful claim. Accurate and often detailed information from both parties is needed to make correct calculations and to issue a judgment which is fair to all. Sometimes the Tribunal can only estimate the loss: for example, for how long a party may be out of work.

Different types of remedy

3) For some claims the only remedy is to order the employer/respondent to pay a sum of money: for example, wages due, holiday pay and notice pay.

4) For unfair dismissal the Tribunal may:

4.1 Order the employer to "reinstate" the dismissed employee. This is to put them back in their old job, as if they had not been dismissed; or to "re-engage" them, which is to employ them in a suitable but different job. In each case the Tribunal may order payment of lost earnings, etc.

4.2 If those orders are not sought by the claimant or are not practicable, the Tribunal may order the employer to pay compensation. This is calculated in two parts:

- a "Basic Award", which is calculated in a similar way to a statutory redundancy payment; and

- a "Compensatory Award", which is intended to compensate the employee for the financial loss suffered.

5) In claims of unlawful discrimination, the Tribunal may:

5.1 make a declaration setting out the parties' rights; and/or

5.2 order compensation to be paid by the employer and/or fellow workers who have committed discriminatory acts. If the employer can show that it has taken all reasonable steps to prevent employees from committing such acts (called the "statutory defence"), the only award which can be made is against the fellow worker, not the employer; and/or

5.3 make a recommendation, such as for the claimant's colleagues or managers to be given training to ensure that discrimination does not happen again.

Mitigation

6) All persons who have been subjected to wrongdoing are expected to do their best, within reasonable bounds, to limit the effects on them. If the Tribunal concludes that a claimant has not done so, it must reduce the compensation so that a fair sum is payable.

7) The Tribunal will expect evidence to be provided by claimants about their attempts to obtain suitable alternative work and about any earnings from alternative employment.

8) The Tribunal will expect respondents, who consider that the claimant has not tried hard enough, to provide evidence about other jobs which the claimant could have applied for.

Statement of remedy

9) The Tribunal will usually order the claimant to make a calculation showing how each amount claimed has been worked out. For example: x weeks' pay at £y per week. Sometimes this is called a "Schedule of loss" or a "Statement of remedy".

10) Tribunals are expected to calculate remedy for each different type of loss – sometimes called "Heads of loss" or "Heads of damage". Therefore the statement should show how much is claimed under each head.

11) If the claimant has received State benefits, he or she should also specify the type of benefit, the dates of receipt, the amount received and the claimant's national insurance number. (See also "Recoupment" below).

12) Typical heads of loss include;

- wages due
- pay in lieu of notice (where no notice or inadequate notice was given)
- outstanding holiday pay
- a basic award or redundancy payment
- past loss of earnings
- future loss of earnings
- loss of pension entitlements.

13) In discrimination cases, the heads of loss will also typically include:

- injury to feelings
- aggravated or exemplary damages (which are rare)
- damages for personal injury (but only when the act of discrimination is the cause of the claimant becoming ill).

14) The Tribunal will usually order the statement to be produced early in the proceedings, as it can help in settlement negotiations, when considering mediation and when assessing the length of the hearing. It should be updated near to the hearing date.

Submissions on *Polkey* and contributory fault

15) In an unfair dismissal claim, if an employee has been dismissed, but the employer has not followed a proper procedure (such as the ACAS Code), the Tribunal will follow the guidance in the case of *Polkey v AE Dayton Services Limited* and subsequent cases. The Tribunal will consider whether, if a fair procedure had been followed, the claimant might still have been fairly dismissed, either at all, or at some later time. This question is often referred to as the "*Polkey*" question or deduction.

16) There are also cases where the dismissal may be procedurally unfair, but the employee's own conduct has contributed to the position they now find themselves in. This is called "contributory conduct".

17) Where either or both of these are relevant, the Tribunal will reduce the compensation awarded by an appropriate percentage in each case. This means that there may be two reductions, which, where there has been really serious misconduct, could be as high as 100%, so that nothing would be payable.

18) Generally the Tribunal will decide these issues at the same time as it reaches its decision on the merits of the claim. Sometimes this will be done at a separate remedy hearing. The Tribunal will usually explain at the start of the hearing which of those options it will follow. If it does not, then the parties should ask for clarification of when they are expected to give evidence and to make submissions on these matters.

Injury to Feelings

19) In discrimination cases and some other detriment claims, Tribunals may award a sum of money to compensate for injury to feelings. When they do so, they must fix fair, reasonable and just compensation in the particular circumstances of the case. The Tribunal will bear in mind that compensation is designed to compensate the injured party rather than to punish the guilty one. It will also remind itself that awards should bear some relationship to those made by the courts for personal injury.

20) The Tribunal will follow guidelines first given in the case of *Vento v Chief Constable of West Yorkshire Police* and in subsequent cases. These guidelines are referred to as the "*Vento* guidelines" or the "*Vento* bands". The President of Employment Tribunals will issue from time to time separate guidance on the present value of the *Vento* bands or guidelines.

21) The Tribunal will expect claimants to explain in their statement of remedy which *Vento* band they consider their case falls in. They will also expect both parties to make submissions on this during the remedy part of the hearing.

Information needed to calculate remedy

22) This varies in each case dependent on what is being claimed. Each party should look for any relevant information which could help the Tribunal with any necessary calculations in their case. They should provide copies of this information to each other and include those copies in the hearing bundle.

23) The types of information that could be relevant include:

- the contract of employment or statement of terms & conditions with the old employer
- the date the claimant started work with that employer
- details of any pension scheme and pension contributions
- pay slips for the last 13 weeks in the old employment
- any other document showing the claimant's gross pay and net pay
- proof of any payments actually made by the old employer, such as a redundancy payment or payment in lieu of notice
- any document recording the day the claimant last actually worked
- any document explaining how many days and hours per week the claimant worked
- any document explaining how overtime was paid
- any document recording when the holiday year started
- any document recording when holiday has been taken in that year and what has been paid for those days
- any documents setting out the terms of the old employer's pension scheme
- any documents showing the claimant's attempts to find new or other work
- contract of employment and payslips for any new job with a new employer
- documents such as bank statements, if losses for bank charges are claimed
- medical reports or "Fit notes" if unable to work since dismissal
- any documents showing that jobs were or are available in the locality for which the claimant could have applied.

24) The witness statements should tell the Tribunal which parts of these documents are important and why. Providing enough information to the Tribunal at an early stage could help to promote a settlement and so avoid a hearing.

Is all loss awarded?

25) For claims such as unpaid wages, holiday pay and notice pay the Tribunal will order the difference between what should have been paid and what has actually been paid. Wages and holiday pay are usually calculated gross, but pay in lieu of notice is usually calculated net of tax and national insurance. The judgment should specify whether each payment ordered has been calculated gross or net.

26) In the case of unfair dismissal there are several limits (called statutory caps) on what can be awarded.

Grossing up

27) The rules on when tax is payable on awards made by Tribunals are too complex for inclusion here. When it is clear that the claimant will have to pay tax on the sum awarded, the Tribunal will award a higher figure, calculated so that tax can be paid and the claimant will receive the net sum which properly represents the loss. This calculation is called "grossing up".

Interest

28) There are two separate situations where interest is relevant

29) First, when a Tribunal calculates compensation for discrimination, it is obliged to consider awarding interest. If it decides to do so, it calculates interest from the date of the act of discrimination up to the date of the calculation. The exception is for interest on lost wages, where the calculation is made from the middle of that period (as that is simpler than calculating interest separately on each missing wage, but leads to a roughly similar result). The Tribunal will then include that interest in the award made.

30) In addition, interest is payable on awards for all claims if they are not paid when due. A note accompanying the

Tribunal's judgment will explain how interest has been calculated. In respect of all claims presented on or after 29 July 2013 interest is calculated from the day after the day upon which the written judgment was sent to the parties, unless payment is actually made within the first 14 days, in which case no interest is payable.

31) The Employment Tribunal plays no part in enforcing payment of the award it makes. That is done by the civil courts, who issue separate guidance on how to enforce payments.

Recoupment

32) For some claims, such as unfair dismissal, if the claimant has received certain State benefits the Tribunal is obliged to ensure that the employer responsible for causing the loss of earnings reimburses the State for the benefits paid. In those cases the Tribunal will order only part of the award to be paid to the claimant straightaway, with the rest set aside until the respondent is told by the State how much the benefits were. The respondent then pays that money to the State and anything left over to the claimant.

33) This is called "recoupment". The Tribunal should set out in the judgment whether or not recoupment applies, and if it does, how much of the award is set aside for recoupment purposes. If either party is in any doubt about recoupment, they should ask the Tribunal to explain how it affects them.

Costs

34) See the separate guidance on "Costs".

Pensions loss

35) The President of Employment Tribunals has issued separate guidance and principles on the calculation of pensions loss. See:

https://www.judiciary.uk/wp-content/uploads/2015/03/Basic-Guide-to-Compensation-for-Pension-Loss-2021.pdf

https://www.judiciary.uk/wp-content/uploads/2015/03/Principles-Third-Revision-2021.pdf.

APPENDIX 2: Sample schedule of loss

Claimant's schedule of loss – Green v XYZ Ltd

Background

Mrs Green, who was born on 14/02/1985, started work with XYZ Ltd on 24/10/2015. Her gross weekly salary was £2,500 and her net weekly salary, after the deduction of tax and employee national insurance, was £2,000. She was a member of the employer's defined benefit pension scheme, the details of which are added below. On 17/04/2019, she was dismissed summarily for gross misconduct and was given £2,000 as payment in lieu of notice. Her contractual notice period was 8 weeks. Mrs Green found part time work from 23/07/2019 until the date of the Tribunal hearing, earning a net amount of £15,523 up until the date of the hearing. This arrangement was expected to continue for the next few months at least. Mrs Green was not eligible to join the pension scheme in her new job until she had worked for them for 2 years.

The date of the remedies hearing has been listed for 03/01/2020.

Mrs Green's claims

- On 28/06/2019 Mrs Green brought claims of unfair and wrongful dismissal and sex discrimination at the ET.
- She maintained it would take a year to find another equivalent permanent job and therefore was claiming future loss of earnings until 17/04/2020.
- She was entitled to a sum representing loss of statutory rights.
- Any award should be increased by 25% for the failure of the employer to comply with the Code of Practice.
- She was entitled to a sum of £850 representing untaken accrued holiday which the respondent had not paid on termination.
- She claimed a sum of £18,000 for injury to feelings and interest on this figure, from 01/01/2017 until 01/01/2019.
- Mrs Green argued that as it would take 2 years for her to become eligible to join the pension scheme in her new job she wants to be compensated for loss of pension for that time.

Pension information

- Her gross weekly pensionable pay at the date of dismissal was £2,500.
- Her employer contributed 12% of its wage bill to the private pension scheme.

Respondent's Counter Schedule of Loss – Green v XYZ Ltd

Counter arguments

- The claimant's schedule of loss does not include her expected earnings, which are estimated to be £3,000 from the date of the hearing to the date when the employer's liability ends. This needs to be recorded.
- The respondent disputes the 25% uplift for failing to follow the Code of Practice for unfair dismissal, submitting that the figure should be closer to 10%.
- The respondent submits that pension loss should be limited to the period up to the hearing date.
- The respondent also submits that the claimant was also partly responsible for her own dismissal to the extent of 10% (for both the basic and compensatory awards).
- A deduction of 2% should also be made for accelerated payment of future sums of compensation.
- The sum of £18,000 for injury to feelings is disputed – there was no discriminatory conduct on the part of the respondent.
- The compensation cap should be applied to the final figure since the dismissal of the claimant was not discriminatory.

IN THE EMPLOYMENT TRIBUNALS
CASE NO: 3452/87

BETWEEN

Green
AND
XYZ

CLAIMANT'S SCHEDULE OF LOSS

1. Details

Date of birth	14/02/1985
Date started employment	24/10/2015
Effective Date of Termination	17/04/2019
Period of continuous service (years)	3
Age at Effective Date of Termination	34
Remedy hearing date	03/01/2020
Cut-off date for future loss of earnings	17/04/2020
Contractual notice period (weeks)	8
Statutory notice period (weeks)	3
Net weekly pay at EDT	£2,000
Gross weekly pay at EDT	£2,500

2. Basic award

Number of qualifying weeks (3) x Gross weekly pay (£525.00[1])	£1,575.00
Total basic award	**£1,575.00**

3. Damages for wrongful dismissal

Loss of earnings: Damages period (8) x Net weekly pay (£2,000)	£16,000.00
Plus failure by employer to follow statutory procedures @ 25%[2]	£4,000.00[3]
Total damages	**£20,000.00**

4. Compensatory award (immediate loss)

Loss of net earnings: Number of weeks (29.3[4]) x Net weekly pay (£2,000)	£58,600.00
Plus loss of statutory rights	£350.00
Plus accrued holiday pay	£850.00
Less payment in lieu	-£2,000.00
Less earnings: (23/07/2019 to 03/01/2020)	-£15,523.00
Pension loss (loss of employer contributions)[5]	
£2,500 x 0.12 x 37.3 weeks	£11,190.00
Total compensation (immediate loss)	**£53,467.00**

---

[1] £525 was the limit on a week's pay at an EDT of 17/04/2019

[2] The ACAS uplift can also apply to damages for wrongful dismissal – see Adjustments and order of adjustments and Schedule A2 of TULR(C)A

[3] £16,000 x 0.25

[4] 29.3 weeks has been calculated by subtracting the damages period of 8 weeks from the total number of weeks between EDT and the hearing date (37.3)

[5] Following the guidance in *Principles for Calculating Pension Loss* which was updated in March 2021

5. Compensatory award (future loss)

Loss of future earnings: Number of weeks (14.9[6]) x Net weekly pay (£2,000)	£29,800.00
Future loss of pension (loss of employer contributions)	
£2,500 x 0.12 x 66.7[7] weeks	£20,010.00
Total compensation (future loss)	**£49,810.00**

6. Adjustments to total compensatory award

Failure by employer to follow statutory procedures @ 25%	£25,819.25[8]
Compensatory award before adjustments	**£103,277.00**
Total adjustments to the compensatory award	**£25,819.25**
Compensatory award after adjustments	**£129,096.25**

7. Discrimination

Injury to feelings	£18,000.00
Plus interest @ 8%[9] for 730 days	£2,880.00[10]
Discrimination award	**£20,880.00**

8. Summary totals

Basic award	£1,575.00
Wrongful dismissal	£20,000.00
Compensation award	£129,096.25
Discrimination	£20,880.00
TOTAL	**£171,551.25**
TOTAL AFTER GROSSING UP AT 40%	**£265,352.08**[11]

---

[6] Number of weeks between 03/01/2020 and 17/04/2020

[7] 104 weeks (i.e. 2 years) minus 37.3 weeks immediate loss

[8] (£53,467.00 + £49,810.00) x 0.25. Remember that accrued holiday pay which has not been paid can be classed as unlawful deductions and thus uplifted according to Schedule A2 of TULR(C)A

[9] The interest rate is 8% from 29/07/2013

[10] £18,000 x 0.08 x 730 ÷ 365

[11] (£1,575 + £20,000 + £129,096.25 + £20,880 - £850) - £30,000 (i.e. the tax free amount) = £170,701.25 - £30,000.00 = £140,701.25. Remember that the £850 holiday pay should not be grossed up since it should be paid gross by the employer. The award for injury to feelings figure is also included here because this will be fully taxable for EDTs after 06/04/2018.

Grossed up at 40% = £140,701.25 ÷ 0.6 = £234,502.08

Add back the £30,000.00 and £850, and the final award comes to £265,352.08

The statutory cap does not apply since the claimant is claiming that the dismissal was for discriminatory reasons (see respondent's counter schedule).

IN THE EMPLOYMENT TRIBUNALS
CASE NO: 3452/87

BETWEEN

Green
AND
XYZ

RESPONDENT'S COUNTER SCHEDULE OF LOSS

1. Details

Date of birth	14/02/1985
Date started employment	24/10/2015
Effective Date of Termination	17/04/2019
Period of continuous service (years)	3
Age at Effective Date of Termination	34
Remedy hearing date	03/01/2020
Cut-off date for future loss of earnings	17/04/2020
Contractual notice period (weeks)	8
Statutory notice period (weeks)	3
Net weekly pay at EDT	£2,000
Gross weekly pay at EDT	£2,500

2. Basic award

Number of qualifying weeks (3) x Gross weekly pay (£525.00)	£1,575.00
Less contributory fault @ 10%	-£157.50
Total basic award	**£1,417.50**

3. Damages for wrongful dismissal

Loss of earnings: Damages period (8) x Net weekly pay (£2,000)	£16,000.00
Plus failure by employer to follow statutory procedures @ 10%	£1,600.00
Total damages	**£17,600.00**

4. Compensatory award (immediate loss)

Loss of net earnings: Number of weeks (29.3) x Net weekly pay (£2,000)	£58,600.00
Plus loss of statutory rights	£350.00
Plus accrued holiday pay	£850.00
Less payment in lieu	-£2,000.00
Less earnings: (23/07/2019 to 03/01/2020)	-£15,523.00
Pension loss	
£2,500 x 0.12 x 37.3 weeks	£11,190.00
Total compensation (immediate loss)	**£53,467.00**

5. Compensatory award (future loss)

Loss of future earnings: Number of weeks (14.9) x Net weekly pay (£2,000)	£29,800.00
Less expected future earnings (04/01/2020 to 17/04/2020)	-£3,000.00
Total compensation (future loss)	**£26,800.00**

6. Adjustments to total compensatory award

Less accelerated payment	-£536.00[12]
Plus failure by employer to follow statutory procedures (ACAS uplift) @ 10%	£7,973.10[13]
Less contributory fault (compensation award) @ 10%	-£8,685.41[14]
Compensatory award before adjustments	**£80,267.00**
Total adjustments to the compensatory award	**-£1,248.31[15]**
Compensatory award after adjustments	**£79,018.69**

7. Summary totals

Basic award	£1,417.50
Wrongful dismissal	£17,600.00
Compensatory award	£79,018.69
TOTAL	**£98,036.19**
GROSSED UP AWARD AT 40%	**£142,826.98[16]**
TOTAL AWARD CAPPED AT LOWER OF GROSS ANNUAL SALARY (£130,000) AND STATUTORY CAP (£86,444)[17]	**£106,311.50[18]**

---

[12] Accelerated payment only applies to future loss. The future loss figure is £26,800 and 2% of this figure is £26,800 x 0.02 = £536

[13] Immediate loss + future loss – accelerated receipt = £53,467 + £26,800 - £536 = £79,731. The ACAS adjustment should now be applied to this figure = £79,731 x 0.1 = £7,973.10

[14] This has been calculated by first adding together the immediate loss, future loss and ACAS uplift, and deducting the sums for accelerated receipt to get £53,467 + £26,800 + £7,973.10 - £536 = £87,704.10

Next, the contributory fault deduction needs to be applied to this new figure but LESS the £850 holiday pay sum because contributory fault does not apply to holiday pay. This now becomes: (£87,704.10 - £850) x 0.1 = £8,685.41

[15] - £536 + £7,973.10 - £8,685.41 = - £1,248.31

[16] (£1,417.50 + £17,600 + 79,018.69 - £850) - £30,000 = £97,186.19 - £30,000 = £67,186.19. Remember that the £850 holiday pay should not be grossed up since it should be paid gross by the employer.

Grossed up at 40% = £67,186.19 ÷ 0.6 = £111,976.98

Add back £30,000 + £850 = £142,826.98

[17] The statutory cap applicable at an EDT of 17/04/2019 is £86,444 (see Table 1). Compare this with the claimant's gross annual salary of £130,000 (i.e. £2,500 x 52) and the smaller figure, in this case £86,444, applies.

[18] First, we need to find out what just the compensatory award is after the grossing up has been done to check if that figure exceeds the statutory cap. £10,982.50 was tax free (because £30,000 - £1,417.50 - £17,600 = £10,982.50). The balance of £67,186.19 (i.e. £79,018.69 - £10,982.50 - £850) is grossed up to get £111,976.98 (i.e. £67,186.19 ÷ 0.6).

Thus the total compensatory award = £10,982.50 + £111,976.98 (excluding the holiday pay) = £122,959.48 which exceeds the lower of the statutory cap and the gross annual salary.

Therefore, the total capped award is: £1,417.50 + £17,600 + £86,444 + £850 = £106,311.50. Remember that the £850 holiday pay does not count towards the compensation cap.

APPENDIX 3: Calculating holiday entitlement

The calculation of holiday entitlement can be a complicated matter. The calculation ultimately depends upon the construction of the contract of employment, and where relevant the construction of the Working Time Regulations. The Working Time Regulations must themselves be interpreted consistently with the Working Time Directive where it is the four weeks of paid leave that derive from the Directive that are under consideration (see *Bear Scotland & Ors v Fulton & Ors* [2015] ICR 221). Subject to that strong note of caution, the following principles will often assist in calculating holiday entitlement.

Working 5 or more days a week

Most workers who work a 5-day week have a statutory entitlement to 28 days paid annual leave per year which amounts to 5.6 weeks.

Note that the statutory minimum is limited to 28 days - even if a worker works 6 days per week, they will still only be statutorily entitled to 28 days holiday per year (not 6 x 5.6 which is 33.6 days).

Working part-time

Part-time workers are also entitled to a statutory minimum of 5.6 weeks of paid holiday each year, although this may amount to fewer actual days of paid holiday than a full-time worker would get. For example, someone working 4 days per week will be entitled to a minimum of 4 x 5.6 weeks which comes to 22.4 days per year.

Working a fixed number of days per week

Number of days entitlement per year = number of days worked per week (up to a maximum of 5 for the statutory minimum) x number of weeks holiday entitlement (5.6 is the statutory minimum although the contract of employment may provide for more)

> *Example 1*: for a worker who works 3 days per week, and who is contractually entitled to 7 weeks holiday per year, they would be entitled to 3 x 7 days = 21 days

> *Example 2*: a worker who works 4 days a week and is contractually entitled to 35 days a year pro rata would be entitled to 4 ÷ 5 x 35 = 28 days

> *Example 3*: a worker who works 4 days per week but has no contractual right to holiday would be entitled to 4 x 5.6 = 22.4 days

Working a fixed number of hours per week

Sometimes it is easier to calculate holiday entitlement in terms of hours rather than days, especially if the worker does not work whole days. It also means it is easier to calculate how much holiday is due to a worker who leaves part way through the leave year.

> *Example 4*: a worker works 20 hours per week, and is entitled to the statutory 5.6 weeks per year.

> Holiday entitlement is 20 x 5.6 hours per year = 112 hours

Working a different number of hours per week and variable number of days per week

This will apply to many casual workers and again it is usually easier to calculate holiday entitlement in hours, with direct reference to the number of hours actually worked. Note that the WTD provides for entitlement to four weeks paid leave.

Statutory holiday entitlement only

For each hour worked, the worker accrues 0.1207 of an hour or roughly 7 minutes of holiday. The 0.1207 is the proportion of the working year that a worker is entitled to have as holiday by statute, and is worked out as:

> 5.6 ÷ (52 - 5.6) = 5.6 ÷ 46.4 = 0.1207 [The 5.6 weeks are excluded from the calculation as the worker would not be at work during those 5.6 weeks in order to accrue annual leave.]

> *Example 5*: a worker works 20 hours in a week.

> Holiday entitlement = 20 x 0.1207 = 2.41 hours, which is approximately 2 hours and 25 minutes.

Holiday entitlement in excess of statutory minimum where holiday is expressed in weeks (W)

For each hour worked, the worker is entitled to W ÷ (52 - W) of an hour.

Example 6: a worker works 25 hours per week, and holiday entitlement is 6 weeks per year.

Holiday entitlement per hour of work = 6 ÷ (52 - 6) = 0.1304 of an hour or about 8 minutes.

Holiday entitlement in excess of statutory minimum where holiday is expressed in days (D)

For each hour worked, the worker is entitled to D/5 ÷ (52 - D/5) of an hour (this divides days by 5 rather than 7, since the statutory formula is worked out on the basis of 5 working days).

Example 7: a worker works 25 hours and holiday entitlement is 34 days per year.

Holiday entitlement per hour of work = 34/5 ÷ (52 - 34/5) = 0.1504 of an hour = approximately 9 minutes

Annualised hours

The following calculations would be suitable for any worker who works a set number of hours per year. The easiest way to calculate holiday entitlement is to treat the worker as a casual worker and calculate the number of hours of holiday accrued per hour of work actually done.

For statutory holiday entitlement

Holiday in hours = hours actually worked x 0.1207

For holiday entitlement in excess of statutory minimum

Holiday in hours = hours worked x W ÷ (52 - W) where W is the number of weeks holiday the worker is entitled to according to their employment contract.

Example 8: a worker works 1000 hours per year and is entitled to 8 weeks holiday per year.

Holiday entitlement = 1000 x 8 ÷ (52 - 8) = 181.82 hours per year.

Compressed hours

Some workers work compressed hours; for example, they may work 40 hours compressed into 4 days instead of 5.

The easiest way in which this is calculated is by working out the number of hours' holiday that is being accrued. This avoids having to calculate the length of a day for the purposes of taking a day off.

Holiday entitlement (hours) = hours worked in a week x number of weeks of contractual holiday (or 5.6 if only statutory holiday).

Shift workers

The easiest way in which holiday entitlement can be calculated in this case is to work out the number of shifts the worker is entitled to take off. To do this calculate the proportion of the entire shift pattern (including days off) that the worker has actually worked to work out the average number of shifts worked per week, and then multiply this number of shifts by the number of weeks of annual holiday entitlement.

Example 9: a worker works four 12 hour shifts in a week and then has 2 days off. He is only entitled to statutory holiday.

First find out the average number of shifts worked per week. The complete shift pattern is 6 days, of which the worker works 4. So in a 7 day week they work on average: 4 ÷ (4 + 2) x 7 = 4.67 shifts.

Then, annual holiday entitlement = 4.67 x 5.6 = 26.15 shifts

Entitlement if a worker starts or leaves part way through the leave year

Starters

You need to work out the proportion of the year left from the day the worker started to the end of the leave year, then multiply by the entitlement as calculated above.

Example 10: leave year is from 1 January to 31 December. A worker starts on 18 September. Full years' entitlement (as calculated using the above formulae) = 28 days.

First, the number of days between 18 September and 31 December, including both days = 105.

Holiday entitlement for the remaining period = 28 x 105 ÷ 365 (or 366 in a leap year) = 8 days

Leavers

You need to work out the proportion of the leave year actually worked, then multiply by the entitlement as calculated above. Finally subtract any holiday actually taken.

> **Example 11**: leave year is from 1 June to 31 May. A casual worker worked a total of 600 hours and left on 24 October and had already taken 20 hours holiday. Statutory holiday entitlement applies.
>
> In this case, because holiday is being accrued for each hour worked, we don't need to work out the proportion of the leave year worked.
>
> Holiday entitlement = 600 x 0.1207 hours = 72.42 hours
>
> Holiday pay due = 72.42 - 20 = 52.42 hours
>
> **Example 12**: leave year is from 1 June to 31 May. A worker, who worked 3 days a week, left on 24 October and had already taken 4 days holiday in that leave year. Statutory holiday entitlement applies.
>
> Annual holiday entitlement = 3 x 5.6 = 16.8 days
>
> Then, number of days between 1 June and 24 October inclusive = 146 days
>
> Holiday entitlement = 16.8 x 146 ÷ 365 (366 in a leap year) = 6.72
>
> Holiday pay due = 6.72 - 4 = 2.72 days

Term time only workers

There is no specific calculation for working out the holiday entitlement for term time workers and the easiest and fairest calculations might be those used for annualised hours or casual/irregular hours .

Calculating accrued holiday pay on termination of employment

If an employee has left employment part way through a leave year, and at the effective date of termination he has taken less holiday than he is entitled to up to that date, the employer should make a payment in lieu to the employee, either according to a relevant agreement (see below) or, if no such agreement exists, then the accrued holiday is calculated according to Reg 14 WTR 1998 which then needs to be multiplied by a day's pay or an hour's pay:

> (A x B) - C
>
> where:
>
> A is the period of leave to which the worker is entitled;
>
> B is the proportion of the worker's leave year which expired before the termination date; and
>
> C is the period of leave taken by the worker between the start of the leave year and the termination date.

What is a day's pay?

The calculation of a days' pay can be a complicated matter. The calculation ultimately depends upon the construction of the contract of employment, and where relevant the construction of the Working Time Regulations and ss221 to 224 ERA 1996. The Working Time Regulations must themselves be interpreted consistently with the Working Time Directive where it is the four weeks of paid leave that derive from the Directive that are under consideration, such that provisions in the ERA 1996 for calculating a days' pay cannot be relied upon at face value (see *Bear Scotland & Ors v Fulton & Ors* [2015] ICR 221). Subject to that strong note of caution, the following principles will often assist in calculating holiday entitlement.

A day's pay for the purposes of working out holiday pay is calculated according to a 'working' year rather than a full 365 day calendar year. This approach was adopted by the EAT in *Leisure Leagues UK Ltd v Macconnachie* UKEAT/940/01. It held that a year's pay should be divided by 233 because this was the number of actual days worked by the claimant in the year.

What is an hour's pay?

For workers for whom it is easier to calculate holiday entitlement in terms of hours rather than days, it will be necessary to calculate the appropriate hourly rate of pay. Where there is a straightforward hourly rate of pay with no variations or additional sums, this will be simple to establish. Otherwise, this may be calculated by identifying the total remuneration over the last 12 weeks and dividing this by the total number of hours worked over the last 12 weeks, in accordance with the calculation of a day's pay, but using hours worked instead of days.

Relevant agreement

Podlasiak v Edinburgh Woollen Mill Ltd is an ET decision where the tribunal held that a clause in the claimant's contract of employment, providing that they would receive £1 in respect of any accrued holiday pay on termination of employment, was unlawful and unenforceable. It was incompatible with the Working Time Directive, even though otherwise consistent with the wording in the WTR.